Creating Strategic Change

Creating Strategic Change

Designing the Flexible, High-Performing Organization

WILLIAM A. PASMORE

John Wiley & Sons, Inc.
New York • Chichester • Brisbane • Toronto • Singapore

Copyright © 1994 by William A. Pasmore
Published by John Wiley & Sons, Inc.,

Library of Congress Cataloging-in-Publication Data:

Pasmore, William A.
    Creating strategic change : designing the flexible, high-
performing organization / William A. Pasmore.
        p.   cm.
    Includes index.
    ISBN 0-471-59729-5
    1. Organizational change—Management. 2. Strategic planning.
    3. Organizational effectiveness. I. Title.
    HD58.8.P366   1994
    658.4'06—dc20   93-39202

To Mary, Brenna, and Kelsey

Contents

Preface

This is a book about designing organizations that are truly flexible and responsive to change. It is intended to help people understand how to manage in turbulent times, how to create learning organizations, and how to change everything that needs to be changed—all at the same time. It presents an antidote to chaos, an alternative to falling into the program-of-the-month trap, and a guide to organizing for the future. It suggests that change is here to stay, and that it is time we started to organize and manage as if change mattered. It makes absolutely clear why our present ways of managing and organizing are hopelessly out of step with the world we live in today and suggests that our only way out of the crisis we are in is to think systemically about change, rather than trying to solve one problem at a time. Creating flexible, high-performance, learning organizations is the secret to gaining competitive advantage in a world that won't stand still. If change is a part of your experience, this book will help you to understand what it takes to get out in front of it. If change isn't a part of your experience, it probably will be soon; so it's best that you do your homework to prepare for change now.

In the past 20 years, we have witnessed the coming and going of faddish efforts to cope with change: quality of worklife, employee involvement, quality circles, total quality, work and redesign, reengineering. None of these has been sufficient to prepare organizations for the changes we are currently facing or the changes yet to come.

This book is intended as a resource to guide the thinking of people who believe that the time has come to move beyond a

ix

firefighting approach to change. It suggests that how well organizations learn, and then use that learning to change, is fundamental to competitive advantage. Learning to learn and learning to change require that we make a conscious effort to transform every aspect of the organization, from the way we think about people to the way we think about management and even to the way we think about thinking. It is a challenge to many of our fundamental beliefs about management and organizing and will no doubt cause some discomfort to the reader. It is not a cookbook, since the primary thesis of the book is that cookbook solutions are out. It is a book about the management of rapid and complex change, about living in the midst of chaos and keeping our cool.

Much of what you will read here is personal. After 20 years of teaching and consulting, I felt a need to pause to reconsider my own journey. I took a sabbatical, retreated to the Maine woods, and thought about life and what I have learned. I hope that reading it is a sabbatical for you as well, and that it inspires you to take some time to think about your own journey. Whether you are a CEO, manager, consultant, or employee, I hope the book will stir action on your part to help your organization become more flexible and responsive to change. Many others are counting on you.

One person I have counted on in writing this book is John Mahaney, my editor at John Wiley & Sons, who encouraged me to follow my instincts in writing a book that would matter, not just fill up space on a library shelf. His comments on earlier drafts spared your having to struggle with thoughts that would have made reading the book more difficult or confusing. You should thank him, too, if you get the chance. He and the other folks at Wiley have been a pleasure to work with on this book, as they were on my last. At home, Mary and Brenna and Kelsey have helped as much as they could, even when it meant that I disappeared from their lives for long periods of solitary reflection and work. Permitting someone you care for to do something that is important to him, when it means that you can't be with them as much as you would like, is surely one of the deepest forms of love. Mary also accepted the risk of providing me feedback on my ideas; many of the breakthroughs in my thinking came during conversations with her. She is a constant reminder to me that our first concern in life should be for each other and that in the end nothing else really matters. Thank you; I love you, too.

I can't thank all of the people who provided me with material for the book, since I have chosen not to reveal their identities in many instances. I think you will recognize yourselves when you read my stories from the road; just know how much your faith in me has meant to my own learning and that of others. Thanks to Al Fitz, Jack Sherwood, and others of you who read earlier drafts of chapters, contributed examples, and helped me find ways to communicate my message more clearly.

Thanks, too, to the good people of Limerick, Maine for their hospitality, friendship, and good cooking during my stay; and to my mother, father, and sister, whose visits during my sabbatical reminded me that life isn't all about work.

CHAPTER

1

Change and Flexibility
Creating a High-Performance Organization

Maine is a good place to write a book. Tucked away in the northeastern corner of the country, its cold winters keep it from becoming too heavily populated. Its main attraction is physical beauty, which is indescribable, and quietude. It's a wonderful place to slow down, reflect, and sort things out.

Change comes more slowly to Maine than it does to some other places. The old weathered, whitewashed churches and the crumbling stone walls that run through the forests and surround cemeteries full of graying granite slabs seem to ward off efforts to modernize. Roads are seldom straight, meaning that you can't get from here to there if you're in a hurry, and people from one town consider others to be "from away" if they were born in the town on the other side of the hill.

1

Given a little time, you settle into the pace of life here and begin to let go of the ties that keep you tuned in and turned on in the city. You watch less news, read fewer newspapers, and stay at home for dinner more often. Pretty soon, you wonder what all the rushing around was about, and why you didn't slow down sooner.

All of this keeps Maine out of the mainstream, sheltered for the moment from the changes that others feel almost instantly, thanks to CNN, car phones, and computer modems. People in Maine choose to live a slower life, and they pay the price for it; they aren't rich, and they don't intend to be. You can still live a good life here on little money, but people are always concerned that the money will run out soon; that a change in the economy will bring a deeper recession, that the mill will close, that new restrictions will be placed on lobster fishing. Somehow, I know that these people would find a way to survive here anyhow; they are flexible enough to bend with the changes. But they resist the changes as hard as they can.

I came here in January for my sabbatical both to get away from the city and to get into the solitude, so that my writing would be as focused as it possibly could be. I do my best work when I can concentrate on just one thing at a time; I'm always shocked when I take time to decompress to discover how little of what I have been running around so frantically trying to accomplish really matters. I wanted this book to matter, to make a difference. It represents more than 20 years' worth of my own effort in learning about management and organizational change and many more years of effort by others. Writing it has clarified for me what I have learned and now believe to be true. It has also surprised me. When you take time to think, you learn things about yourself that you weren't aware of before.

When I discovered an old photograph of myself the other day, I was surprised to notice how much I have changed in the past few years. I'm always surprised by old photographs, letters, an antique car that wasn't considered an antique when I was driving one. I know that my life is progressing, and that time is moving on, but I supress it so that I can focus on the present and enjoy what I'm doing today. And then, when I am reminded again of how much I have changed, I'm surprised.

Change is happening to all of us, and to our organizations as well. Most of the time, however, we manage as if change isn't happening or doesn't matter very much. We keep doing the same things we did yesterday, and when changes occur that force deviations from what we expect, we try to force things back into the old patterns again. We have a hard time admitting that change really is happening, and that it matters. Change that matters means that we have to change the way we do things, or the way we think about things, and that can be expensive or difficult.

We prefer to imagine that change is gradual and insignificant, that while there is change, it is change around some comfortable equilibrium; and therefore our best strategy is simply to continue doing what we have been doing until things return to normal. This strategy works until we look at an old photograph of ourselves and discover that the process of change is unidirectional and irreversible. Or look at changes that have occurred in the world and recognize that business will never be the same. Or get hit by the full force of a change in our environment that we didn't expect, which produces the need for sudden and dramatic responsiveness, for which we are not prepared. Then, we wish that we were more aware of change, more able to respond to it, more flexible. We are all more like the people of Maine than we might imagine.

Like love, change is a deceivingly simple word. Easy to say, easy to understand, at least on the surface. I've spent most of my adult life trying to understand change. I know more about it than I once did, but am still learning and still changing. Apparently, so are leaders of organizations. How else can we explain the constant surprises revealed in our daily reading of the *Wall Street Journal*: the fluctuation of the markets, the closing of the gates of another factory, the failure of another new product, the amazing success of a young entrepreneur who raced around the conventional wisdom to get ahead of her seasoned competition, the shift of wealth and power to other nations. *Change.* Unpredictable, unrelenting, ubiquitous, surprising change. Full of promise and opportunity for those willing to embrace it, but so frightening to the rest of us.

It would be one thing if we wanted these changes to happen, or even accepted them as the way things have to be; if we saw in them the natural workings of an evolutionary force that moved slowly over time to remove the less fit from the ranks of the *Fortune* 500 and replace them with younger, stronger stock. But it is clear that the forces of change are often not welcome, at least among managers of organizations soon to become extinct. And it is just as clear, in retrospect, that leaders of organizations that have become extinct had no way to cope with the changes they were facing, even though the signs of change coming were clearly visible on the horizon. Braniff Airlines, American Motors, Republic Steel, Ameritrust Bank, The May Company are examples.

But change hasn't been all bad, or equally troubling for everyone. For those who saw change as an opportunity, the chaotic period that began in the early 1970s provided many options for applied creativity. Names that weren't even in our vocabulary then are a part of the every day scene today: Microsoft, Apple, W. L. Gore & Associates, Genentech, Wal-Mart, Humana. Some established organizations recognized the changes affecting them and were able to make themselves over completely: Xerox, GE, Walt Disney, Motorola. What separated these organizations from their floundering counterparts was their willingness to accept change gracefully, and respond flexibly, not simply with more of the same.

Like the superficial simplicity of change, the thesis of the book appears patently obvious: The more flexible an organization becomes, the better it can respond to change. But, like many common-sense propositions, this one is more easily imagined than put into practice, judging from the upheavals occurring in almost every sector of our economy. Preparing people and organizations for change must be more difficult than it seems; if managers already knew how to do it, they certainly would have done it by now. In truth, what we witness, for the most part, is more intensive firefighting: more drastic, short-term cuts, another program of the month, another change in top management, another buyout, merger, or collapse. Firefighting is being done for the sake of survival, not for the sake of flexibility or preparing for change. The aftermath of downsizing, as demonstrated through recent research conducted by Lou Harris & Associates, is in fact to *weaken* the ability of the organization to respond to further change.[1] A majority of companies surveyed reported that downsizing resulted in lower morale among the remaining workforce, and four out of 10 companies reported that downsizing efforts resulted in undesirable consequences for the organization, including losing the wrong people, needing to retrain the remaining workforce, and more use of overtime. So, short-term cost cutting provides no apparent guarantee of long-term survival. Another strategy must be employed, one that prepares the organization for continuous change in a world that provides no stability and accepts no excuses for being unprepared; a strategy based on *Flexibility*.

Flexibility isn't constant across organizations. Managers may presume that their organizations will be flexible when they need to be, but the fact is that some organizations are more flexible than others. Those that are flexible have worked at developing flexibility, usually over a long period of time. Flexibility requires more than quick, top-level strategizing; it is far easier to change strategies than to change organizations. Flexibility requires that, when strategies need to change, the focus of the organization is able to change, too. This requires that the systems of the organization are able to change, and how people are managed, and what people do, and even what they think. Being flexible means being able to change everything, all at the same time. That's what makes responding to change difficult.

When managers misunderstand what change really requires, they issue edicts, make bold cuts, and provide new marching orders for people to follow. In this flurry of their own activity and in their deep desire to help their organizations survive, they believe that their actions will indeed produce change. In fact, very often, change is only superficial, temporary, or imagined. Real change requires dramatic, committed, insightful leadership, to be sure; but it requires much more. Becoming aware of the need for change and holding a vision of the future are only the first steps in the process of achieving real organizational change. Much more work must be done to change the structure of the organization and how it operates. How much more depends on how flexible the organization is to begin with; which in turn depends on how much attention managers have paid to building flexibility into their people, technology, systems, and thinking. Flexibility is also a function of how change has been handled historically and how members of the organization feel about their leadership. Change is easier to accomplish when people are working with you to make it happen than when they are resisting change, or just busy trying to avoid being burned again. In the final analysis we must admit that organizations aren't flexible or inflexible, only the people in them are. Improving organizational flexibility starts with the recognition that organizational change and human change are one and the same.

Change isn't always positive; but it can be handled in ways that strengthen rather than diminish the commitment people have to an organization. The first rule of change, therefore, is to begin any process of change with concern for its impact on people. The second rule is to prepare people for the change by educating them in what they need to know in order for the change to be successful; the third, to involve them in the change as much as possible; and the fourth, with their involvement, to change what really needs to be changed about the entire system in order for the effort to produce real results.

In one case where change was handled with these rules in mind, the leaders of a Michigan firm knew that, given uncontrollable economic pressures, they would need to reduce their labor force by a third. Rather than decide who should leave, management gave the decision to the people in the organization. Management explained the economic problem, its consequences, and the outlook for the future of the business. They explained how they arrived at the number of people who would need to leave and that they were very concerned about the impact the cutback would have on people—both those forced out and those left behind. They wanted to maintain the excellent relationship between labor and management in the organization but recognized that a layoff like the current one, unprecedented in the organization's history, would change forever how people felt about their association with the organization. Faced with the unavoidable problem, *but caring about the impact of the change on people*, management explained why it had decided to share the decision with those directly affected.

The result was surprising even to management: People met in groups, developed criteria for deciding who should go and who should stay based not only on seniority but also on family and financial obligations, other opportunities available, and personal choice; and decided among themselves who would actually go. In the end, both those leaving and those left behind *grew* in their admiration for the company; the social contract was stronger than it had ever been. Trust was intact, and emotional energy was available to help the organization confront its new business environment. The organization possessed the flexibility it needed to respond to the change, and approached change in a way that preserved flexibility for making future changes.

In another organization, a similar set of economic circumstances necessitated the closure of 14 manufacturing plants in a division with a total of 44 plants. In the past, closures had been announced on the Friday of the last week of the plant's operation, out of fear that employees would sabotage operations if they were aware of the decision. This time, led by an enlightened human resources manager, the closures were announced as much as *three years* in advance; and despite many dire predictions from corporate headquarters about worker unrest and lowered productivity, the productivity in each of the plants actually *increased*! People reported that they wanted to leave with dignity and pride, that they were sorry their careers with the organization had been cut short, but that they were pleased that the organization trusted them enough to alert them to the changes ahead and allowed them to plan what to do once the change took place. When we approach change more flexibly, we find that people are able to be more flexible as well.

When the rules aren't followed, things don't go so smoothly. Recently, I was invited to visit the research division of one of this country's largest companies to discuss the need to revamp the design of the organization to enhance product-development processes. In the morning, I had a pleasant chat with the young man assigned to be my liaison and his boss, the director of organizational effectiveness. Together, they provided me with a historical background of the division and laid out their hopes for the day.

Unfortunately, their hopes were far out in front of the readiness of top management for change. The internal change agents had imagined that a visit by an external expert would prod top management into action. The change agents knew that the design of the organization was interfering with its effectiveness and that redesigning it was the right thing to do; but they also knew that redesign would disturb empires, power bases, job descriptions, and much more that was deeply entrenched. Yes, the managers agreed, dramatically improved levels of performance were absolutely essential. Yes, they recognized the wisdom of what was being said; but this year's change budget was already committed to diversity training. Maybe next year. Flexible management? Hardly.

There's nothing wrong with doing diversity training. But it wasn't going to solve the problems the organization was facing in the market. And doing one program at a time, instead of changing many things at once, usually produces awareness but not change, because too many aspects of the system force behavior back into old patterns. Diversity training is necessary but not sufficient. Managers in the division would need to do much more, eventually; but for the moment, a single program occupied their entire attention.

When the world is changing quickly and in many ways simultaneously, responding with one program at a time won't make a difference. Complex changes require complex responses, which in turn require a great deal of organizational flexibility. Organizations that respond to complex changes with single programs aren't committed to change; they may *wish* for change, but they are *committed* to maintaining appearances; to the old adage "doing something is better than doing nothing," and, mostly, to the status quo. They may not want the status quo, but they don't know what else to do. And when they are told what else to do, they find reasons not to listen, at least for now. Flexibility begins with the courage to face reality.

An alternative scenario calls for managers to engage in learning, using what they discover from sensing the changes in the world around them to constantly alter the way the organization does business. Because learning and change are considered important, managers take steps to keep the organization flexible so that it can adjust to new conditions with minimal trauma, cost, and lost commitment to the future. Flexibility becomes the source of competitive advantage, as the company's products, services, and ways of doing business evolve more quickly than the competitions'. The organization becomes an industry leader and remains in a leadership position by virtue of its ability to adapt. Examples? Merck, 3M, Procter & Gamble.

What does this kind of management look like close up? After visiting the company doing diversity training on Monday, I spent the next three days of the same week in Springfield, Massachusetts with a group that was finishing up a 3-week effort to redesign their production unit. Some members of the group had 39 years of experience in head-banging with management. The union was skeptical of the redesign process. So were the people it represented. But this was something new for them: union and management, including representatives from upper management and the union leadership, meeting to figure things out. Not one side at a time, but both sides in cooperation. *For three whole weeks.* Initially, a lot of behaviors on both sides slowed down the redesign process and limited its creativity. We would remind people of the need to be globally competitive (this unit had almost closed twice already) and to think at least five years into the future. Thirty-nine years of history is a lot to overcome in three weeks. Changes in attitudes came slowly, incrementally, amidst heated discussions. My colleagues and I were concerned but realized that real change involves this kind of hard work. At first, it appeared that no progress was being made at all; certainly not the kind of progress likely to produce changes that could wind up as an example in Tom Peters' next book. Just an old, hardened, traditional-thinking dinosaur of an organization plodding along for a few more paces, trying to deny that its ice age had come. But beneath the surface, things were changing. People were raising tough questions and listening to the answers, some of which they would rather not hear. Both sides were giving it their full effort, leveling with one another, telling it like it is. By Thursday of the third week, the group began to coalesce; people who had not been sitting together now huddled around one table, planning what to do next to move things forward. Time was running out and they knew it. They had said what needed to be said about the past and were ready to work together to create the future. The group designed an organization that would be flexible and responsive to the kinds of changes that had knocked it off balance before. Because they were involved throughout the process, the leadership of the union and the company approved the recommended changes made by the members of the unit *that same day*. Implementation of systemic changes began the next day. While still facing a tough market, the unit is geared for the future, and people are committed to working together to make the best of the opportunity they have been given. They also learned a lesson in what it takes to create flexibility. It's more than a program.

Programs tell people that they need to change. But we shouldn't confuse telling people they should change with actual change. Actual change takes real participation, not just listening. It takes real emotion and understanding and commitment, not euphoric hopes that things will be better. Change is more than training, more than slogans, more than creating a design team, more than appointing a reengineering czar or a quality council. It's a cognitive *and* emotional shift, at the core of our individual and organizational being. It's a new way of looking at the world, a new way of living. We haven't understood this very well in the past. Without understanding what change really takes, we go on doing what we know how to do, hoping that this time it will be different; knowing that soon, it will *have* to be different. We were pretty sure total quality was *it*; the focus on the bottom line, measurable results, and the customer made a lot of sense. But total quality *programs* weren't enough. So now we're hoping that reengineering is *it*; but unless we change the way we are going about it, I'm afraid reengineering will disappoint people as well.

What we know is that the best change processes are those that people invent for themselves. There's a big difference between self-initiated change and change that comes at people from left field. We should begin to design change methods that reflect what we now know about the process of change. Our current approach to change typically combines teaching with coercion, even though we call it *participative* change. Self-initiated change based on authentic participation is something else entirely. It is change from within. That's why programs don't work. They are change from without; somebody else's idea of how change should happen, how change should feel. Often the someone isn't even a member of the organization; it's an author or consultant who knows nothing of the lives and experiences of the people involved. Yet, people are asked to follow the advice of the guru, in a blind and cultish way. Just do the program, and don't ask questions. *We should never assume that just because we have completed a program , we have produced change.* Programs don't increase flexibility. Programs don't help people learn how to learn; learn how to respond more appropriately the next time, how to create their own programs for change that are better suited to their needs.

* * *

I talked recently to a manager who said, "The older I get, the more cynical I become about organizational change. I just don't think we can expect to see results unless we change systems as well as trying to change behaviors."

I don't think there's anything cynical about his view. What he said makes sense. We can ask people to change, but when we fail to redesign the structures and systems around them, a lot of old behavior gets reinforced and new behaviors go unrewarded. Pay systems, leadership styles, job boundaries, technology, policies;

if these aren't also changed, they merely serve to pull people back to where they were before the change process started. What the manager was lamenting was that so few change processes ever get around to changing these things. The union is too skeptical to allow the contract to be rewritten. Managers are afraid they will run into all kinds of problems if they relax the policies. People are afraid they won't be treated fairly if the old rules aren't followed. When such fears dominate a change effort, behavioral change alone just won't produce lasting bottom-line results. We can train people in facilitation skills until we are blue in the face. Or give more stirring speeches. Or redesign the process one more time. But in most cases what we really need to do is to change everything at the same time, as if we were designing the organization from scratch. It's hard to sell, but it's the only way it really works.

* * *

Early in my career, I had the opportunity to work with an organization that undertook two change efforts simultaneously at the same location. In one case, a product failure led to the introduction of a new product, new technology, and a chance to try out a new organizational design based on sociotechnical systems principles. It was like starting from scratch, except that the existing labor force was used, and the union's cooperation in permitting experimentation was crucial. In the second case, there was no new product, no new technology. The change effort consisted of administering an attitude survey, following which discussions were held with every group of employees to determine how the operation could be improved. The same union represented both groups, and the same top management was responsible for the overall operation of both units.

Despite the commonalities of the union, management, and labor force, the results of the two change efforts were dramatically different. In the first case, productivity soared by more than 30 percent, quality was uniformly high, and management and the union agreed that satisfaction, commitment and cooperation had never been better. In the second unit, attitudes and cooperation improved as well; but productivity, costs, and quality remained the same. What was the difference?

In the first unit, there was agreement that new ways of working should be explored. Employees were given training to allow them to perform a broad range of technical tasks, and teams were formed with responsibility for controlling interdependent production processes, not just independent pieces of equipment. The supervision of the unit, its pay system, and even its technical layout were designed to foster teamwork and self-direction. In the second unit jobs, pay systems, supervision, and the technology remained the same. People *talked* about improving the performance of the unit, but they didn't *do* anything to make it happen. Control of the overall process remained with the first-line supervisors. People *wanted* to do a better job but ultimately found that there was little they could do within the design of the organization to change things. Responsibility for the performance of the unit remained with management, and shortly afterwards the hard feelings that had existed between management and labor prior to the intervention reemerged. The first organization was truly flexible; the second wasn't.

Making cosmetic changes within an existing system won't produce dramatic improvements in performance. "Touchy-feely" interventions that are intended to make people feel good are like a narcotic. They make people feel better, but only for a short time. Then, when the drug wears off, they feel worse.

If we are to avoid overly simplistic programs, we must help people develop other processes that produce the flexibility our organizations need. We can't just manufacture emotion and hope that it leads to improved organizational performance; the events that must be set in motion are too complex and interrelated to hope for a miracle like that. It's true that people know much more about what needs to be changed than we sometimes give them credit for knowing; but to simply fan the flames of enthusiasm and then stand back waiting for results is folly. Changes in organizational flexibility require emotional change, but they require much more. Increasing flexibility requires an elaborate orchestration of factors, some human and some not, which ultimately coalesce into a heightened capacity of the system to respond to change. The system needs to be understood and human relationships and behaviors transformed. The nature of work must change as well as the tools used to perform it. So must our managerial practices, organizational systems, and even the way we think.

Organizational change is not a simple process, and it should never be treated as such, despite our familiarity with it. A rational, logical cookbook approach devoid of emotion won't do the job, and a whole troop of cheerleaders urging people on won't either. Change affects people in all kinds of ways, some of them good, some of them bad, all of them irreversible. It makes sense to think that people will be curious about what is happening to them, interested in understanding what is going on and why, and perhaps concerned about what it will do to their lives. It makes no sense to think that change is mechanical, simple, and without impact on people, and that it can therefore be undertaken without anyone even noticing that it is happening. Change can be forced on people, and life will go on; but it will go on differently, and people will feel *done to*, and they will remember. And the next time it won't be the same; once you have trampled over people, the damage is done, innocence is lost, trust is shattered. The social contract is forever changed, with suspicion a constant fuel for the examination of its fairness. Emotional investment, faith in the future, the willingness to risk in the hope of a better future are all weakened by change attempts that are poorly conceived and managed, as was demonstrated by the research on downsizing. The ironic truth is that the faster and more thoughtlessly we leap at change, the more careless we are in regard for its side effects, the less flexible we become.

Let's stop doing what's simple, cookbook, and cheap; let's recognize that there is a lot at stake here, and that winning the competition is going to take some real effort and require challenging some vested interests and sacred cows. Let's begin to approach change like we mean it, investing enough in the process to do it well, and not letting go until we achieve real bottom line results. Let's stop confusing making people *feel* good with real change. Feeling good and developing effective relationships are important to people and essential to organizations, but making people feel good isn't the place to begin an organizational change process, and it certainly isn't the place to end one.

Organizational change is about *changing organizational perfor-mance*. The clearer the tie between what we are doing and results, the more energy, commitment, and excitement we will generate during the change process. If the tie to results is fuzzy, what we are up to will eventually meet with resistance, apathy, or support from the lunatic fringe—none of which we need. Instead, we should *start and end every change effort with performance improve-ment as the goal*. And then change everything that needs to be changed to make it happen. That's what flexibility is about.

* * *

The unfolding interplay among all these factors makes the process of change mysterious if not miraculous, as dynamic an achievement as any mankind could hope to accomplish. The process is beautiful to behold, enchanting in its shifts between subtlety and storminess, no more predictable in its course than the cutting of a river through granite. With its origins in our spirit and our primal acquaintance with it, change in human systems remains as thrilling to experience as the wind of a thun-derstorm sweeping across an open lake. Slightly apprehensive, forever expectant, we approach change in organizations with our heads and our hearts fully engaged, straining toward the goal like a horse pulling a heavy carriage. We will succeed; we will make the organization better; we will arrive at the moment of fulfillment in which we can look back upon our work and rest, at least momentarily, with pride. *Real* change means changing *everything*; not just hoping that better feelings will lead to miracles. When we really change things, we are also changed.

* * *

I laid out the mechanics of systems change in *Designing Effec-tive Organizations*.[2] Here, I want to go beyond the basics in order to address the factors that distinguish successful from less suc-cessful change efforts and to talk about novel applications and advances in the state of the art.

In Chapter 2, I address the trajectory of change: where all this change is coming from, and why I think we have to give our organizations more flexibility to respond to it. I'll also discuss what all this means in terms of a new approach to change orga-nizations.

Chapter 3 details the importance of preparing people to change. In our haste to make life better for people, we sometimes forget to ask them what *they* want, and what help they need to get it. Helping people become active participants in their own change process is another essential element in achieving success. Making citizens out of people who have lived in hierarchical organizations their entire lives is not simple, but this chapter will help demonstrate what needs to happen and how to get it done.

Chapter 4 is about making technology more flexible. I go beyond just talking about flexible manufacturing to address broader issues concerning the advancement of technology, such as how organizations, designed to support one technology, become barriers to adopting another. I'll also talk about knowledge technology, since inflexibility in our thinking is just as dangerous as inflexibility in the way we create products and services.

Chapter 5 is entitled "Flexible Work" because it's time that we recognized that the basic nature of work is changing in fundamental and inalterable ways. The era of mindless, unchanging, individualized, highly repetitive work has already given way to new ways of working that involve more change, more thoughtfulness, and more collaboration for most people in organizations. Our methods for analyzing work and our goals in organizational design should change as well.

Chapter 6 addresses flexible thinking in more depth. I'm convinced that there are tremendous gains to be made here by all organizations, not just those that are devoted to the advancement of knowledge, like R&D organizations. It seems that there is more than a bit of thinking involved in management and marketing and manufacturing, too. I introduce the *polynoetic* organization, which I promise is the only new jargon I'll force upon you in this book. I just don't know any way to talk about an organization that is entirely different from anything we know without calling it something new.

Chapter 7 addresses the question, "What happens to the leaders?" In this age of collapsing hierarchies and broadening spans of control, are leaders becoming extinct? Do we really need leaders if we're serious about self-management? I hope some of my answers surprise you.

Chapter 8 deals with flexible organizing and introduces a powerful new concept to replace the traditional organizational chart. Organizational designs based on the new physics, in this case fractals, may provide the flexibility our era demands. There are some really exciting new ideas here, which I think you will find provocative.

Chapter 9 reviews the essential elements in achieving success in organizational change. I talk about the concept of *changing everything all at once,* by which I mean approaching the change process in a systemic fashion rather than through the program-of-the-month method. To change everything all at once we need to approach change more open-mindedly than we have in the past and involve more people in it more completely.

Chapter 10 puts change in a personal perspective. Too often, we try to manage change through a series of mechanical exercises, straight out of the consultant's cookbook. We forget that change is ultimately a human experience and that managing change requires an understanding of human emotions. There can be no flexibility without consideration of the feelings that change induces in all of us.

* * *

The approach to change described in this book is still evolving, just as management itself is evolving. It is evolving toward greater awareness of what change really requires and how to meet those requirements. Among the requirements are better education and preparation to allow people to be more fully involved in helping the organization to change; more understanding of the relationship between the core work of the organization and the support required to maintain and improve it; more contact and skill in dealing with the external environment; more awareness of the multitude of factors that must change if organizational change is to occur and persist; and more attention to the changing palette of work itself, which continues toward complexity and variety and away from simplicity and routine. The ideas expressed here are intended to be flexible, to change as the need for change in organizations becomes apparent. There can be no cookbook solutions nor one-size-fits-all recommendations if we believe that change really matters. Some of these evolutionary directions require reinventing our methods; others require that we reinvent our thinking. The shift from static to dynamic management is fundamental and important. I hope that, in addition to being the right thing to do, it opens up possibilities for people and organizations that make it exciting and worthwhile. In the chapters to follow, I address the changes in methods and thinking that are required to help our organizations become truly flexible and responsive to change.

The Trajectory
of Change
Designing Flexible Organizations

Personally, I'm sick of change. It seems that there has been altogether too much of it lately, and altogether too many people writing about how much of it there is. In the newspapers, on television, at work, at home; we try tuning out, but we can't hide for long. Even here in a distant corner of Maine as I write this book I catch glimpses of the news, and at the local eatery I hear people in thick plaid jackets and hunting caps talking about the latest events. All too frequently, the fax rings and whirrs, delivering a little bit of news via its infinite network of connecting wires right into my office, like an unwelcome but undeniable guest. These messages of change would have gotten through eventually; they just reach me faster now. And as much as I would like to escape them, I can't. Change is real.

Seemingly, just when we get things the way we want them, we receive news that things have changed. And *we* have to change. Running to keep in place, running faster than the competition to stay ahead. Out-inventing, out-investing, out-maneuvering the other guy, the other organization, the other country. We set off chain reactions that we can't even imagine, but that are real and that come around to kick us when we least expect it. Dealing with change is not a one-time event for our generation; it has become our way of life.

Some of the changes we experience are slow and gradual, almost imperceptible as we go about our daily routines. Others are lightning fast, shocking, upending. Slow change is like a nagging toothache; it keeps reminding you that it's there, and you keep wishing and hoping it will just go away. It doesn't. Fast change is brutal but there's no denying it. In a crashing split second of realization, you know it's hit you, and that you must respond. Set everything else aside until you have a chance to deal with it because, like a screaming child, it won't be ignored.

Organizations will need to deal with both kinds of change. And because responding to change must be an *organizational* act, not just an individual one, the challenges ahead are great. Change is hard enough to handle on our own; organizational change is many times more difficult to manage. Some organizations are better at managing change than others; the good ones expect change to happen and are proactive in preparing themselves to respond. The really good ones provoke change, knowing that they can gain ground over their slow-footed competitors who struggle with change.

In fact, many of the changes we face are self-initiated. We are a social species; we have instincts that cause us to seek one another out, get organized, and try to do things that we can't do by ourselves. Our feats of organizing are legendary, at least to us: The Great Wall of China, the beauty of a ballet, our telecommunications system. We are amazed at what we can do and always surprised by what we think of next. We keep on thinking, exciting each other with our ideas, and then finding ways to do the impossible. We can fly, explore space, breathe underwater, and sprinkle fertilizer on our lawn that kills dandelions, too.

With all that we have done, you would think we would be smarter about organizational change; that we would learn to control change so that more of what happened around us is expected and positive. But we don't seem to have our hands on the tiller; we're constantly surprised at our destination and unable to discover who has been setting the course. Organizational change can be frustrating and frightening; many people would prefer to avoid it altogether. I suspect that this is a human feeling, one that comes with the territory.

Part of the problem with organizational change is simply that there are so many of us. Each of us wants a good life, and we work as hard as we can to create the life we want. We are called social animals, but that doesn't mean we are sociable. We think independently, band together with people we like, rush forward with our plans, and worry about the fallout on others later, if at all. When we *experience* the fallout, we react—and not always in a friendly or understanding manner. We stake out our turf and defend it, and in so doing we overlook the myriad benefits of cooperation as we resort to actions based on our instinctual kill-or-be-killed mentality. We atone on Sunday, and then go out and do it all over again on Monday. Survival of the fittest, domination of the weak by the strong. We don't want to acknowledge our fundamental character, our basic instincts, our deepest fears; but there they are, all over the front page, where it's hard to ignore them.

Buried in the middle of the daily paper are bits of evidence that we can rise above our animal instincts; that we can work together cooperatively to improve our communities, assist each other, and invent medicines to prolong life. We can be a wonderful species, at least at times. When we are working together on changes that we hope will make things better, we aren't as frightened or frustrated as we are by change that is out of our control. It's not that we hate all change; we just don't like to be threatened.

Our desire to avoid pain causes us to learn from our experience, and our learning comes at a high price. So, naturally, we want to use our learning when opportunities arise. When we come together to do something with others, we share our experience. Sometimes our experience is valued, and sometimes it isn't. We would like others to see things our way, but they don't always. They have their own experience, their own learnings. Each of us is trying to avoid an unpleasant experience by using what we have learned from managing earlier change. We resist change not because we are against change in general, but because the change being suggested threatens us in a way we have learned to defend ourselves against. It's all very rational, even though we often regard resistance to change as ungrounded. In an organization, we must deal with everybody's needs and everyone's past experiences with change. It's likely that any change will be perceived as a threat by somebody; and that the resistance they demonstrate will cause concern in others who may not have been concerned before. Organizational change is a social phenomenon. If organizational leaders become impatient with the resistance they encounter, and the change that must be made is important, it is likely that they will use the authority of their positions to dictate change. Change by fiat is the most feared type of change and causes the greatest distress among the troops. This type of change can be successful, but too much of it may incite revolution. There is only so much threat that people can endure. More successful change efforts begin with education and patience and provide opportunities for people to buy into the idea and even shape how the change will affect them. This is not a new discovery.

All of this has been happening since the beginning of recorded history. The saga of human change contains a story that is still played out today. The etchings of this story on the composure of man are as evident in history as the effects of wind and water and erosion are on rocks. Human progress consists of individual and organizational efforts to cope with change. Many of the efforts are crude and brutish, involving the use of force to effect change in others. History books are full of it. Absolute rulers with absolute power, weakened in their excesses, overthrown by those who were smarter, craftier, hungrier. The record is there to see: much of it is a record of conquerors and vanquished, of victors and victims.

But there are other stories, as well. Stories of bold adventurers and nation-builders, of people who devoted their lives to helping others prosper in the face of change. Change doesn't have to be managed in crude, brutish ways; we decide how we will respond to or, better yet, *anticipate* change. We can be crude and brutish about it if we wish to be; but we don't have to be. The choices we make determine how we and others experience change. We can try to ignore change altogether, only to have its effects surprise and dismay us. We can respond to threatened change with our prehistoric instincts and create battles where battles need not have been fought. Or, we can think our way through changes together, and figure out how to make happen what we want to happen, collectively. The third approach is representative of human society at its highest level of development, and what I believe we should aspire to in organizations as well. It may be that we have no other choice.

The trajectory of change is taking us toward an age in which we must rise above our base instincts in order to deal effectively with the types of changes we are facing. We can't afford to be simple or backward in our thinking about change and our methods of responding to it. As change has accelerated and become more complex, our old ways of managing it have become less effective. We issue orders and edicts, and joust at change with the force of all our human and material resources; but we discover that the changes are faster and more complex than we are able to control, and that our motivation to continue the fight is weakened by so many failed charges at the enemy. Just as we pour our resources into dealing with one problem, another pops up, equally important and potentially devastating. And when we need the help and commitment of others the most, we find that they are alienated or burned out by the way we handled the past 10 efforts to change. In the future, we cannot afford to deal with change in these reactive ways. We need to develop new ways of preparing people and organizations to cope with the fast and furious changes we are currently experiencing and that are yet to come.

THE PAST TWO DECADES

The past two decades have been full of change for all of us. Some would argue that the rate of change we are experiencing is greater than in earlier eras, but since we weren't around then, it's difficult to say. What we can say is that the following changes have transformed our lives and our organizations, irreversibly.

Globalization

Think of the changes that have occurred in just the past two decades, first at a global level and then a bit closer to home. It was only two decades ago that an oil embargo changed the way we drive and live, as well as the fortunes of U.S. automakers and all of the companies that supplied them with parts and services. Over the past two decades, we watched Japan's economic power grow, through advances in its auto, electronics, and consumer goods industries. We witnessed the emergence of other Asian countries as major trading partners: Singapore, Korea, China. Much later, we would experience the economic and political collapse of the Soviet Union at almost the same time as new strides in cooperation were being taken in Europe and North America.

The globalization of trade has had impacts on our economy that are all too evident and familiar. Even so, not everyone has been affected directly, and, until they are, some will have a hard time understanding what all the fuss is about. A plant manager I know had difficulty getting his people to understand the need for organizational change and productivity improvement. His was the flagship plant in his corporation, certain to be the last affected by hard economic times. And his people knew it. When he held communication sessions in the cafeteria to warn people of what was coming and the need to be out in front of the changes, the response from almost everyone was an unenthusiastic yawn. Using his Yankee ingenuity, he traveled around his northeastern town taking pictures of all the textile mills and other plants that were closed, their windows broken and their parking lots covered with weeds. He had these pictures projected onto the screen behind him when he held his next communication session. He asked people to think about the people they knew who had worked in those plants and to recall how complacent they had been about their jobs and how certain that the mills would be there forever. He asked them to think about what those people were doing now, where they were working, the quality of their lives. And finally, he declared, with real tears in his eyes, that he wanted to provide a chance for anyone who so desired to retire from his plant rather than being thrown out on the street as those others had been. His message got through. They started planning how to create the future they wanted instead of just waiting for their own gates to close.

Most people are feeling the effects of global competition on our economy. Those organizations that aren't threatened with closure or significant downsizing are fighting harder for customers who demand much more and have less to spend. Most of us are learning how to get by with less; the current generation is said to be the first since the Depression that can expect to have a lower standard of living than the one before. And most of us are being asked to do more at work, for little or no extra pay. Having a good job is more important than it was a few years ago, when it seemed that good jobs were plentiful and benefits were guaranteed for life. Today, the heat is on to make every job and every dollar count. This translates into pressures for effectiveness and efficiency, for creative redesign, for better service, for continuous improvement, for flexibility. And for speed.

Time

Time has become a more important competitive lever than ever before in our history. Perhaps it is because the speed of life has become so fast, so many things instantaneous, that the desire for speed has carried over into organizations. Everyone seems to be in a hurry these days. We have fast food, express mail, fax machines, instant coffee. All around us, the pace of life seems to be speeding up; it's almost as if we are worried that if we waste a second, we are wasting our entire lives. We can't imagine living the way our grandparents did: walking to school, doing dishes by hand, baking our own bread, handcrafting our own furniture. We have come to value speed for speed's sake; and we have come to live our lives as if speed is more important than the quality of our experiences. We idolize people who are the fastest at racing and running and swimming and flying; we buy time-saving devices for our homes; we read newspapers that provide short, punchy descriptions of what is going on in our world. We want instant gratification and minimum downtime. We hate being inefficient, waiting, or having to follow time-consuming instructions. We speed on the highways, write notes instead of letters to our relatives, and fly instead of drive. We are the fastest generation ever to inhabit the earth.

So it makes sense that we would carry our passion for speed into our organizations. That we would want our organizations to do their work quickly, and that everything that we do concerning our organizations be as fast as possible. After all, as the old adage says, time is money.

To learn to compete on the basis of speed will force us to change some old habits: to quit demanding 17 signatures on every work order; to stop processing five copies of every invoice; to not allow ourselves to keep inventories of partially finished work stacked up on different priority lists in each department. We will see more streamlining, more empowerment, and more reengineering.

Technology

Technologically, we have advanced significantly in the past two decades in computers and medicine, and to a lesser but still remarkable degree in chemicals and telecommunications. The list of items found in many homes today that were not available 20 years ago would include microwave ovens, fax machines, personal computers, VCRs, personal copiers, and cordless phones.

The impact of technology on our lives is a frequent topic of cocktail party debate. Is it too great, or is technology our only hope for survival? Should we condone genetic engineering, nuclear fusion, the space station? Or should we try to stop the juggernaut of technological progress, forcing our scientists to heel to a jury of their peers? How could a jury of their peers ever begin to understand what they were talking about? How can we ever hope to control science if we can't even learn how to program our VCRs?

We could carry on the cocktail debate, but other than amusing ourselves, it wouldn't do much good. Technology will continue to advance. If not here, elsewhere; and there is no sign that we are willing to forfeit leadership in technological development to anyone else, even for a moment. We take our technology seriously, almost as a symbol of our nation's strength and an indicator of its future well-being. Even though we trail other countries, most notably Japan, in the number of patents we are filing, we continue to believe that technological dominance is our underlying source of competitive strength, our trump card in the increasingly unfriendly international card game of business. Only the future will tell us if we are right.

As technology develops, it often enters the business arena first, where its advantages help shave costs when applied on a large scale. Computers, copying machines, facsimiles, and cellular telephones all were aimed at business first and later found their way into the consumer market. When these technical advances enter our organizations, they change things. They change what is possible; and, when people begin to understand the new possibilities technology provides, people begin to change their behavior. Work is reconfigured to fit the new technologies, and as work changes, so do roles and responsibilities; and with changes in roles and responsibilities come changes in status and power. Eventually, this power is used to change things even more; until, before long, people are talking about the good old days and wondering how things got to be so different.

Today, the talk is about virtual organizations and global alliances, made possible by the wonders of telecomputing and telecommunications. We can be anywhere in the world in less than a second, virtually. To be there and to make a difference still takes a lot longer, since relationships are involved, and they haven't been automated—yet. But it's nice to think about being able to be anywhere we would like to be in the wink of an eye; even if we can't actually sip the espresso in a Paris cafe.

Technology is also speeding up the pace of product development; not only is new technology finding its way into products at a faster rate than ever before; technology is changing the way we develop products so that we can do it all faster. The arrival of CAD CAM systems, tied to flexible manufacturing equipment and automated material handling systems, means we can fly in a new Boeing aircraft in three years instead of 10. Or find that our new computer is obsolete by the time we get it home.

Technology won't allow most of our organizations to stay still for long, either in the products they make or the way they do business. Customers and competitors will see to that. The race for technological leadership will continue, and even intensify, if that's possible. As the old song goes, "We ain't seen nothin' yet."

It used to be that we could manage the introduction of new technology by simply installing it and then training people in how to use it. But technology is becoming so complex, and the amount of technology we need to introduce becoming so great, that we can't keep up with it all anymore. We learned in the '70s that we couldn't just install computer systems without taking into account the impact on the human system; too many systems were sold with promises of huge returns on investment that were never realized because people never fully understood how to make the systems work. We still have difficulty in figuring out how to keep up with technical change, even when people who will be using the technology are involved in planning its introduction. Maybe they will invent technology that helps us keep up with technology; until then, we will need to spend more time and money to keep ourselves and our products current. I don't know where the time will come from; I just know that we'll need it. Technology will continue to demand greater flexibility on the part of the workforce, product designers, customers, and, of course, managers. No one is immune, and the epidemic is spreading, even to the world around us.

The Environment

As a society, we have grown conscious of the natural environment and have begun to take actions to preserve its integrity for future generations. It was less than 100 years ago that people such as John Muir began to point out that mankind could actually create irreversible changes in the state of the planetary ecosystem. Before then, we acted as pawns of nature, part of a larger play of evolution in which we had only bit parts. When we awoke to the fact that *we* were the invisible hand guiding the destiny of the planet, it was a shocking realization. What were we mere mortals doing driving the bus? What did we know about running this whole, big, complex planet? We felt as if we were being asked to assume direct control of our autonomic nervous system; our hearts had been beating just fine, and we didn't want to have to think about it. But we do have to think about it, and we still haven't begun to figure it out. The state of our planet, and the species and peoples who inhabit it, will continue to be a driving force for change in the way we design, market, and dispose of our products. Volvo will recycle your car for you; the Body Shop will make you feel good about your soap; and many companies are touting "all natural" ingredients in their prepared foods. (What was in there before?)

Business is being held accountable for everything, by everybody. Take care of the planet; provide product liability insurance; support the community schools; train our workers who can't read. In an increasingly litigious society, ignoring accountability has become more expensive; and, with "60 Minutes" on your tail, ignorance, even if affordable, simply isn't good for business anymore. The only choice is to become more agile, more responsive; to be better prepared with a positive offense rather than a stodgy defense.

Diversity

The challenge isn't just an external one. Internally, managing diversity has gone from requiring only lip service to real action. Diversity management used to mean EEO; and it used to be mostly about women and blacks. Now, diversity has widened our spectrum of concern to all people who wish to be known as different in some way, even as individuals. The Americans with Disabilities Act is the latest in the list of rulings that tell us that differences cannot be dismissed or overlooked. Differences are real, and when people feel that differences are causing unfair treatment, it's a foul.

Managers can't treat everyone the same anymore; the new law says that being fair isn't fair. People who are different need to be treated differently, if that's what it takes to make them equal. The logic isn't easy to follow, but the court rulings make it necessary. We need to see employees as individuals, and pay attention to the individual's welfare for as long as each is in our employ. Some organizations are giving up, turning to contract labor where they can, believing that the liability of having a person on the payroll is getting to be greater than the benefit that comes from years of uninterrupted service. But although we may run, we can't hide.

The question of diversity is a global issue, as people from less developed nations raise more loudly legitimate questions concerning the actions of the more developed nations of the world. Free trade agreements, economic communities, and joint ventures will continue to thrust diversity issues into the business press. We will need to learn to live with diversity, and even to embrace it. We cannot return to a world where our boundaries provided us a false sense of identity, an image of ourselves as a single-minded people. We are who we are; we are who we *all* are. While bumper stickers proclaim, "Love it or leave it!", there's no place to go. The world is a diverse place, and becoming more so every day. Doing business in the next few decades will require a degree of cultural flexibility we have never known; the winners, as always, will be those who learn the fastest.

Quality

Then there's the consumer's demand for quality. Enough has been written about quality in the last few years to fill a small library. I don't need to waste more trees repeating what we all know: Concern about quality in our products and services is high and growing, and it's not going away. Customer expectations have been transformed forever. A few years ago, organizations could decide whether or not to have a quality program. For many, it's no longer optional. ISO 9000, the new international quality standards, will make doing international business impossible without attention to quality. Local consumers will ask, if it's good enough for the world, why shouldn't it be good enough for me? Global standards will become local standards, and the stakes will continue to rise. In an era where costs must constantly be cut just to continue playing the game, we also have to find ways to make things a lot better and to provide still more improved service to customers, before and after their purchase. It won't be easy, and we'll need to learn to be flexible to get the job done.

Downsizing

Organizationally, the most noticeable trend during the past two decades has been one of retrenchment and concurrent downsizing. While there are notable exceptions to the rule among some older companies, and signs of hope in newcomers such as

Microsoft and Ben & Jerry's, the general experience of the past 20 years has been one of adjustment to heightened international competition. A round of expansion through diversification was followed by the selling off of noncore businesses, and then by joint ventures and alliances with former adversaries. Quite recently, cuts in defense spending have sent contractors scrambling for ways to convert guns to butter, in a market where opportunities seem limited in the face of stumbles by steel, autos, airlines, and even excellent companies such as Boeing and IBM. The long-term impact of downsizing is yet to be determined; but, in the short run, one impact is that organizations have to do more with less, utilizing each resource and every person as fully as possible.

Participation

We once viewed managing change as a managerial responsibility; we assumed that employees had nothing to offer in the way of ideas or strategies for coping with changes that they knew very little about. Over the past two decades, managers have pushed for competitive advantage through a parade of participative programs spawned by the success of Japanese companies: quality circles, total quality, just-in-time inventory, Kaizen. Other programs also became prominent: work redesign, sociotechnical systems, gainsharing, flextime. Today we see the value of involving people in change to gain both their ideas and commitment. When organizations operate with fewer people, as many are today, it is imperative that each person perform effectively and flexibly. Increasing participation has been called for by almost every management guru since the 1950s; but the movement toward total quality in the 1980s solidified our belief that employees really can make a valuable contribution with their heads, not just their hands. It's no longer enough just to show up and do one's job; we expect employees to do their jobs and figure out how to do them better, too. Businesses are increasing training budgets and setting aside time for learning both inside and outside of the organization. People work on task forces, quality action teams, committees, and design teams. It all adds up to greater participation, in things that matter more and more to the success of the enterprise.

In the future, we will go beyond participation within prescribed limits to more equal influence over issues that affect the well-being of the organization and everyone it employs. We will move beyond participation as a *program* toward participation as a *method* of managing continuous change.

THE FUTURE

Now think of the changes likely to affect us and our organizations over the next 20 years. Twenty years is not too long a span of time for executives to consider, even though most will hold their positions as CEOs for considerably less time than that. Following are 10 trends based on my reading of various futurists that will have dramatic impacts on organizations over the next two decades.

The Liberalization of Trade

As barriers to economic cooperation continue to fall, we will become increasingly involved in efforts to capture shares of important global markets. This will require that we rethink who our customers are, what they want from us, and who we are as an organization. In order to serve a wider variety of global customers more effectively, we must allow for greater decentralization of authority over product, marketing, and pricing decisions. Eventually, it may be difficult to find a common identity in the products, marketing, and managerial practices of different segments of the same multinational organization. National borders will blur as consumer-preference clusters occupy greater attention. As trade barriers fall, organizations will need to become more flexible in how they recruit, train, manage, and deploy people. Organizational structures will become more complex and alliances more common, necessitating managerial strategies that are nonhierarchical in character.

The Aging and Shifting of the Population

As the U.S. population ages, and the population of the developing countries continues to rise in comparison with that of developed countries, the center of wealth will continue to shift to foreign markets. The role of the United States will become less and less that of providing goods, and more and more that of an agent for organizing trade and advancing technology. Employment in nonskilled jobs, other than the service sector, will shrink as manufacturing moves offshore and more highly skilled employees are in greater demand. Organizations in the United States will not grow rapidly, but they will go through tremendous changes in the work they perform and the people needed to perform that work.

Technological Leaps

The current barriers to communication and transportation will be removed so that travel and shipment of goods can be accomplished more cheaply and quickly. Geographical distance will no longer be a significant factor in determining market accessibility or influencing organizational design. Improvements in medicine will offer significant advancements in the quality of life, although living longer will necessitate further reforms to the social-security and health-care systems. Advances in the material sciences will provide us with alternatives to nonrenewable natural products and simplify manufacturing of many goods. Energy production will shift more toward nonpolluting, renewable sources. Manufacturing will continue to become less labor intensive and more fully integrated with customer systems that enable faster design-through-delivery of products. Technological advances in every field will necessitate the constant reeducation of the workforce at all levels. Media vigilance will continue to force reexamination and readjustment of social patterns and international issues.

New Standards

The globalization of trade will bring with it new rules and standards for everything from product quality to corporate legal conduct. Many of the issues we currently struggle with, such as product liability, the constraint of trade, and corporate social responsibility will become global issues. Eventually, such issues may be resolved in a more powerful world business governance organization springing forth from combined efforts of large multinational firms and the United Nations. New standards will necessitate changes in organizational processes and designs to compete successfully in the global marketplace.

Environmental Recovery

The emphasis on the environment will shift from mere protection of the environment to recovery of what has deteriorated. Sustainable development will become the rule for business expansion, and global attention will be given to the future of the oceans and other common resources. Organizations that shift from polluting to recovery technologies will gain significant competitive advantage.

Ownership and Equality

Employees will respond to invitations to become more involved in making their organizations successful by taking ownership positions; their involvement and understanding will in turn lead to more equal roles with managers. The continued downsizing of middle management and increase in self-direction will shift the boundary between employees and managers from the first level to the top level of the organization. As employees express interest in taking a more active part in setting organizational strategy and determining organizational design, participation will shift from occasional involvement in insignificant issues to regular involvement in critical organizational issues.

Work Patterns

Flexibility in work locations and assignments will continue to increase, aided by the development of expert-based computer systems that make it easier for people to perform tasks that were traditionally reserved for the highly specialized or highly skilled. Learning will occupy a greater part of people's time, and employment by several organizations simultaneously will become a fact of life for a majority of professionals. To avoid relocation and retraining costs, professional labor pools will be developed regionally to service the needs of organizations.

Societal Patterns

With greater diversity and fewer social constraints, society will become more fractionalized in its character. Opportunities will be made more equal, but the price of admission to good jobs through education will also become higher. Adult education and retraining will become more prevalent. Organizations will expect more flexibility from employees and also provide more opportunities for people to retrain themselves both on and off the job. Global concerns will continue to grow in intensity, meaning that society will expect more from organizations in the way of participation in global improvement efforts.

Management Trends

The evaluation of executives by boards and external agencies will intensify, as will upward evaluation of all managers by employees. Performance demands will become more broad, emulating the criteria in the Malcolm Baldrige quality award. Managers will be expected to be better managers, not simply to produce better results.

Future Compression

The time it takes for us to do things and then feel the effects of them will become shorter. We will become faster at everything, and better at organizing ourselves to get things done. The net result is that we will live in a faster age, in which ideas that used to take 50 years to become reality now require only five. Because all the trends and forces affecting organizations will be subject to future compression, the rate of change will intensify. Furthermore, the advances in our communications abilities and in our increased interdependence globally will mean that small changes create large reverberations throughout every segment of our society and in every aspect of our organizations almost instantly. Knowledge, technology, and managerial practices that provide competitive advantage will become more short-lived, as efficient innovation becomes more important than efficiency or innovation alone. The interrelatedness of changes will be more apparent, since the time for feedback from the effect of one change on another will be shortened. While future compression will create short-term chaos, the good news is that we will learn how to manage more systemically so that we can become more capable of creating the future we want.

Whether the assessment of these trends is right or wrong is not as important as the conclusion that significant change is in the making. As long as people have existed, they have dreamed; and dreams ultimately fuel change. We are better at turning our dreams into reality than we were a million years ago; and as we continue to enhance this uniquely human ability, we become both the victims and beneficiaries of more rapid change. So, we can count on two things: 1) The pace of significant change will accelerate; and 2) the complexity of change will increase. As a consequence we can presume that in the future, even more than today, how organizations respond to change will largely determine their effectiveness and survival.

If the trajectory of change is toward greater frequency and complexity, our responses to change must become more continuous and thoughtful. We must utilize our resources more effectively and respond in ways that strengthen our motivation and ability to make the next change and the next one after that. To do these things, we need to engage people more fully in thinking about the future and in helping us to decide how to make the future what we would like it to be. Managing change needs to become an organizational priority and a part of each person's job, and rather than viewing changes as disparate and discontinuous, we need to view them as interrelated and continuous. Rather than responding to each change with a whole new strategy or program, we must develop methods of responding to change that are systemic, effective, and sustainable. Meeting these challenges will require: 1) that we prepare people for roles in managing change different from the roles they have held in the past, and 2) that we put intentional effort into making organizations more flexible and adaptive than they have ever been before.

Some executives will choose to respond to the changes as they occur, in a firefighting fashion; but fighting fires is a risky business in which the fire sometimes gets out of control. Firefighting also leaves little time for planning how to prevent future fires or to apply knowledge gained in fighting the last fire. In the high-pressure, short-term, densely interconnected, globally competitive markets faced by many firms, firefighting has become the *modus operandi,* even though the fires of change continue to spread. Firefighting can work if bold fire lines are cut, as they were at GE under Jack Welch; but firefighting still leaves the long-term well-being of the organization in doubt unless supplemented by a prudent fire-prevention program. Furthermore, the same firefighting techniques that were effective in dealing with change in the past may not be effective in dealing with the faster, more complex changes organizations will face in the future.

Other executives will view the next 20 years differently; they will concern themselves with learning and make certain that their organizations develop the flexibility needed to take advantage of the opportunities change will provide. They will not allow the momentary crisis to distract longer term efforts to build the capacity of organizational members and organizational units to respond to rapid, complex change. They will invest in training, in research, in organizational improvement. They will slaughter sacred cows that create rigidity and introduce new ways of thinking about their markets and customers. They will reach out to others instead of pulling in, in order to take full advantage of what others have learned and can contribute. They will take time to read, to think, to retrain themselves in the service of reinventing their organizations. They will find ways to draw upon the intelligent resources within their own organizations to assist them in making progress, despite the difficulties inherent in doing so. They will view everything as open to change, and settle for nothing less than constant improvement through innovation in every aspect of the system. They will be dreamers, to be sure, but they will also be pragmatists and doers. They will be the empire builders of our modern times, our best hope for a bright future. Unlike their firefighting counterparts, they won't just *run* their organizations; they will *transform* their organizations by recognizing the need for change and building the flexibility internally to respond to that need. This is a book for the empire builders; in a metaphorical sense this book is about fire prevention for organizations; about preparing organizations to be flexible in the face of change; about managing as if change mattered.

CHAPTER

3

Flexible People
Helping People Take
Responsibility for Change

My neighbors in Maine are ordinary people. They don't know much about the goings on at Microsoft or the Tokyo stock exchange, but they know what they know. You can get good advice on fishing, learn how to predict the change of seasons, and taste some delicious blueberry pancakes. Most of my neighbors would feel uncomfortable working in one of today's large corporations; they just wouldn't fit in. Many of them would rather work on an old pickup truck than a computer, and wear plaid wool shirts instead of business suits. Someone from New York or Boston might think of them as backward, unable to participate in modern society. Probably ineducable, and certainly not managerial material. But Maine people fool you, as do people from almost every other rural area of the country. They're a lot smarter than you think; maybe smarter than all the rest of us. Certainly, the quality of their lives is about as good as it gets, despite their lack of conspicuous wealth.

The mistake we make when we become educated is that we see clearly what it is we know that other people don't know. Then, instead of remembering that we were uninformed at one time ourselves, we begin to believe that we are somehow superior to everyone else; that they could never learn what we know. George Bernard Shaw's *Pygmalion* reminds us that we shouldn't underestimate the Elizas of the world. But we do. We see people for what they are, not who they could be. We make judgments about them based on their current and past behavior, and project more of the same into the future, never expecting them to change, or allowing them the opportunity to change.

Once our expectations are set, we use our power to create a world that preserves the status quo. We don't expect people to be capable of learning, so we don't invest in training for them. We don't expect our union opponents to understand our point of view on company finances, so we don't bother to explain it to them. We keep people in their place, at least in the place *we* think they belong. We form people into rigid statues instead of into flexible players who can help our organizations adapt to change. And then we blame them for the problems we have in competing with other workforces around the world. It isn't fair, but it has been going on for so long that we don't even recognize our part in creating the pattern anymore. We just assume that things are the way they have to be. They aren't.

It used to be that when I heard a supervisor tell me, "My employees aren't ready to participate." I felt the problem was with the supervisor's view of people. The supervisor, I thought, was a theory X manager who needed to learn about theory Y. But more recently, I have come to respect the supervisor's appraisal; most of the time, supervisors are right about this; their people *aren't* ready to participate. They have never been invited to participate before, and they lack the basic skills and self-confidence to participate in important decisions affecting the future of their organization. Even when they are forced to take part in employee involvement activities, they sit silently, hoping that someone else will carry the conversation and make the big decisions. It's not that they don't *want* to participate; it's that they don't *know how* to participate, and they don't want to make bad decisions that could screw things up.

It doesn't take long for supervisors to remind employees of how much they don't know, and for employees to withdraw from involvement. None of us likes to be reminded of our ignorance; and, particularly in the early stages of employee involvement activities, employees are reminded far too often. We do a terrible job of preparing people to participate in change, and of preparing our supervisors to help people participate. Eventually, participation in change will allow people to develop the knowledge and skills they need to become real contributors to organizational success; but the early phases of participation can sour people's views of the process, causing them to give up before they learn how to make a real difference.

If all people understand is how to do what they have always done before, their flexibility is limited. If employees begin to understand the business and its customers, broaden their knowledge of technical systems, and start to develop the social skills needed to participate effectively; and supervisors learn to understand employees as people rather than just cogs; together they will help the organization achieve the flexibility it needs in a changing world. But our approach to change hasn't recognized this simple truth. We continue to limit workforce participation to relatively trivial issues because we view them as unable to take part in more meaningful discussions. We view participation as a gimmick to increase their satisfaction and motivation, rather than as a potent force to enhance organizational survival. We look to grab a few quick suggestions from people who have been told to keep quiet in the past, and then pronounce ourselves to be participative managers who understand the value of our human resources. But we haven't even come close. We haven't developed people to be our equals, because we view them as employees rather than as partners in the enterprise. We have kept people in their place and, by so doing, have denied them opportunities to learn and to use what they learn in helping our organizations to become more flexible. In the end, we limit their horizons and thereby limit the growth of our organizations as well.

Until we learn to counter this trend, the path ahead is one of falling further behind countries that provide better education for their citizens, and whose managers understand the meaning of lifelong learning. The fact is that we are a nation run by elites, and that our desire to retain our elitist power is interfering with our wish to become globally competitive. There is vast competitive potential locked in our human resources but it cannot be released until we understand how to set it free. What passes for employee involvement and human resource development today were steps in the right direction, but they fall far short of what is possible. It's time to take a fresh look at people and their role in organizational change.

In what has now become the traditional approach to redesigning organizations using the sociotechnical systems method, I often work with a design team composed of a cross section of representatives from all levels and functions of the organizational unit we are trying to change. Regardless of the eventual outcome of the redesign effort, using this approach means that one thing is almost always guaranteed to happen: The people who serve on the design team will be changed as a result of their participation in the process. They are transformed by the experience. They learn to think about the organization in new ways, to speak out when they have an opinion, to deal with conflict within the team, to survive battles with management, to communicate with their peers, to be creative, to read, to make presentations, to write, to participate. In a word, they become *citizens*. Active, powerful, well informed, conscientious citizens bent on improving the system in which they live and work.

Members of design teams may be the closest thing we have today to our founding fathers; politicians today seem more intent on working within the constitution than in rewriting it. Design team members question what the organization is about, why it is the way it is, and how it could be. They question their own capabilities and the capacity of others to learn and change. They examine alternative systems of organizing and governance and often recommend a whole new way of doing things. They are appointed revolutionaries, and they take their job seriously.

But there's a problem with the design team approach: While the people on the design team are becoming active citizens, everyone else is staying the same. Doing the same old job, holding the same old beliefs, practicing the same old skills. When the design team springs its thinking on the rest of the organization, it learns that others aren't where the design team is; and, what's more, they don't want to be.

I recall working with a design team that did a marvelous job of analyzing its organization, learning about alternatives, and putting together some excellent recommendations for change. Some of the recommendations were revolutionary and would have resulted in changes in the entire management system of their plant. The plant manager, who had chartered the design team, had stated clearly in the beginning that he expected the design team to challenge his thinking. When he heard the recommendations, however, he said that he hadn't expected to be challenged *that* much! He hadn't been involved directly in the design team's process; and therefore he hadn't been transformed by it. He knew that he wanted a new design for his organization that would be radically different, but he hadn't done anything to prepare himself to *think* differently. I had overestimated his openness to change because of his bold challenge to the design team during the chartering process.

Eventually he accepted most of the recommendations of the design team, but the battle was harder than it should have been. And then when he did approve the changes and presented them to everyone in his organization in a plant-wide communication session, he was surprised to find that others didn't accept them readily. His middle managers were the most resistant because their jobs were most threatened by the proposed redesign. The middle managers hadn't been involved in the process, so their thinking hadn't been transformed either. The plant manager believed that his position gave him the authority to implement change, at least in a caring, compassionate way. He didn't demand that people change; he just said that this change was necessary for the good of the organization and that he hoped everyone would do their best to make it happen. When they didn't, he became angry with them. Why didn't they accept his decision? What happened to their loyalty? How could they go against his authority in such an important matter? He still didn't understand. And I didn't understand, because I thought I could hold a session with the middle managers to answer their questions and provide whatever support was necessary to help them through the transition. *But they didn't want to go!* They weren't involved in the process of creating the new design and they didn't like it. No amount of help *getting* there would make *being* there better for them. I finally understood. It was too late to get the supervisors on board. People involved in the process of deciding what the changes should be are transformed by the process; those who aren't involved aren't transformed and may *never* be, even with a good deal of force applied from outside or above.

If we want to create more flexible organizations, we need to do a better job of preparing people to participate in the process of change and then involving them in making decisions that really matter to them. The more important the decisions, the more preparation is required. You wouldn't want a student pilot to fly your 747; so why would you want someone who has no knowledge of organizational design or management deciding how the organization should run? Neither employees nor managers are prepared for this task at the beginning of a redesign effort. Most have never worked in a flexible organization of the kind I am describing or read much about alternative ways of organizing or how to approach change. Some have never thought about these things before, and a few don't ever *want* to think about them. The more I've done this kind of work, the more I have come to recognize how great is the distance between where people are and where we are asking them to go. Whether they are employees or managers, the need for learning is clear; unfortunately, the process for helping them learn what they need to know is not. It follows that the more we help people learn about redesigning their organization, the better they will be in participating in the process. If people know only what history has taught them, they are prisoners of the past. Flexibility requires learning new and different behaviors; flexible organizations require flexible people.

WHAT ARE THE ATTRIBUTES OF FLEXIBLE PEOPLE?

Flexible people are open-minded, willing to take reasonable risks, self-confident, concerned, and interested in learning. They are creative and willing to experiment with new behaviors in order to make better choices about what works for them in a given situation. They are able to learn from their own experience as well as from the experience of others. They are not opposed to new ideas or bound by tradition. They possess basic skills that allow them to adapt readily to new circumstances, and they view themselves as able to make the best of opportunities that come their way. They are active, resourceful, and curious; they are good communicators and good listeners.

Most of us are born with a good deal of flexibility; it's a helpful trait that allows our species to adapt to the wide range of habitats and circumstances we encounter. But the process of growing up in a hierarchical world teaches us to become inflexible. We learn first in our families that authority is not to be questioned and that our parents' way is the right way. Then we attend hierarchical schools in which we are taught to obey our teachers and regurgitate their views of the truth. If we attend church, the sanctity of authority takes on religious significance; we are told we will go to Hell if we fail to follow the rules. Then, either the military or institutions of higher education polish off our remaining square edges so that we are perfectly prepared to fit into a comfortable, obedient square hole in some hierarchical organization. Throughout these experiences, we are taught to follow directions, color within the lines, and avoid taking risks. We lose the flexibility we once had to ask innocent questions and see new possibilities all around us. We find ways to fit in, to accept our role, and to play the game within the rules. Then, when the rules of the game are changed suddenly and dramatically, we find that we are at a loss; we don't know how to respond; how to be flexible. We look to authority figures for answers, but we find that they, too, are baffled by the turn of events and can offer no assurances of safety. We try to do more of the same harder, but we soon discover that the same old routine produces the same old outcomes. We need to learn, to be creative, to innovate; but we don't remember how.

In a country widely recognized to be the greatest democracy in history, we have forgotten how to participate in shaping the systems that control our destiny. As recipients of our forefathers' great wisdom, we have lived comfortably within the framework of our constitution for more than two centuries. We believed that their work would last for all time, and that only minor modifications to the system they created would be required. We stopped training ourselves to be actively involved and trusted that a few representatives would take care of things while the rest of us earned our daily bread. We stopped being active citizens and became wards of the State, knowing that any misfortune would be handled for us by the appropriate government agency.

In organizations, we went through a tremendous period of growth, fueled by the great entrepreneurs. We created railroads and automobile manufacturing firms, phone companies and pharmaceuticals. And as these organizations grew and become more bureaucratic, we become "organization men," fitting into the jobs advertised in the classifieds. We forget how to be entrepreneurial, to grow organizations, to think for ourselves. We understood less and less about the business as it grew. We became narrow in our skills, and our creativity became smothered by the weight of layer upon layer of management. We trusted the system to provide for our needs and our security; we followed the rules and were paid well for doing so. But then things changed.

The government couldn't pay its bills and told us that it could no longer promise to take care of our every need. And our businesses fell upon hard times as global competition made our organizational faults glaringly apparent. Flexibility was needed but, by now, nowhere to be found. We were in trouble.

We needed active citizens who could take care of their own needs; and in our businesses we needed people with the flexibility to respond to change. We needed to question the old system and to create one more fitting to the world we now live in. We needed greater levels of participation, more people involved in efforts to improve things. And we jumped at employee involvement programs and quality circles, applying them to everything from manufacturing to government. But they didn't work well enough; our downward trend continued, and we turned to more radical solutions, such as downsizing and reengineering to cut costs.

Now, we are trying to run our organizations with a skeleton crew, made up of people who aren't sure whether they are winners or losers in the big game. Is it better to get laid off and start all over again, or find that you're working yourself to death because you are one of the remaining few on the payroll? And the news still isn't getting better.

Of the 1979 *Fortune* 500, 37 percent don't even exist today. More innovation is called for, but now there are fewer people around to make it happen. It's harder to take people away from their jobs to concentrate on improving work processes, because the backup isn't there. And it's harder to get people excited about helping out when they sense that there may be a pink slip as their reward for increasing efficiency. We need more participation and more flexibility than ever; but, as Einstein noted, we can't get out of the mess we are in with more of the same thinking that caused the problem in the first place. We need new strategies for increasing the flexibility of our human resources. We need to be flexible in order to create flexibility.

INCREASING HUMAN FLEXIBILITY

How do we help people become more flexible? The answer, I think, is to help them learn to participate effectively in decisions that really count. And to do this, they need to develop the business, technical, and social skills that effective participation requires.

Just as we wouldn't trust a new medical student to perform a serious operation, we can have no confidence that the average employee will make intelligent business decisions in critical areas. We are comfortable with employees planning the annual picnic, because not much is at stake; but when it comes to making important business decisions, we are less trusting. We tend to restrict participation to "safe" topics and, by doing so, fail to develop people's understanding of important business issues. For participation to matter, to really make a difference in the bottom line performance of the firm, participative decisions must involve substantive issues. Participation, no matter how widespread, will return little to the organization if the issues addressed are individually insignificant. Understanding the business, and what influences its success or failure, is the first prerequisite of effective participation.

Employees need to know what managers know: how to read the income statement and the balance sheet; what makes the numbers on each get larger or smaller; what the numbers really mean; where the company stands today compared to where it's been historically and versus the competition. Employees need to know the threats to the organization and the plans to deal with them. They need to know why the plans make sense and what other alternatives were considered before deciding on this course of action. They need to understand decision-making processes and criteria and how much risk is acceptable. They need to understand the consequences of making poor decisions and what to do when the unexpected happens. They need to understand customers' expectations and how to better meet them. They need an introduction to global economics, and why it costs so much more to do business in the United States than in Mexico or Korea. They need to know about health-care costs and about workers' compensation, about the costs of carrying inventory and liability insurance. Because there is so much to learn, it may be impossible to convey all of the information to everyone immediately; in the short run, a few people can learn about one subject while others learn about different subjects. It won't take long for all the information to be shared with everybody.

Once employees understand the business, they can begin thinking along with managers, using their ideas and creativity to offer practical solutions to important problems. They begin to question decisions that don't appear to make sense based on what they understand. Often, they are right: The decision doesn't make sense. Eventually, as employees and managers learn how to think together about the business, flexibility begins to creep in; employees suggest new alternatives for increasing competitiveness, many of which involve cost-cutting or methods changes that increase production or enhance quality. I've never worked with an employee group that lowered its production rate when given the opportunity to do so; all have found ways to raise their rates, knowing that, in the long run, what's best for them is what's best for the company. Surprise. Why didn't we know this all along? Employees *want* to be partners in the business; they *want* to influence decisions that affect their future. When employees act like opponents rather than partners, it's usually because they don't trust management to really involve them in decisions that count. If partners treated each other the way some managers treat employees, the partnership wouldn't last for long. Partners need to know what's happening, whether the news is good or bad; and they need to influence decisions, *especially* when the news is bad.

Participation is easy when times are good and the available options all have positive consequences. Encounter a crisis and employees look for the truth to emerge; will managers "walk the talk" or revert to theory X? During a crisis, there's a lot to lose and little time for participation. But there's also a lot to gain, both in terms of worthwhile input and in building trust and flexibility. It's hard to be flexible when you are simply told to be flexible and don't understand the need to change; it's easier to be flexible if you helped to define the change for yourself. I'm not suggesting that we make employees into managers, although I'm fairly certain that most could do a good job of managing in a relatively short time. I'm only suggesting that participation not connected to knowledge of the business is necessarily limited in scope, an academic exercise rather than a practical solution to organizational problems. True flexibility is the product of meaningful participation, which requires full knowledge of its business consequences.

In addition to understanding the business, employees also need to understand the technical system used to produce goods or services; they must know how it functions and why it was designed as it was designed. Employees must understand what technical alternatives are possible and what would be involved in applying them. Employees are powerless to improve the performance of the system if they don't understand how it works or are denied the authority needed to change things.

In conducting the technical analysis of organizations, we usually look for variances: things that go wrong that shouldn't. We then ask what causes these things to go wrong, and who deals with the situation when problems do occur. Often, we find that the people who know what to do about technical problems are not the same people who create them. Engineers or maintenance specialists usually descend upon the scene of a problem, pushing the machine operator or front-line employee aside as they make repairs. When the specialists leave, things return to normal— until the problem occurs again. The machine operator remains unable to correct the problem or, sometimes, unaware of what he did to cause the problem to occur. Everyone assumes that the job of the operator is to operate the equipment and the job of the specialist is to effect repairs.

In some plants, such as Exxon's Baytown refinery, the line of demarcation between maintenance and production has been eliminated. Each person in the plant learns maintenance skills and most are able to make basic repairs to their equipment. This allows people to keep the process running more smoothly and to be more aware of the causes of technical problems. In order to prevent variances from occurring, employees need to be able to detect conditions that cause variances; they need to have the skills, knowledge, and tools to effect changes in the system; and they need the authority to act. If any of these components is missing, variances will continue to occur, and the technical system will operate suboptimally.

Achieving variance control requires more training and delegation of authority than most organizations provide; achieving technical *flexibility* requires yet another level of effort. To make the technical system flexible, employees must know what the people who designed the technology know; they must learn how to change the system without damaging its integrity, how to take it apart and put it back together again so that it works better than before. At the Zilog plant in Nampa, Idaho, engineers spent a great deal of time educating employees about how the complex semiconductor manufacturing process worked. In a short time, employees were offering improvements to systems that in most other semiconductor manufacturing firms were understood by only a handful of engineers and PhDs. Employees catch on readily and start to provide a return on the investment in their technical training more quickly than one might expect.

Once employees understand the system, they can help to make it more adaptable. Employees who understand the technical system can recommend small changes in their own part of the operation and participate in more significant changes to the entire system through membership on organization-wide technical improvement teams. The idea is a simple one: Get the information out of the heads of a few experts, where it is difficult to access, and place it in the minds of the people doing the work, who can apply it to improve the system. Flexibility is driven by understanding, not simply by watching others make changes in technical systems.

In knowledge-intensive organizations, where work consists primarily of thinking rather than doing, understanding the technical system may mean broadening one's knowledge base. Knowledge workers tend to specialize into narrow areas of expertise in order to develop the depth of understanding needed to make advances at the leading edge of their field. The problem comes in fitting what they discover into everything else that is going on; the whole system needs to understand their thinking before it can be applied to improve products or processes. Narrow specialties make learning about the rest of the system difficult; in extreme cases, people may not even know how to speak the same technical language. Developing technical knowledge helps with the communication/integration problem, which may be the biggest barrier to flexibility in knowledge work settings. I'll say more about knowledge work in Chapter 6.

Finally, employees need to develop the social skills that allow them to take part in participative activities: to speak up in front of others, to confront differences, to understand how to reach consensus, to facilitate the participation of others, to listen. A poll once indicated that public speaking ranked higher than death or illness on a list of human fears; I believe it. I've seen burly truck drivers almost faint when asked to address a group of their peers, and accomplished academics nervously read their papers word for word to their colleagues, never looking up. Participation is no easy thing.

Most employees have no training for participation, and few have had opportunities to practice participation, inside or outside the workplace. Training courses in interpersonal relations are often ineffectual because they are taught at times other than when they are really needed, in an atmosphere removed from real issues and concerns. Participation, particularly concerning things that matter, touches people's emotions. Dealing with real emotions coming from people who we know we will have to work with in the future is always difficult. Some people refuse to participate when given the opportunity to do so because they are afraid of the repercussions following a confrontation with a boss or powerful coworker. Some don't trust the motives of the people they work with, and figure that if they don't participate, maybe others won't either. Dealing with issues of poor performance is one of the most sensitive topics that can be taken on in a participative forum; but improving performance is what participation is all about, and sometimes this involves dealing with some hard cases involving truly inflexible people.

Every time I think about the framing of the Constitution, I marvel at what the fathers of our nation must have gone through: the debates, the threats, the risks. Few of us would have the courage to stand up to the strongest military power in the world and declare our freedom. Fewer still would have the patience to work together long enough to overcome the many obstacles inherent in forming a single nation from a patchwork quilt of colonies with such different interests and goals. And they did it all without training in interpersonal skills or conflict management. Perhaps there is hope for the rest of us. Maybe, given time and opportunities, people in organizations could learn how to participate in decisions affecting their common future—decisions on a much smaller scale than those involved in framing the Constitution, but just as important to those directly affected. Maybe. If we choose to involve people in important organizational decisions, we shouldn't expect to see anything close to the quality of a constitutional convention in the short run. Learning to participate takes time. In fact, we should probably expect to see people struggle with the process; to be frustrated with one another; to mistrust management's intentions; to sit quietly for long periods of time; to make recommendations that won't work; to avoid confrontation; to withdraw after not getting their way; to badmouth the whole process of involvement; to decline invitations to participate. It's a normal part of the learning process. We feel the same way when we try to learn to ice skate or play golf or speak a foreign language. We feel awkward; we question the benefits of learning and recalculate our motivation. Sometimes, we give up.

We can help make learning to participate easier for people if we look at it from their perspective. For example, I ask people to try juggling in front of others when they have never done it before. There's usually a lot of nervous laughter, a half-hearted attempt, and a quick exit stage right. Research in human learning tells us that it's harder for us to learn new behaviors when others are watching us than if we are alone. It's part of being human. As humans, we are concerned about how others perceive us because we know that their perceptions affect how they will interact with us in the future. Most of the time, we try to look good to others; we avoid doing things that are likely to be awkward or embarrassing. We don't learn to juggle in public. After people have tried juggling once, I ask them to try again; but before they begin, I tell them that their job depends on not dropping anything. Most won't even try to juggle the second time. And this is precisely how people feel about learning to participate. Learning to participate has to be done in front of others; there's no way to learn to participate in private. In organizations, learning how to participate is not only public, but it involves performing in front of people who will form judgments about you based on what you say or don't say. It can literally cost you your job, or a promotion, or an opportunity that you desire. No wonder people are reluctant to try.

We can help people learn how to participate with less fear if we begin by providing them with some of the basic skills involved: speaking, reading, writing, listening, reaching consensus, observing groups, facilitating others, managing conflict. We can make it easier for them by allowing them to practice on less important issues before insisting that they get involved in job-threatening discussions. We can make it safer for people to talk about their fears, and to help each other deal with them. We can provide people with training and feedback, allowing them to accept more responsibility as they feel ready for it. We don't need to force people to juggle in public, with their futures on the line.

The more that employees develop business, technical, and social skills, the more ready they will be to participate. The more they participate, and the more significant the issues they participate in, the more their self-confidence and potential for making a real difference will grow. The more they participate, the more they will begin to see new possibilities as real opportunities, and know what it will take to achieve success. The more they participate, the more they will be willing to take steps toward the future, to try something new; and the more they experiment, the more flexible they will become. To expect people to be immediately flexible or to jump into participation without these skills is like expecting them to leap from the high diving board before they know how to swim. People, in turn, must gradually develop, through firsthand, group-based learning experiences involving significant real issues, the skills and courage to be active and knowledgeable participants in change. These learning experiences must be voluntary. As Rita Weathersby notes, doors can be opened for people, but they must walk through them themselves.[1]

At the same time, we also need to help managers learn how to allow people to participate. Participation is a threat to authority based on strict top-down control of decision making. When we ask managers to accept responsibility for results and also to be participative in their approach to decision making, we don't fully appreciate the depth of the struggle they encounter. Promoting active citizenship in organizations means allowing participation by people in a wide range of decisions and issues that affect the organization. The impediment to this is the question of whether it is feasible for people to participate objectively in decisions regarding changes that affect themselves.

Managers question the ability of employees to participate in important decisions based upon their perceptions of employees' behaviors in the past. Managers often view employees as less knowledgeable, less willing to sacrifice for the good of the company, and less articulate in stating their positions than other managers are. They doubt whether employees have anything of value to contribute and fear that if employees are given access to decision-making power, it will be abused. None of this is news. What is surprising is that the dynamics are recreated from one century to the next, from one society to another, when the pattern is so obvious—and so obviously wrong. Why can't we break out of our own prison? Why can't we recognize the need for people to become more flexible in order for our organizations to respond to change? Why can't we see the role we play as managers in keeping them inflexible? What are we really afraid of?

These questions are as old as civilization itself. The struggle between our desire to involve people in meaningful decisions that shape their lives and our doubt in people's capacity to participate in these same decisions has been a part of human history. In addressing this struggle in *The Republic* and other writings, Plato held that the best interests of the city-state would be served by the direct participation of citizens via the *polis* in matters of governance. Laws developed by citizens themselves were more likely to be understood, accepted, and obeyed. At the same time, Plato held that ordinary citizens, due to intellectual limitations and vested interests, should not participate in *all* decisions; he would reserve certain critical decisions to philosopher-kings, who would be supported by society so that they would be freed of personal interests and trained from an early age to be impartial and wise. The Greeks restricted access to the polis to citizens, those they felt had the right and capabilities to participate in heroic dialogue. Barbarians, slaves, and those who did not hold land were excluded. Of course, women were automatically ineligible. The Greeks feared that should the polis become too large, it would become too difficult to allow each person to be heard and to create the conditions for conferring upon each speaker the respect due to him by other "true" citizens. With a few minor exceptions, the modern boardroom could easily be mistaken for the Greek polis.

So while democracy was born in ancient Athens, it was a democracy of the few. Not until the American Revolution was there an experiment in more equal participation in governance.

Alexis De Tocqueville in his observations of early democracy in America, clarified the premise of our system, in which potentially every citizen could be a full participant.[2] He observed that citizens respected laws that they themselves helped to create and administer; that the active involvement by many in government avoided the manipulation of the government by the few; and that a true belief in the equality of self-interests resulted in a state of mutual concern and the avoidance of anarchy and oppression. As a consequence, De Tocqueville perceived American citizens to be more actively involved in government, more energetic, and more concerned about the welfare of others than in other democracies. Still, it took many years for women and minorities to receive the right to vote, and true equality has yet to be attained.

Those of us who are interested in organizational change did

not create this controversy, but we have inherited it. Research on the benefits of participation by employees in organizational decision-making has produced equivocal results.[3] These mixed results support the views of those who argue that participation is no more than a way to manipulate peoples' feelings, and that we shouldn't look to employees for input on matters of organizational importance. While our values typically include that participants at all levels of organizations be empowered to take part in decisions that affect them, we cannot conclude based on any reasonable review of the literature regarding participation in organizations that simply involving people in decision-making will produce positive benefits to either those involved or the organization as a whole. We simply don't seem to understand enough about participation to make it work. Managers are right to be suspicious of participation, at least as it has been practiced historically. What do we know?

Many credit Kurt Lewin[4,5] with discovering the importance of participation in changing attitudes. In a series of experiments involving changes in food preferences, Lewin demonstrated the superiority of participative discussion over lectures or direct appeal as a means of changing attitudes. After Lewin's experiments, and following the classic Hawthorne studies,[6] participation became the focus of a number of early experiments in organizational change, the most noted of which were those conducted in the Harwood Manufacturing Company by Lester Coch and John French.[6] The explicit goal of these studies was to investigate what could be done to reduce workers' resistance to job changes. It had been observed that workers in the plant who were transferred to a new job learned at a slower rate than workers who were hired and placed on the same jobs for the first time. Alex Bavelas demonstrated in the same plant that group decision techniques resulted in very marked increases in the rate of relearning. Building on this finding, Coch and French assigned workers to participative and nonparticipative experimental groups to determine whether group discussion concerning the new jobs had an impact on relearning. In analyzing the results of their experiments, Coch and French concluded:

It is possible for management to modify or to remove completely group resistance to changes in methods of work and the ensuing piece rates. This change can be accomplished by the use of group meetings in which management effectively communicates the need for change and stimulates group participation in planning the changes. (p. 531).

The effects of participation, however, were not without variation. Coch and French noted, as did Lewin, that the degree to which individuals in the work group identified with the goals of the group influenced the rate of relearning achieved following group discussion. Since the Harwood experiments, the investigation of participation has involved a search for additional variables that could explain the mixed outcomes observed in practice. The strong bias on the part of researchers in favor of participation has supported continuing research and theorizing despite the lack of convincing evidence that participation works.[8]

Victor Vroom investigated the impact of personality variables on self-reported effects of participation using a sample of 108 middle managers in a parcel delivery company.[9] Vroom noted that individuals with a high need for independence and a low need for authoritarianism seemed to benefit most from participative opportunities. He also argued strongly that participation was most beneficial when combined with programs designed to increase individuals' skills and abilities. Aaron Lowin, in reviewing laboratory, observational, and field experiments involving participation, added other variables to consider.[10] His list included

- The extent, relevance, importance and visibility of participative activities
- The difficulty of issues being addressed
- The extent of social pressure for participation
- The clarity of goals to be achieved through participation
- The linking of financial rewards with participation
- The amount of directly useful information available to individuals
- The extent to which individuals control the factors that influence outcomes

- The lack of pressure to make a decision
- The number of levels included in the process.

H. Peter Dachler and Bernhard Wilpert, in a review of participation a decade later, reached similar conclusions and noted that the results of participation research seem confusing because researchers approach the subject with different interests in mind.[11] Dachler and Wilpert also noted that there is evidence to support doubt about the ability of individuals to engage in effective participation, although the research in this area leaves much to be desired.

Ed Locke and David Schweiger, in a comprehensive critical review of experiments involving participative leadership, group decision making, goal setting, and organizational change reached the conclusion that support for the positive effects of participative decision making is at best mixed.[12] As did Lowin and Dachler and Wilpert, they concluded that success in participative decision making is not guaranteed and that mediating factors must be considered.

Thus, even those managers who *do* seek to employ participation for organizational improvement often find themselves frustrated with the results they achieve and even with the willingness of organizational members to become involved in these activities. What's wrong? Is participation a good idea in theory, but one that doesn't work in practice?

The answer is that participation works, but only when people are prepared to participate. The problems that managers encounter are problems that stem from failure to make effective participation a priority in our society and in our organizations. The hit-or-miss track record of participation has more to do with how we have attempted to use participation than whether participation works.

In a study of an organization in which a majority of people opted not to participate in employee involvement activities when given the opportunity, Jeanne Neumann discovered that the reasons for not participating far outweighed the potential benefits of getting involved.[13] The supervisors in the organization attributed the poor participation record to people's personalities;

the supervisors believed that "these people just don't like to participate." In interviewing people at length, however, Neumann discovered that there were a number of reasons why people chose not to participate that had nothing to do with their personalities. Neumann found three "clusters" of deterrents to participation: (a) structural, including organizational design, work design, and human resource management policies (*e.g.*, the "real" decisions are reserved for those at the top); (b) relational, including how participation is managed, the dynamics of hierarchy, and the individual's stance toward the organization (*e.g.*, rank and status continue to be more important than knowledge or competence); and (c) societal, including primary and secondary socialization experiences, ideology, and politics (*e.g.*, deeply held values of not demonstrating disloyalty are confronted by participation).

Neumann pointed out that a combination of these factors can lead to a situation that is overdetermined *against* participation by the majority of people, even though the intention of those designing participative programs is just the opposite. The solution to this problem, according to Neumann, is not to blame the victim, but instead to examine the system of participation that has been created to see if managers really want to walk their talk regarding employee involvement.

A similar conclusion was reached by Dachler & Wilpert, who contend that participation cannot be expected to produce positive results when the issues discussed are irrelevant to task performance, when people don't understand the organizational context, and when the effectiveness of performance is beyond the control of the employee.[14]

Even Douglas McGregor, who made theory Y a credo for the modern manager, held deep concerns about participation:[15]

> Some proponents of participation give the impression that it is a magic formula which will eliminate conflict and disagreement and come pretty close to solving all of management's problems. These enthusiasts appear to believe that people yearn to participate, much as children of a generation or two ago yearned for Castoria. They give the impression that it is a formula which can

be applied by any manager regardless of his skill, that virtually no preparation is necessary for its use, and that it can spring full-blown into existence and transform industrial relationships over-night. (p. 124)

The bottom line is that participation doesn't work when our organizations are not designed and managed to make it work. As long as we make half-hearted efforts at participation, we will get half-hearted buy-in from employees and mixed results. If we want people to participate fully and achieve success through participation, we have to act like we really mean it.

Even when we do mean it, and even when we do provide people with the training and support they need to develop participative competence, we will notice variation among people in their willingness to participate. Some people are more flexible than others. Those who lead the way will be more self-confident, more willing to take risks, more articulate, more extroverted; in short, they will demonstrate more of the traits of flexible people. Those who lag behind will be more inflexible by nature and require more time and support to become fully involved.

In the literature on the development of individuals, authors have said that people progress through stages from infancy to maturity. Even as adults, there are stages of personal growth that take us from being impulsive and self-protecting to conscientious and autonomous.[16]

Full participation would require the development of individuals to at least the stage of conscientiousness, but more advanced developmental stages would add greater quality and meaning to participative acts. Prior to the conscientious stage is the conformity stage, wherein individuals are more concerned with "fitting in" than with establishing their individual identities or standing up for their own points of view. Individuals in the conformity stage are easily influenced by stereotypes and cliches, winning and losing, and blaming external circumstances for failure; they demonstrate little introspection or emotional awareness and tend to ignore or suppress individual differences. As Eric Fromm notes, the freedom of speech is meaningless if all we carry in our heads are the thoughts of others.[17] Individuals in the conformity stage would hardly fit the mold of *organizational citizens*. Developing conscientiousness and autonomy is a prerequisite to real flexibility.

In the conscientious stage, people begin to live according to their own standards, seeing rules as general guidelines rather than absolutes, recognizing exceptions and contingencies engaging in complex reasoning, being concerned with mutuality in relationships, valuing achievement, seeing real choices having long-term goals, and being more aware of oneself and the broader social context. Even higher stages of development are characterized by the ability to recognize inner conflict, respecting others' autonomy, viewing life as a whole, responding to abstract ideals such as equality and justice, tolerating a great deal of ambiguity, and reconciling inner conflicts in order to develop a consolidated sense of identity.

Chris Argyris viewed participation primarily as a means to an end—the integration of individual and organizational needs.[18,19] Argyris noted that the needs of normal, adult human beings and the arrangements in traditional organizations are opposed, at considerable cost to motivation and effectiveness. The needs of normal, healthy adults, according to Argyris, are to develop from passive infants into active adults, to move from dependence to independence in relationships, to increase one's range of effective behaviors, to understand complex problems and opportunities and to see them as challenges, to devel-op a long-term time perspective, to move from a position of subordinacy to equality, and to gain autonomy over one's behavior.

What most individuals encounter at work, however, is a situation that does not meet their needs. Argyris reviews the impact of principles of formal organization on the adult. These include task specialization, which lacks of challenge; chain of command, which increases dependency and shortens time perspectives; unity of direction, which reduces ego involvement; and span of control, which produces passivity.

Lowin also notes also that pattern maintenance in hierarchical organizations tends to work against effective participation.[20] People are selected to fit into the existing hierarchical structure.

(Lowin suggests that their attitudes must match those of the supervisors who are doing the hiring.) Information on standard operating procedures and policies will reinforce the power of the system over the individual. Messages that would change the power structure have a difficult time working their way up the existing hierarchy. Parallel communication channels are usually either not available or ineffective. Lowin points out that, as a consequence, subordinates often lack information necessary to participate in a competent fashion.

Argyris suggests that the conflict between healthy adults and traditionally designed organizations will grow as individuals mature. The eventual result is withdrawal, apathy, and disinterest. To avoid or overcome these consequences, Argyris advocates changing the structure of the organization and increasing opportunities for meaningful participation. Argyris views participation as a means of helping individuals to become more active, more independent, and more equal. Along with changes in job responsibilities and time orientations, these changes help to close the gap between individual needs and organizational experiences, leading to greater self-actualization and higher levels of performance.

What would be required, based upon models of adult development, to prepare people for participation? Clearly, in order to reach the conscientious stage of development or beyond, people must be provided with opportunities to test their reasoning and judgment skills in the context of decisions that matter. These opportunities should create conditions similar to those for adult development: namely, (a) varied direct experiences and roles; (b) meaningful achievement; and (c) relative freedom from anxiety and pressure. Thus, opportunities to develop participative abilities must be in the context of direct participation in a wide range of decisions that affect people's lives in organizations; must provide people with feedback that helps them to gauge their level of achievement; and must be done in an atmosphere of trust and support that eliminates unnecessary risk or pressure. Lectures on participation will not substitute for the real thing, as noted by Lewin:[21]

To understand what is being talked about the individual has to have a basis in experience—as a child in a student council, in the hundred and one associations of everyday life; he has to have some taste of what democratic leadership and the democratic responsibility of the follower mean. No lecture can substitute for these first-hand experiences. Only through practical experience can one learn that peculiar democratic combination of conduct which includes responsibility toward the group, ability to recognize differences of opinion without considering the other person a criminal, and readiness to accept criticism in a matter of fact way while offering criticism with sensitivity for the other person's feeling. (p. 52)

Few employees have reached the higher stages of adult development in hierarchical organizations because the organization expects them to be less developed and denies them true developmental opportunities. Some, even when given the opportunity, won't be able to reach the conscientious stage; they lack the motivation or the intellectual capacity to achieve the highest states of development. But the vast majority of people are capable of at least some further development; and most, when given the proper support and opportunities, are capable of reaching the highest levels of development.

The steps needed to prepare people to participate depends upon their level of development. People who have never spoken in front of a group need coaching on basic skills; but those who are experienced participators may find that coaching in alternative modes of engaging others in change is more useful. Although no single program or activity is right for everyone, nearly ideal conditions for the attainment of higher levels of participative competence may be found in new methods of engaging whole systems in self-examination through what are called search conferences.[22,23] Search conferences bring everyone into the room at the same time to participate in the process of defining both the need for change and how changes should be achieved. All levels and all functions of a system are typically represented, as are important external stakeholder groups such as customers, shareholders, and suppliers. The power of search conferences is that they bring together a tremendous array of resources in an active, real-time dialogue where understanding can be achieved and commitment to change nurtured. Search conferences have been used to redesign organizations, school systems, and communities, as well as to resolve heated debates among multiple interest parties over water usage and development objectives. The forum provided by the search conference is the closest thing we have to a true polis, where individuals can engage in acts of courage by speaking their beliefs in a situation of some consequence.

Bob Rehm, Gary Frank, and I have developed a method of introducing change in organizations that we call *fast cycle full participation change*. It utilizes a combination of search conference and sociotechnical systems design methods. With it, we have shortened the time it takes to analyze the organization and recommend design alternatives. More than that, however, we have made the process more meaningful for many more people than the traditional design team approach, as well as increased their commitment to implementing change. We hold search conferences involving as many representatives of the system as possible for each of the three major analyses (environmental, social, and technical) and also for the redesign of the system. We support people in the process with facilitation, materials, and information that help them work together in redesigning their own system. Neither we nor a small design team are responsible for the outcomes; everyone owns what happens. What's more, everyone understands why things were decided *and* knows what can be done to reconsider decisions that don't work out as planned. The fast cycle full participation approach helps create the participative competence that is required to make employees active organizational citizens. The only limits on the outcomes of this process are the creativity of individuals and the readiness of leaders to accept the recommended changes. Sometimes, people are out in front of the system, proposing more than the leadership is prepared to accept; and at other times, leaders expect more from people than they are prepared to give.

Managers are sometimes viewed as different from employees; managers are *expected* to behave as mature adults, to think conscientiously and autonomously, to question the status quo, to take responsible risks. These expectations are translated into opportunities for managers to think and act independently in matters of significance, which in turn allow them to develop the maturity that can only be gained through such experiences. With a few notable exceptions, most people become what the situation allows them to become.

For organizations to develop flexible people, expectations of people must change. Managers must view employees as capable of becoming flexible and provide them with opportunities to develop flexibility, just as they do for other managers. Because the going will be slow and difficult at first, neither employees nor managers should expect to see tremendous growth in the short run. If managers expect too much from people too soon, people will be overwhelmed by the opportunities they are presented, and become disillusioned with themselves. They will doubt their own ability to participate in meaningful issues and even fear that they will cause inadvertent harm to the organization or to others around them.

On the other hand, if managers expect too little, employees will view the participation opportunities they encounter as insincere, reflecting the control needs of managers. When greater opportunities to participate are subsequently provided, employees will doubt their authenticity and fear that the outcomes are predetermined and that participation is being used as a manipulative tactic. According to Rosabeth Kanter, inauthentic participation is very likely to occur when leaders create participation programs to be "nice to people."[24] She notes that such efforts are easily identified by the fact that they are undertaken in conjunction with currently faddish programs and that their expected outcomes are vague.

For flexibility to grow, managers and employees need to strike a balance between the importance of the changes in which people are asked to participate and the abilities of people to participate in change. As people develop greater flexibility, skills, and understanding, the scope of participation should increase commensurately. After some time, managers will learn to expect people to participate effectively and employees will come to trust management's intentions. The learning process involves both sides taking an active part in the process, which is precisely what has not happened throughout our civilized history. One side always seems to be ahead of or behind the other, which leads to disenchantment with the whole process of participative change. The use of force through top-down control or bottom-up revolution is an easy fall-back solution when our desire for change outstrips our patience. In the long run, force begets force, and the cycle of imbalance in development is fueled again.

If the proper balance between readiness and participation is maintained, people in organizations should encounter a series of recognizable stages in the development of participative competence. The lowest level acts of participation involve simply joining and participating in the system (*conforming*), while the highest level participative acts involve redesigning the system itself (*creating*). In between conforming and creating are several other levels, including *contributing* (helping to improve the existing system), *challenging* (attempting to change the system slightly while retaining the existing structure and distribution of power), and *collaborating* (redistributing power in the system while retaining its essential characteristics). Each of the five levels of participation asks more of a person and carries with it both more risk and greater potential rewards.

Employee involvement has typically involved only the first two levels of conforming and contributing. Because employee involvement activities are sanctioned by those in power, they rarely involve an invitation to change the essential nature of the system or the distribution of power within the system. Higher levels of participation require a greater leap of faith on the part of top-level decisionmakers. The higher the level of the participative act, the more likely it is to result in both systemic and individual transformation; hence, it is not surprising that the success of employee involvement has been limited, since its effectiveness is predetermined by the level of change permitted by those in control. As in the stock market, the biggest gains are connected with the biggest risks. Conservatism in investing lowers potential risks, but also potential gains; conservatism in participation reduces threats to the status quo and eliminates flexibility.

ONE PLUS ONE

In the past, the development of individuals and the development of organizations have been two separate activities; but organizations are composed of people, and people determine the pace of change. Despite decades of relying on people to participate effectively, it is only now becoming clear how much our efforts at change are affected by the abilities of individuals to engage in participative activities. The time has come to focus more attention on helping people to be more flexible by preparing them to participate in change.

It is impossible to imagine a significant organizational change that does not affect the lives of individuals; or to think of a meaningful opportunity for participation that doesn't require tremendous courage on the part of individuals to risk leaving their spheres of security to advance ideas supporting change. Individual and organizational change are not two separate activities. They are one and the same. To the extent that we treat them separately, we are at best ignoring the reality of what we are about and the potential power of linking the two together more closely; at worst, we frustrate individuals by asking them to undertake acts of courage they are not prepared for or that the organization is not prepared to reward. When we approach these activities together, consciously and explicitly, we tap into the emotional energy that is the required catalyst for all human change to occur and use that energy to support organizational transformation.

Organizational change and individual change are synonymous and complementary. When approached together consciously, they provide the potential for a synergistic reinforcement of one another that can produce truly significant and lasting changes in the thinking, feeling, and sense-making of individuals as well as the practices, structures, processes, and arrangements of organizing. Our interventions should create processes that allow individual and organizational development to occur simultaneously, continuously, and in the context of a fluid set of structures and arrangements that allow individuals to develop and test their new skills against real and important evolving organizational challenges and opportunities.

Managers who cling to theory X and point to limitations of their employees as justification are only admitting to the difficulty of developing employees as flexible organizational citizens. The difficulty of the task does not negate its importance or value, however. Consultants have let managers and employees down either by selling interventions that expected too much from people too soon or interventions that expected too little for too long.

The developments in the arena of global competition have caused us to tighten the slack in our organizations and taken our current organizational arrangements to their limits of performance. To compete in the future, we need to tighten our belt one more notch; not by cutting more jobs out of our organizations, because there are no more that can be cut; nor by working harder, because there is no more to give. The next notch requires that we finally achieve the promise we have held out all along—to develop and tap the potential of organizational members. Training is a part of this process, to be sure; but the only way to retrieve the value of knowledge placed in the heads of employees is to create systems that support people in finding their voice and sharing their wisdom. For this, we must turn our attention once again to participation and to the creation of processes that support the development of true organizational citizens.

CHAPTER

4

Flexible Technology
Designing the Organization
To Take Advantage
of New Technology

The computer I am using to write this book is an amazing piece of technology. It has far more capability than I am able to take advantage of: programs it will gladly run that I don't understand, statistics it will calculate that I don't know to ask for, and software it will eventually accept that hasn't even been written yet. There is little doubt that my computer ranks near the top of the list in technological flexibility.

But what if you're manufacturing automobiles or chemicals? Or processing insurance claims? How flexible can your technology really be before it becomes inefficient? Should we be producing a different automobile for every customer? And not just a different color or interior or options, but one designed from the ground up specifically to meet each buyer's driving needs? Seems a little extreme.

We may not achieve the same flexibility in mass production that we currently see in computers any time soon, but there can be no doubt that we are moving in that direction. In order to be responsive to our customers and still efficient, we are searching for ways to make technology smarter and more flexible. In order to maintain long term competitiveness, we are trying to find ways to make our technology easier to upgrade as new technology is developed, and less costly to own and operate. Technology is also becoming friendlier to the environment, safer and better designed ergonomically. The classic scene from the movie *Modern Times*, in which Charlie Chaplin loses his battle with the assembly line, is hardly modern at all. The remake would feature a distraught Bill Murray unwittingly sabotaging a computer system or Robin Williams mistakenly mixing together two different strains of genes in a biogenetics lab. Technology has advanced to meet nearly every dream we had a century ago and continues to amaze us with its latest feats. Some are afraid that technology will be our downfall; that we will blow ourselves up, or pollute ourselves to death, or even that technology will become intelligent and take over. Barring these catastrophes, the most likely scenario is more of the same: greater advances in technology that add to the speed, ease, quality, affordability, and customization of the goods and services we consume. It follows that the firms that learn to take advantage of technology and its ever-increasing flexibility will be the most successful in the long run. Simply buying the latest technology, however, isn't enough; *what matters is how the whole system works.*

I'm a good example. The computer I own has tremendous power. I bought it thinking that I would learn to utilize all that power someday; but life has been a little busier than I had planned, and most of my computer's power is untapped. How many firms make the same mistake? The salesman demonstrates the advantages of the new computer system over the old, which are obvious to anyone; the sale is made, and the system is installed; but it doesn't work. Not because the technology is broken, but because no one thought about how much time and training would be required to get the computer users up to speed in using the new technology. Far more often than not, we forget to take the human side of the equation into consideration.

Everything said about flexibility in participation in the last chapter applies to individual technical flexibility as well. People start with few technical skills in life and acquire more as they grow; and each time they are confronted with a new technology, they build on what they know. Some are more open to experimenting with new technology than others. Like becoming comfortable with participation, the development of skills for dealing with new technology takes time. And, just as some people who are naturally extroverted find participating easier than do those who are naturally introverted, so it is with technology. Some of us are technical junkies while others are techno-phobic. Most of us obey the law of large numbers and fall somewhere in between the extremes of the bell curve, which means that, with proper care and feeding, we have at least a chance of keeping up with what is going on.

Lesson One: *If you want your technology to be more flexible, you have to make your people more flexible, too.*

But not just employees need to learn; customers do as well. In doing some work with a computer software engineering organization, I learned that the number-one problem software engineers face is the user of the system they are designing. Customers would ask for things they didn't need or want, make the systems much more complex and costly to develop than necessary, and then get promoted or transferred before the system was fully developed. A new user would be appointed, with a new set of criteria to be met, and everyone would go around the track again. By the time the system was ready to go, it was over budget, difficult to maintain, and required far more intensive training to implement. Guess who got blamed—not the buyers, but rather the software engineers. Flexibility carries a hidden cost: the cost of educating customers on the advantages and disadvantages of utilizing all the flexibility that the system allows.

Lesson Two: *People need to be aware of the impact of their decisions concerning technology if they are ever going to learn to use technology effectively.*

So it's not just people inside the organization who need to learn how to use technology flexibly; it's people outside, as well. And how do organizations educate large numbers of people who are not under their direct control? How can I as a consumer learn everything that my bank, the IRS, the grocery store, my doctor, and the computer salesman want me to know? Where do I go for consumer education courses in all this stuff?

And how do we as a country keep up with the rest of the world? If taking advantage of the advancement of technology is key to competitive advantage, and it's not just people who use the technology who have to learn but everyone, how do we all learn everything we need to know? Should we expect more from our school systems than we are getting? Should we expect more from ourselves in pursuing adult education and lifelong learning? Who has the time and resources to invest? Who should pay? When the bank introduces a new technology such as automatic teller machines, who should bear the cost of teaching me to use it? These kinds of questions must be asked before we simply accept the challenge to make technology more flexible. The global competitive marketplace is driving us to develop and utilize more advanced technologies; and so ultimately are our own demands for convenience and lower costs as consumers. But is learning a new technology really more convenient than continuing to use the old, and are we prepared to accept the costs of introducing and maintaining the new system? Until we answer these questions, the benefits of technological flexibility will be limited.

Lesson Three: *New technology may affect every level of a system, from the individual to the whole world; how well the relationships among* *levels of the system are managed determines how much the new technology can do.*

To create flexible organizations capable of responding to changes in their external environment and taking advantage of internal opportunities, we need technology that allows us to be flexible in what we do and how we do it. Rarely is a lack of technical flexibility due to the limits of technology; much more often, technical flexibility is lacking because human beings ignored the need for it or simply failed to design flexibility into the system. More often still, technical inflexibility is due to our failure to think systemically, thereby allowing ourselves to become trapped in systems that aren't as responsive to change as they could be.

Lesson Four: *Technical inflexibility shouldn't be blamed on the machine alone. Instead, we need to look to people, organizations and the larger systems in which they exist.*

THE INVARIABLE HUMAN

There's an old joke about the fellow who returns his chain saw because it doesn't work well. When the clerk starts the saw to check it out, the fellow asks, "What's that noise?" Although it sounds like this fellow is really dumb, I feel the same way each time I learn to do something with one keystroke on my computer that used to take four or five. I have a sort of inner calculus that tells me when my frustration has built up to a point that it's time to read my manual. If I'm in the middle of something important, I'll wait a bit longer; if I have free time, I may look at the manual just out of curiosity. I'm sure that my learning would be faster if I took a concentrated course, many of which are available at the university for a nominal fee. But that much concentrated time is hard for me to find. So I waste time by seconds and minutes instead, which I'll bet in the span of a year add up to a lot more than the time I would spend in the course. If there are any advantages to doing it my way, they are that I control the rate of my learning and that I don't make too large an investment in a system that will change in a few months anyway. Or so I tell myself. The truth is that I'm not taking full advantage of the technology at my fingertips. If the manuscript I write is a few weeks late, it probably won't mean the end of the world; there is little penalty for my inefficiency. But in business, it's another story.

The capital investment I have made in equipment is minuscule compared to what the average firm invests in technology on a per-worker basis. I remember walking through a plastics manufacturing organization and seeing big signs posted on each of the forming presses, indicating the cost of each piece of equipment. The amounts were into six and sometimes seven figures. The message was clear: "You people better take good care of our expensive machinery!" I thought it was strange that the people didn't have signs on them, too; after all, the organization had probably paid each of the workers in the plant as much money over the course of their career as they spent on a machine. That way, supervisors would get the message: "These people are expensive assets; take good care of them!" All that expensive equipment wouldn't do much good without those people to operate it. But that's beside the point.

The point is that the *total* capital investment in people and technology in this plant is tremendous; and every minute that the *system* of people and technology operates less effectively than it could is a minute lost, a cost incurred, another dollar of interest accumulating on the company's debt that could have been paid off by higher productivity. I'm not an efficiency freak; but the cost of owning and operating equipment is too high for most firms to support if they are running inefficiently. Global competition simply won't allow most organizations to slide by on what was good enough last year. As my colleague, Jack Sherwood points out, the Japanese consider the first day of a piece of equipment's operation its *least* efficient day; through continuous improvement, the Japanese expect to see more output from the machine each day it is in operation. Therefore, the value of the asset appreciates over time. The American mentality is one of *depreciation*: We expect our assets to produce less and less over time until it's time to replace them with something new. Our whole mindset is that the asset produces as much on the first day as it ever will; to increase productivity, we go shopping for a new asset.

Incidentally, this analysis applies equally well to human assets; we hire most people to do a specific job; once they are trained (operational) we don't expect to see much change in their productivity. We expect them to stay the same or get worse; we don't expect people to learn, develop entirely new skills, invent new ways to do their work, perform completely different activities, willingly accept more responsibility, or to change their opinions. Once a union member, always a union member—whatever that stereotype means.

If we took the Japanese point of view, we would be investing in people's education; allowing them to learn new skills, expecting them to help invent new ways of doing their jobs better, *expecting* that every day on the job, the person would get smarter and better and more valuable to us. Most of our organizations are a long way from there.

Even more powerful than the Japanese model is to think about the *whole system* getting better at the same time. Not people or technology, people *and* technology. *And* information systems, *and* reward systems, *and* management, *and* decision-making, *and* quality, *and* human resource management, *and* finance, *and* planning, *and* maintenance, *and* engineering, *and* products, *and* accounting, *and* safety, *and* training, *and* performance management, *and* governance systems, *and* organizational learning, *and* organizational design, *and* customer feedback, *and* scheduling, *and* timeliness of delivery, *and* inventory management, *and* cooperation, *and* innovation, *and* order taking, *and* claim processing, *and* recordkeeping, *and* community relations, *and* environmental responsibility, *and* leadership, *and* communication, *and* customer service, *and* anything else that matters.

Clearly, this can't all happen if we only focus on one thing at a time; changing one thing, like the scope of a subordinate's job, changes something else—in this case, the supervisor's job. And maybe changing one thing changes a lot of other things. If we try to change one thing at a time, we wind up chasing our tails and getting nowhere fast. We may check another program off our "to do" list, but the chances of the program making a significant difference in the long run is nil if our focus shifts to something else, and then to something else, and then to something else again. The trick is to focus on everything at the same time. Impossible? Absolutely—for one person or one group. But not if *everyone* gets involved. The reason we go from one program to the next is that one program is all our current management structure can accommodate; the same few people need to oversee every new effort *and* keep the operation running too. By involving many more people in more meaningful ways in improvement activities, lots of things can receive attention at the same time. And, strangely enough, when programs are designed, conceived, and executed by the people who actually have to live with the results, the results are better and longer lasting. I hate to say it because I have a lot of respect for the managers I have worked with and taught over the years, but the truth is that one of the biggest contributions most managers can make to organizational improvement is simply to get out of the way. This doesn't fit the Japanese model of traditional authority and respect for elders; but there are fewer levels of management in most Japanese firms, so managers tend not to slow up the improvement process so much. You would think that everyone being involved in improvement is very consistent with the American culture and spirit; but I'm afraid we talk more about democracy, involvement, and independence than we practice them.

Technical flexibility requires a revisiting of our assumptions, our underlying beliefs about people, technology, and control. The old model of nonthinking work for the masses and thinking work only for those in high positions needs to be set aside in favor of a model of organizing in which everyone is expected to think. And in which each person knows enough about what is going on elsewhere that he can make independent contributions without screwing up someone else's contributions or destroying the effectiveness of the overall system.

I talked to a fellow who packed light bulbs in boxes for a living. It wasn't a very demanding job, but it paid well. The job could have been done easily by most children, but it so happened that this fellow had a high school education. To keep himself from going insane, he would think of ways to improve his job. Now there wasn't very much to improve; most of us would have to be pretty creative to think of any way at all to improve the effectiveness of our efforts at this task. But he did, and pretty soon, he knew he had become the company's best light bulb packer. By working quickly, and placing the light bulbs in just the right way, he was able to pack three times as many light bulbs into a box as he had previously, and reduce breakage as well. No one had asked him to think about this; he simply did it on his own. He didn't expect a reward for his innovation, even though he calculated how many fewer trucks the company would need to ship light bulbs in one third the number of boxes, and how much the company would save on boxes, drivers, insurance, maintenance on the trucks, and reduced light bulb breakage. He would have liked some recognition, but he didn't expect to receive any. He just did it to keep himself from becoming as boring as the job he had been given to do. One day, though, he did get some recognition—although not from the source or in the form he had anticipated. An industrial engineer observing him work started screaming at him, "It's you, it's you! You're the one who's screwing up our whole system!" Shocked, the fellow asked what the problem was; and the engineer told him how people in the planning department used to be able to predict approximately how many light bulbs there were in a box, and how many boxes it would take to fill an order, and how many trucks they would need to ship those boxes. Now, because everyone didn't pack light bulbs in the same way, the variability in number of bulbs per box was upsetting the whole system. It had even resulted in widening fluctuations in production planning because sometimes the plant seemed to make too many light bulbs and sometimes too few, and no one could determine why. The engineer was tempted to have the fellow fired on the spot, but upon reflection thought better and said to the worker, "Just do the job the way you were told, and for God's sake, don't think!"

So the fellow went back to work, doing the job the old way. In fact, he noticed that other workers weren't as careful as he and tended to break more bulbs than he did during packing; so, just to make sure he wasn't screwing up the system, he started to break a few extra bulbs each day. Within a few years, he and everyone else at the plant lost their jobs; the plant couldn't compete with more efficient facilities in the United States and overseas. I think this fellow knew why; I wouldn't blame him for being bitter.

What should the engineer have done? Clearly, it was important to have a workable system for controlling inventory and upon which to base production planning. But the mentality of the engineer and other managers in this plant was, "Run the system the way it was designed to be run." Instead of the relentless pursuit of improvement, there was a relentless pursuit of perfecting the current system—right down to the way light bulbs were packed. Improvements were constantly under way, but under the control of the engineering department. An improvement wasn't valid unless it emanated from the engineering office, the keepers of the technology. The guardians of the system. Protectors against unplanned change.

Faced with the real need for a quantum improvement in the performance of the plant, the engineers couldn't respond; they reasoned that an investment in new technology, extensive training, and higher wages would make an all-out effort unattractive from a cost–benefit standpoint. Better to close the place down.

How many thousands of improvement ideas had they stifled? How many ideas passed into, through, and out of people's minds without even being uttered because people sensed how their input would be treated? How many chances were missed to improve the efficiency of the operation without a huge capital investment or an all-at-once retraining effort or demands for radically higher wages to fit radically new responsibilities? Thinking about improving technical flexibility through one engineering project at a time just won't make it happen. The whole system needs to change—all at the same time, and continuously.

For this to work, the light bulb packer needs to understand a little about the inventory control system. He needs to know that planning is based on how many light bulbs there are in a box, and that changing that quantity will require changes in the inventory control system. He also needs to understand that he can't just do his own thing, and have everyone else do their own thing. There needs to be a single system, and people need to understand it and be committed to making it work. Just because the system appears simple doesn't mean that only a few people need to really understand how it all works; to unleash the power of each person's creativity, everyone needs to understand how the system works. Then flexibility is possible.

Sometimes, people aren't educated about the whole system because the system is complex and it is assumed that people can't understand it, or that the effort put into bringing them up to speed wouldn't be worthwhile. But that is rarely if ever the case. Engineers at a Zilog plant were perplexed by the job descriptions they were given. The descriptions called for them to spend most of their time providing training to people in the plant rather than actually doing the kind of engineering projects they were accustomed to doing. The engineers protested at first, because the technology involved in semiconductor manufacturing is extremely complex. "Wouldn't it be faster and easier for us to just do the work ourselves? If people have problems, we'll be around to fix them," they said. But the plant management team was resolute: Training was what they should do. The same was true for the quality assurance manager, the human resource manager, and others; their jobs were to train the people, not do the thinking for them. In no time the plant was performing better than any semiconductor manufacturing plant in the world and employees were recommending changes in the technology that the engineers never dreamed of. Although things have not gone smoothly since at Zilog for a variety of other reasons, the philosophy of training people to do their own thinking was fundamentally sound. It is impossible to improve the efficiency of a technical system if it can't be changed; the more people know about the technology they operate, and the more they understand the way the whole system operates, the more they can contribute to technical improvements. Flexible people enable flexible technology.

Another dimension of human flexibility is represented by diversity; not just diversity in skin color or sex, which are important and can sometimes be the basis for different perspectives on the same situation, but diversity in ways of thinking. My colleague, David Kolb, has devoted his life to understanding how people learn and think. What is very clear from Dave's research is that different people do think and learn in different ways. What is also clear is that our educational system, and in fact our entire society, has a preference for certain ways of thinking and learning over others. In organizations, people tend to surround themselves with people who think as they do themselves. What this all adds up to is the danger, if it hasn't already happened, of our organizations and society falling into a gigantic rut, which limits our ways of thinking about the world. For example, we have a very elaborate system set up in the government to prevent us from taking medications that have not been "properly" tested. What do we mean by "properly?" Most of us would automatically think of synonyms like "scientifically" or "repeatedly"; and, when asked what these terms meant, we would again think of certain kinds of cued-in responses, probably left over from our days of watching "Ben Casey" or "General Hospital." The truth is that we don't know what these terms really mean and even the people in the FDA and in the pharmaceutical industry argue over what they mean all the time. Nevertheless, we are taught to be naturally suspicious of drugs that aren't "properly" tested and to ignore altogether alternative treatments or forms of healing known to other cultures for generations. When we hear about the power of mental imaging in fighting cancer, for example, many of us are skeptical and demand proof; and only proof in a familiar form will convince us. The point is that we have been trained to think in certain ways, and that these ways of thinking often block us from learning about something that we really should know. We reject information if it doesn't fit our views or come from a reliable source or help us justify the position we have already taken. We may even ignore what we are feeling physically or emotionally if it doesn't jibe with what our eyes or ears tell us to be true. In the final analysis, we are the greatest enemies of flexibility; perhaps our comfort with the status quo, as fragile and illusory as we recognize it to be, is the product of generations of evolutionary craving for just one chance to sit still for a moment, to stop looking over our shoulders, to rest. But that time has not yet come; and, for our generation at least, developing even greater flexibility is still key to our survival.

ORGANIZATIONAL CHOICE: RIGIDITY BY DESIGN

Many people are aware of the pioneering work of Eric Trist and his colleagues in the British coal mining industry. Those who have heard just a little bit about Trist's work in the mines draw the wrong conclusions about what he discovered. They assume that he discovered that teams work better than individuals, or that self-supervision works better than traditional supervision, or that multiskilling works better than single skilling. All of these things are often true; but the real point, the one most often missed, is right there in the title to the book in which the coal mining studies are described: *Organizational Choice*[1].

Other researchers at the time were still hot on the trail of the ideal organization design. Most had abandoned the search, like the quest for the holy grail, but a few persisted and were the more influential voices of the day. Joan Woodward, more creatively than some of the rest, reasoned that the optimal design for a given organization might have something to do with the type of technology it used to produce goods.[2] Assembly lines, according to her theory, required a different organization design than required by custom job shops or chemical processing plants. After collecting data on a large number of organizations, the statistics supported her contention: Those organizations that were designed to fit the median characteristics of others in their industry outperformed others in the industry whose designs were more extreme. Woodward's research was repeated by others, and questions were raised about her methods and conclusions; but the quest for the perfect design continued. The only debate was over how to determine when one had really found it and what dimensions and determinants of design were really the most critical. But Trist chose his title with care; he didn't call his book *Teams in Mining* or *The Discovery of Self-Directed Work Groups* or *The Effectiveness of Multiskilling versus Single Skilling in Industry*. The title *Organizational Choice* was chosen deliberately, perhaps to say to the rest of the world, "You're all barking up the wrong tree!"

Organizational choice meant that the organization had many choices available to it in terms of how it arranged people, even around the same technology. Some choices were much more effective than others, but the real difference in effectiveness was not due to any single organization design characteristic. Rather, it was due to the way the entire system of people and technology functioned together. The best technology available could perform miserably if it didn't fit the social system; the best and smartest people couldn't make a poorly designed technical system competitive; and variations in span of control or number of management levels or the degree of work specialization in and of themselves would never make up for problems in the basic relationship between people and technology. It was as if Trist had picked up the prevailing academic paradigm, shaken it, and set it back down on its ear. There was no perfect organizational design. Each organization needed to find its own best design, based on an analysis of its people and technology working together in the context of a particular environment.

When the coal miners needed to respond to unexpected problems due to geological conditions they encountered, those mining organizations that had been designed to allow for flexibility in people's roles and activities were able to respond far better than were organizations that elevated all problems to management or engineering for resolution. In the inflexible organizations, if a problem required a different set of skills, the whole system waited until the person with those skills arrived to fix the problem. In the more flexible organizations, each team possessed all of the skills necessary to tackle any problem encountered, and management delegated decision-making to the experts within the teams. Action was immediate and effective. It takes no time at all to choose the system in which you would rather risk your life, or which system would make you feel more valued for your contributions. So multiskilled, self-managing teams worked better in the coal mines. But Trist would be the first to say that he didn't intend the example of the coal mines to become "the one best way." The same solution wouldn't work for football teams or cab drivers or computer engineers. The same solution wouldn't even work for all coal mines; the system worked well because it fit the preexisting culture and current technological configurations in use at the time. New technologies, new miners, or new underground conditions might require an entirely different method of organizing.

The generic principles for meaningful work laid out by Fred Emery included such things as variety, feedback, and elbow room; these characteristics were not a part of inflexible mining organizations.[3] But Emery's principles were broad enough to allow a great deal of latitude in design even among the more flexible mining organizations. So while the general principles of sociotechnical systems design are clear, the specific results in each case are not. Even if they were, an important element in sociotechnical systems analysis and design is the involvement of people who will work *in* the system to change the system. Only through direct involvement do people develop a working understanding of the important choices to be made in designing organizations. And it is this understanding, and experience of having created the system, which gives people confidence that they can change the design again whenever they feel the need to do so.

On a larger scale, the principle of organizational choice can be extended to business units or even multiunit or multinational organizations. Today, many organizations trying to establish a lasting foothold in the global marketplace are in search of the "perfect design for a multinational organization." As always, there are pundits who will argue strongly for a business-dominant matrix, others for a geographical-dominant matrix, and still others for a traditional functional organization. In whatever disguise, the desire for a simple, convenient, take-me-off-the-hook, one-size-fits-all answer continues to dredge up the modern day equivalent of snake oil salesmen. The truth Trist and Emery discovered is that each organization is a unique entity, and that the design that fits it best will be one of its own creation, taking into account its particular environment and in keeping with some very simple but straightforward principles of organizing.

In the search for the perfect answer, organizations give up a great deal of technical flexibility. The battles over who should have the right to control the development and marketing of which products where overshadows the more pressing long-term need to evolve the design of the organization as the environment evolves. In the globally competitive battle that is currently raging, it is possible that the most powerful offense may be to seek collaborative alliances with current and former competitors. Anthony Badarroco's analysis of alliances is informative; he points out that successful alliances are frequently formed under conditions that allow each party to "win."[4] In the case of GM and Toyota, for example, GM got a firsthand look at Japanese manufacturing techniques while Toyota received assistance with its image in the United States and its market penetration here. Both organizations felt that they gained something, even though it is unclear how long the alliance will last or if it will spread to other operations. Even in the highly secretive and closely guarded arena of upstream R&D, multinational corporations are finding it advantageous in certain cases to pool scientific efforts to achieve technological breakthroughs. The *knowledge alliance* may be the greatest organizational innovation of the decade or even the century, given its vast potential to speed the development and implementation of technology in areas that are beyond the knowhow or financial grasp of even our largest single organizations. Sit tight but stay tuned.

The invention, implementation and deployment of new technology represents a slightly different type of technical flexibility than we have been discussing so far. How rapidly they can develop, manufacture, and market new products has become the source of competitive concern for many R&D-based organizations. Whereas it used to be more acceptable to perform research in a campus-like setting, completely detached from the pressures of life elsewhere in the organization, this is seldom the case today. Technology developers are being pulled inside and downstream in many organizations. Basic research is often more difficult to fund in these organizations because of the perception of greater return on investment being gained by having technical people working closer to the customer. In the long run, the answer cannot lie simply in diverting upstream research dollars to applied problems, any more than downsizing alone can restore lasting competitive advantage. Instead, R&D organizations need to learn to do research better and faster, just as other parts of the organization have been forced to consider continuous improvement in practices and procedures that went unchallenged previously.

Technical flexibility in products and processes begins with alternatives to choose from; and developing alternatives requires an investment in internal or external research. How can you do something different when what you are doing now is all you know how to do? Achieving technical flexibility through more effective R&D will require just as large a shakeup in R&D as that which has taken place in manufacturing. New, more flexible organizational arrangements are already enabling a few R&D organizations to cut cycle time drastically and increase the flow of marketable new products. Traditional R&D organizations are under attack and showing signs of losing their fight to remain unchanged. They too are being forced to do more with less. What won't work for them, anymore than it did in manufacturing, is either to deny the changes in the world around them or simply demand that people work harder. Doing more of the same faster won't produce the breakthroughs that are needed in product development speed or success. Things have to be done differently.

One R&D organization I worked with was facing this kind of pressure and needed desperately to respond. If it did not, there was a high probability that its sinking parent corporation would divest the entire business unit of which it was a part, with no guarantees of safe landings to those jettisoned overboard. The R&D organization had a policy of promoting its most favored scientists to the positions of team leaders. With this promotion came the right to set the scientific direction for the team to follow. Junior scientists labored, sometimes for years, on projects they felt no investment in while waiting for their own turn at the wheel. Once given the opportunity to lead, they thrust their ideas upon their teams with insensitive abandon, ignoring pleas from their former peers that their ideas would never work. After years of this practice, and very few successes to show for the investment, the organization had unintentionally created a culture in which the majority of scientists felt their projects would be unsuccessful and were pessimistic about the organization's future. Some of the brightest fled to competitors, and a few others sounded as alienated and frustrated as any union member I have heard.

The organization created a number of teams of scientists from various project teams to study the way they conceived of projects and carried them out. To their credit, managers of the organization listened to what the teams had to say and made significant changes in the way its new projects were organized and managed. While it is too early to report major scientific breakthroughs as a result of the change, they are still in business and much more optimistic about the future.

Once technologies are developed and implemented, rigidity can actually become designed in to the organization by the creation of roles, budgets, and policies designed to support the current arrangements. Functional boundaries may be drawn around technical systems (plating, coating) and multiple levels of supervision installed to micromanage operations according to the grand plan. Employees may be trained in a narrow set of technical skills that makes it difficult to shift them to other tasks without large investments in additional training. Labor and management negotiate contracts that further define and rigidify the rules of the game. Eventually, the government becomes involved by regulating safety, conditions of employment, and other aspects of the system. Once all the supports that maintain the current technical system are in place, it seems inconceivable to start all over again with a blank sheet of paper. Even though humans put the system together, the accumulation of rust has frozen the parts of the system together to the point where humans no longer possess the strength to loosen them.

At one time, Sweda was the leading manufacturer of mechanical calculators. We all know what happened when Texas Instruments introduced the electronic calculator; but in the face of this competition, rather than reading the writing on the wall or waiting to see where the technology was headed, Sweda sunk a huge investment in increasing the efficiency of its mechanical calculator manufacturing facilities. Higher efficiency wasn't the answer, and mechanical calculators may find their only future to be as display items in museum collections. Knowing how to do something very well, and especially being the best in the world at it, creates narrowed vision, over-confidence, and organizational xenophobia.

Clearly, inflexible organizations are found everywhere, at every level, and not just in assembly line or sweat shop operations. Organizational inflexibility in roles, decision-making, functional responsibilities, and other aspects of design can affect the development, deployment, and overall flexibility of technical arrangements. The goal is not to be the best railroad in town; it's to stay in the transportation business.

YOU CAN'T FIGHT THE SYSTEM

Like most others, when I began graduate school, I was expected to help teach a course in exchange for tuition support. And, like most others, I welcomed the opportunity to teach, since I planned to spend a good portion of my life doing it and I wanted to learn to do it well, as soon as possible. But to my shock and dismay, the course I was assigned to help teach was introductory accounting. I had taken accounting courses, and had done well in them, but I would have listened more carefully had I known that I would have to remember the difference between debits and credits for more than one day after the final exam. I had less than one week to get up to speed again. After walking into a lecture hall filled with 500 students, and explaining the difference between debits and credits, I never feared standing in front of a class again. At least not as much.

In addition to learning something about teaching that semester, I also became more fond of accounting. I got to know some of the accounting faculty and accounting graduate students and discovered that they were unexpectedly likable. I nearly switched fields; but the next semester, my duty was in economics, and the semester after that, I received my own course in organizational behavior. There was no turning back.

Today, when I hear people in organizations complain about accountants, I try to tell people it's not the accountants, it's accounting. When I hear of the seemingly stupid reports, approvals, policies, and procedures emanating from accounting departments, I'm certain that none of the accountants I knew would ever have created such a system. Not if they could have avoided it. But sometimes good people can't seem to avoid doing bad things, things they know won't help in the long run. Like setting up separate profit-and-loss statements for segments of a business that should be working together interdependently; or finding ways to depreciate assets as rapidly as possible; or forcing everybody to pay attention to a number that has nothing to do with the strategy of the organization or customer satisfaction. People down in the organization, faced with day-to-day choices about technology, are forced to choose between doing what's right (such as investing in technology to enhance its flexibility) and doing what the accountants are measuring (such as maximizing immediate returns on capital investments). They would like to do the right thing, and their managers would like them to do the right thing. And if the stockholders understood what was going on, even they might like them to do the right thing. But from the perspective of the lowly individual decision-maker, the system is too big and too difficult to change. Better to do the wrong thing and live to fight another day. Blame the accountants for the failure of the business; after all, it's their system.

If it's not the accountants, it's human resources. Especially labor relations people or compensation people or EEO people. Human resources has inherited every policy, every grievance, every corporate program; and with all of this, human resources has also inherited a reputation as being a pain in the neck and keeper of the status quo. When manufacturing wants to introduce new technology, or train people to be more flexible in operating existing technology, who is standing in the way? Human resources. Why? Because the last time manufacturing pushed ahead without consulting human resources, it led to a grievance over job descriptions that almost caused another strike. Manufacturing gets measured by results, so you can't trust them to do the right thing by people; human resources gets rewarded for slowing manufacturing down and thereby avoiding a possible catastrophe. It's a crazy system. Things have gotten so bad that I expect the greatest resistance I will face in working with organizations to create more flexibility to come from human resources. These people are supposed to be on my side, to think like I do, to care about people, to be interested in demonstrating their ability to help the organization become more progressive; but instead, they are guardians against change, keepers of the status quo. I know it's the nature of the role, but, sometimes I can't help but begin to formulate a theory that these people wouldn't be in human resources if they were interested in change. They would be in manufacturing, or information systems, or marketing—somewhere closer to the action, where the goal is to make something good happen. I don't hear many line managers putting in their bid for assignments in human resources. In fact, most line managers would just as soon see human resources disappear. But when line managers become business unit managers or CEOs, they begin to see the value of the human resources function. Everyone else is trying to break the rules, but you can count on human resources to be a hall monitor for potentially truant line managers.

I think that someday, we will recognize that it makes no more sense to separate human resources out as a function than it does quality control; the line has to think about people and technology at the same time. As soon as we appoint someone to a staff position, the rest of us stop thinking about that area of concern. We figure that if we don't hear any bad news, we must be doing OK; we can concentrate on doing what's really important. When we do hear bad news, we initiate a crash program to turn things around, promise never to do it again, and then go back to business as usual. In the case of introducing new technology, this means that we proceed in fits and starts, have to back up, renegotiate the contract, go forward again, experience more problems, fight a few grievances, then recognize the need for training, start that, and finally climb slowly up to near full capacity, but with a labor force that is more alienated than ever. Nonsystemic thinking: It's human nature, but it's not particularly good for flexibility or long-term organizational effectiveness. If managers could just learn that all work systems are *socio*technical systems, and that no introduction of technology should begin without the involvement of those affected, we could save human resources a lot of work, and a bad reputation.

The funny thing about human resources is that it is also the favorite place to stick internal organization development practitioners. Change involves people, so that must mean anyone who deals with change should sit in human resources. But being in human resources is the kiss of death for an OD consultant; human resources seldom has the respect or the clout it needs to make things happen. And besides, change isn't really *caused* by human resource issues most of the time; change is more often driven by new technology or competitive pressures. The people who have the most to gain from successful change are the people who want to see the new technology work or the business meet its sales goals. Rather than creating a special function for powerless internal consultants within human resources, it might make more sense to provide training in change management to engineers, business unit managers, or marketing people; people whose careers are on the line if change doesn't happen. I know this sounds strange coming from a person who has helped to train hundreds of internal consultants, but I'm really tired of hearing the people I train complain that they don't get to use half of the skills they have on the job. I'm tired of hearing how they are belittled, ignored, and openly kicked around by the clients they want so desperately to serve. These are nice people, for the most part; they deserve better treatment. But they aren't going to get it if they are part of human resources.

Someone once said to me that it's a lot easier to teach a good engineer people skills than it is to make a liberal arts major into a good engineer. They may be right, but having been trained in engineering myself and working with engineers over the years, I'm pretty sure it isn't *that* easy. Given almost any opportunity, most engineers will be attracted to technical issues rather than people issues. They can think about people when they are reminded to—it's just not a natural first instinct. So new technical systems usually get pretty far along in development before questions are raised such as, How many people will we need to operate this system? What kinds of jobs will they have? What will it feel like to do this kind of work? Can they lift that much weight for eight hours? Is the terminal interface user-friendly? How long will it take to train people to do this? How difficult will it be for people to fix this system when it breaks? How flexible will this system need to be if our projections are wrong? Many of these questions aren't answered until the equipment is bolted to the floor and the production schedule and profitability goals already have been established. By then, it's hard to involve people in decisions that really matter: decisions that affect their day to day experience of work and their ability to control the system they have been given to operate.

When Ben & Jerry's built a new plant recently, they put ordinary shop floor employees to work on the design job. They sent them out to benchmark against the best manufacturing systems they could find, provided them with technical information on options and alternatives, gave them a budget to stay within and a blank sheet of paper. The plant is extremely successful, and you can bet that the people who work in it are dedicated to making it work as well as it possibly can. No wrenches thrown into the works here. Later, when it comes time to update the technology, workers won't panic at the prospect of what management might be thinking about doing to them next; they can relax knowing that if there are important changes to be made, they will be involved in making them. In the midst of all our technical specialization and advanced training, we forget how simple life can be; and how flexible a system can be; and how flexible people can be when they work in a flexible system that involves them in decisions instead of coercing them into going along with what someone else thinks will be good for them.

Sometimes organizations get caught up in systems that are bigger than they are. The steel industry is a classic example. Shareholders viewed the mills as cash cows and opted not to invest in new technology; the Japanese entered the market with newer and more efficient technology, which allowed them to produce and sell steel for less than U.S. manufacturers. By the time U.S. steel industry managers could get through to their shareholders, it was too late; no one wanted to invest the huge sums of money that would be required to make the industry competitive again, if it ever could be, given costly government-imposed requirements for pollution control technology. The unions were used to high wages and refused concessions; an expectation on everyone's part of lifetime employment delayed downsizing efforts; arrogance during the period of market dominance resulted in a lackadaisical attitude toward customers. There were so many people to blame for the decline of competitiveness that it was hard to blame anyone. Yet it seemed that someone should be to blame, because it was obvious that the wrong actions had been taken and that the industry could have been saved if *someone* had been more on top of things. Once the whole system gets on your back, it's difficult to carry it uphill. As the old proverb goes, it's easy to help an elephant get up when it's getting up, but it's hard to help an elephant get up when it's in the process of sitting down.

TRADING IN YOUR STEAM ENGINE
FOR WARP DRIVE

What does it take to enhance technical flexibility? Flexible people, flexible technology and flexible systems. Sounds easy; but if it were, I'd know how to use my computer better by now. What's required, I think, are some important shifts in the way we think about people and technology.

First, we need to place real emphasis on developing people and rewarding them for efforts in acquiring technical skills that enable technical flexibility. Pay for skill systems are entirely consistent with this objective, but they often stop short at rewarding people only for learning skills that are needed to get the job done today. Just as important to long-term flexibility is building up people's requisite variety: skills they don't need right now but which may be vital tomorrow. This should start in our school systems and carry on through life; keeping up with technology is something we are all going to have to do for a very long time.

Work assignments and staffing decisions should take the need for technical updating into account, allowing people to spend meaningful time learning about systems that they may use to enhance the performance of their work. In the case of high-tech organizations, longer term sabbaticals or classes for every person may be beneficial. When someone says the cost of such training is prohibitive, they need to be put on a plane, sent to Cleveland, and told to stand in the middle of a deserted steel mill until they gain a new perspective.

Technical system designers need to learn change management skills, especially those associated with employee involvement. Then, like the engineers at Zilog, they need to teach other people enough about the technical alternatives to empower them to make intelligent technical system design choices for themselves. These design alternatives should emphasize flexibility in technology, to allow for unforeseen changes in customer demands, industry developments, or technological upgrades. People should take ownership of the technology they operate by understanding enough about its design and operation to maintain it and even to improve it.

Systems of hierarchical control can be eliminated when control is achieved through commitment rather than reconnaissance. Systems of control should be owned by the people responsible for producing results. Let the fox guard the chickens? Why not? Isn't that the lesson we learned through total quality? Build quality in to every job, don't try to inspect it into our products; build responsibility into every person, don't try to catch them if they break the rules; it's expensive and inefficient. And which of our managers don't we trust?

Develop systemic thinking, including the ability to think about every technical system as a sociotechnical system. And develop the capacity to recognize when the system is in trouble sooner by *expecting* change to be necessary. Put more time into thinking about how to make the system better than trying to figure out who is to blame for screwing up the light bulb inventory system. Reward people for taking risks, for trying something new, for helping us to understand ideas that don't work. Better yet, set a minimum number of mistakes quota for every manager; if we're not making enough mistakes, we aren't trying enough things that are new and daring.

Let people who don't understand the technology look it over. They often ask questions that lead to new insights and improvements. Get ahead of the technology curve; be an early adopter on a small scale rather than waiting for everyone else to decide that the technology is worth investing in. Move people around internally, and send them out to observe others frequently. And don't just send them to others in the industry or who use the same technology; try to find companies that are in similar businesses in entirely different areas. Interested in logistics? Visit Wal-Mart. Want to know about distribution? Talk to UPS or Federal Express. New ideas in plant design? Try Ben & Jerry's. Then try their ice cream; you'll be even more impressed.

Develop a customer education program; you can't move ahead without taking customers along with you. And while you're at it, let the shareholders know what is going on—and not just via the annual report. Understanding the need to invest in technical flexibility requires more than looking at some nice pictures and reading a suspect explanation of the profit-and-loss statement.

We're much better at responding to a crisis than we are to incremental change. We have been in the midst of a technical revolution for the last century and a half, and the revolution isn't over. Yet we are still pretending that whatever this latest advance is, it's the last we will ever have to assimilate. We set up special one-time budgets, one-time training efforts, one-time customer information briefings. When we finish, we tear up the change infrastructure—until we need it again, and then we have to start all over. Enhancing technical flexibility begins with finally accepting that we are living in a whirlwind of change that will only grow stronger. The best companies will be those that learn to bend with the wind; or, perhaps, to bend before the first breeze is felt by others.

CHAPTER
5

Flexible Work
Getting Things Done through Teamwork and Collaboration

One of the things I enjoy the most about being a professor is being left alone. Not literally, but in terms of deciding what work I should do. Many people make suggestions to me about what I should write or teach or research, but, in the final analysis, I don't have to listen to any of them. I get to decide for myself.

There are some requirements I must meet: teaching classes, attending faculty meetings, spending time with students; but, for the most part, the actual work I do is up to me. And because I like variety, my work is always changing in ways that I want it to change. I never teach a course exactly the same way twice; and what I do outside of the classroom is constantly evolving in the directions I desire. I'm allowed to formulate my own hypotheses, design my own research, decide what papers or books to write, and develop my own approach to consulting.

All of this makes sense; as a professor, my job is to try to stay on top of my field—in fact, ahead of it if I can. I'm supposed to be the expert on my work; no one is supposed to know more about it than I; and so, at least theoretically, no one should be able to supervise me in doing it. I'm supposed to be able see the opportunities that exist for furthering knowledge and then ask the right questions, find the right answers, and convey what I have learned to others. It wouldn't make sense for me to research what is already well understood or write about what others have written. The nature of the work I do is always changing, and so is my job. The same approaches I used to answer the last question probably won't fit the next; the same consulting strategy I applied to one organization may not be right for another. My work needs to be flexible to remain relevant, and I need to be flexible in order to do it.

The life of professors has always been a life of flexible work. Society is willing to gamble on supporting universities in their dual mission of research and education; and universities rely on professors to advance the state of knowledge in their chosen fields. The number and quality of publications turned out is the primary measure of professorial performance; publications provide an objective reference point in an arena in which very few people speak one another's technical language. Teaching is important, too; but in most large universities, the specifics of course content are left to the professors to decide. Students evaluate courses, and truly awful teachers get some counseling; but rarely is poor teaching the primary cause for denial of tenure. Advancing the state of knowledge is what keeps the whole system going in the long run. Without new knowledge, there would be nothing new to teach; and, after a while, no real need for the university. Professors understand that they must return enough value to society to continue earning their freedom. Or at least some do. Society trusts the university, the university trusts the professors, and professors guard their self-interests by doing work that is new and important.

The same level of trust exists only in relatively few other jobs in our society. For most people, work feels much more constraining. Objectives are handed down, sometimes along with instructions on how the job is to be performed. Job descriptions define what a person is or isn't supposed to do, where they are supposed to work, what tools they are to use, what they are allowed to touch or not touch, and even when they can go to the bathroom. Even though almost every job description ends with the phrase, "Other duties as required," neither the person nor the organization expects the job to vary greatly from day to day.

The thinking that produces this system of strict definition of detailed job descriptions and activities makes work inflexible. When new technology is introduced, or a customer wants something special done for her, the job description may represent a barrier to change. If change really is here to stay, either job descriptions will need to become more flexible or a lot more time will be needed to keep them current. I think the former makes more sense. It seems to me that the evidence in favor of flexibility over rigidity is everywhere and growing. Even jobs that people thought would never change are in fact changing today: the postal clerk, the electric utility meter reader, the assembly line worker. And what's more, people are changing jobs.

It's harder than it used to be to find someone who has been in the same job for more than a few years. Even those who hold the same job are doing work today that they could never have imagined doing a few years ago; many are doing work that didn't even *exist* a few years ago. Yet, in many companies, job descriptions remain virtually static.

In a world of fast-paced, competition-driven change, the last thing an organization needs is an organization chart that is immutable. In times of rapid change, more organizations will fail because of failure to redirect key roles than because of failures in maintaining the status quo. Whether it's new markets, new products, new technologies, new regulations, or new competitive strategies, the one thing that is common to all significant efforts to enhance organizational success is that some, if not many, roles will need to change as well. Change doesn't happen by simply planning for it or wishing for it to happen; it requires that people engage in new behaviors, in *new work*.

Let's take an example from customer service. Many organizations these days are talking a good game about being responsive to customer input; far fewer really do more than talk. One that does is RR Donnelly, the printing company. In some RR Donnelly locations, major customers are a part of cross-functional work teams that encompass all the jobs needed to serve the customer, beginning to end. Now it's one thing to *talk* about customer feedback; it's another thing to actually *listen* to it. RR Donnelly folks not only listen, they figure out how to *respond* to their customers, in real time. If the customer asks for something new and different, people on the team sit together around a table until they figure out how to do what the customer wants done. Eventually, the team will figure out the answer, sometimes after contacting support groups such as engineering or engaging the supplier of ink or paper in the discussion. Once the answer is known, the group plans how to implement its solution. It's here that jobs begin to change. Someone on the team, and often everyone on the team, needs to do something new and different. Being involved in the discussion of what needs to happen is tremendously helpful. People start out on the same page; they don't just receive orders from a supervisor to act differently or a notice from production control to turn up the ink supply on the next job. They know what the customer wants and what their part of delivering the new product will be. They may need to retrain themselves, experiment with some new processes, or develop some new process measures to ensure that they can maintain quality during a run. But then they get on with the job. The time spent planning and discussing as a team what the customer wants may seem wasteful at first, but the ideas and the commitment that are generated during the discussion make the time spent meeting as a group worthwhile and result in tangible resource savings. The customer-focused work system creates significantly higher customer satisfaction than the way things used to be done. In the past, there was a single point of reference between the customer and the organization—often a marketing person who had little idea of what would be required technically to give the customers what they wanted. Now, the technical experts are getting it straight from the horse's mouth. The customers may miss some of the expensive lunches, but most are a lot happier at the end of the month because they have received what they asked for—instead of what the salesman thought they needed.

To enable this responsiveness to customers, work needs to be made flexible; tight job descriptions and carefully prescribed functional boundaries would interfere with the ability of the team to implement solutions to the customer's problems. Because doing something different involves learning, over time employees become more knowledgeable and more able to understand how the whole system works. And the system works better because the employees know what needs to be done. It's a win-win.

WHAT IS FLEXIBLE WORK?

Fred Herzberg said it a long time ago: There's a big difference between job enlargement and job enrichment.[1] He advocated *vertical loading* as one antidote to boring work; and by that he meant adding tasks of greater responsibility—often tasks formerly performed by supervisors—to employees' roles.

Today, Herzberg's point seems to be often misunderstood. Multiskilling, intended to produce job enrichment, may produce only job enlargement. When multiskilling involves no more than learning the jobs of other people who do similar work, the job has gotten larger but no more meaningful. It isn't until a new multiskilled group responsible for a whole task meets to *think* about their work that multiskilling actually becomes enriching. When management asks people to multiskill but not to think, employees have a right to ask what is really behind the change. Chances are, it's cost cutting, not concern for the employees, or for the long-run success of the business.

Flexible work begins with developing flexibility in technical skills. But increasing technical skill flexibility is only the first step. The real benefits from creating flexible work are achieved when people are able to examine the work they are performing and decide that it isn't the work they *should* be performing—and do something about it. This reexamination may be driven by customer demands, as in the case of RR Donnelly, or it may be driven by awareness of relevant technical advances, or by benchmarking against work arrangements used in other companies. Regardless of the instigating force, true flexibility requires that groups possess both highly developed technical skills *and* problem solving capabilities.

As technology becomes more complex and the environment more turbulent, information-processing demands increase and the acquisition of high levels of technical and social skills becomes more difficult. At some point, the work becomes too much for the group to handle, at least as a whole group at the same time. The group is forced to consider alternative ways of staying on top of learning agendas, information needs, customer feedback, work system design issues and alternatives, and, not incidentally, production.

I recently visited a company that had undertaken a work redesign effort a few years earlier. I was being brought in to review the progress to date and to make some suggestions concerning some difficulties that had been encountered. One of the difficulties was fulfilling the training schedule that had been set during implementation planning. The site manager felt badly that not everyone on every team had been able to receive training opportunities. The work that people in his organization performed was highly technical in nature, involving decisions crucial to revenues and safety, so cross-training people took a very long time. The system had to be kept running, so training had to fit in around the edges; and, given lean staffing, the training had proceeded more slowly than expected. There was an ambitious schedule for other types of training as well: training in quality, safety, teamwork, diversity, and problem solving. The training backlog was growing, and people at the site were frustrated with their inability to implement the system fully.

As I listened, it became apparent that the training agenda would *never* be met under the constraints that people mentioned. Given that fact, the only choice was to reduce the amount of training being offered. At first, it appeared that reducing the amount of training would jeopardize the design; if everyone didn't learn every skill, how could the group function as a self-directed team?

The answer to the training problem was that everyone *didn't* need to learn everything; that it was OK for some members on the team to be more knowledgeable about certain things than others on the team! When I suggested this, there was an expression of disbelief on the faces of most people around the table. "Doesn't sociotechnical systems design require that everyone learn everyone else's job?" they inquired. My answer, clearly, was "No!" This organization had studied designs in less complex and more stable settings in which every person *did* learn every other person's job. At the Gaines Pet Foods in Topeka, for example, each production employee eventually learned every production job in the entire plant. But the organization I was visiting was different; its work required much longer periods of training to master, and its environment was changing more rapidly, both technically and in terms of customer demands. The design that had been suggested was actually making work *less* flexible by insisting that everyone go through the same training, instead of recognizing that a greater depth of expertise was required on the part of a few people to help others understand technical alternatives. Others on the team could specialize as well, in *different* areas of expertise. In that way, the knowledge of the whole team would be much greater, and the team could be more flexible when asked to change. Flexible work requires a base-level understanding of the whole task or system; but it doesn't require that people become completely interchangeable parts.

Increasing flexibility also requires time; it's hard to redesign an airplane while it's flying and it's almost as difficult to redesign a system while it's producing. In order for groups to consider new ways of working, develop the new skills they need to implement the new system, and discuss the outcomes of their efforts, groups need time off-line. Improvements pay for themselves *in* time; but they don't happen *without* time. The fallacy of traditional thinking about improvement is that a few experts can think of all the improvements themselves, and then simply tell people what to do differently. Not only is this an arrogant presumption, it overlooks the tremendous value of the creativity that exists among those doing the work. And it fails to build people's commitment to make the innovation work. In a large organization, providing time for groups to think about innovations in work can release thousands of creative minds to assist in improvement efforts. Research on group decision-making consistently demonstrates that four or five people can think of more ideas and better solutions than the same four or five people working alone. We have to ask ourselves, how much better can 100 or 100,000 people do at thinking than just one? Using everyone's creativity will be the sustainable source of competitive advantage in the future; but only if creativity can be coupled with flexible working arrangements. As noted earlier, quality circles had relatively limited impact on the organizations that used them because tight boundaries were placed on what people were allowed to think about. Usually, improvements had to fit within the system as it was currently designed. Pay, information systems, marketing research methods, supervisory practices, technology, and company policy were off limits in many cases.

Apparently, some believe that significant improvements in performance can be made without changing the system very much, the theory being that the system and the people are two independent entities. People can change what they do without changing the system; and the system can be changed without impacting what people do. However, this simply isn't the case. Even seemingly insignificant changes, such as rearranging the furniture in an office or removing a wall here or there can produce dramatic changes in communication patterns; and when communication patterns change, so does the content of work. People talk to each other, think about what they say and hear, and change what they do because of it. The impact of the change is magnified when the changes in the system affect the technology used to perform work, or the ways in which people are rewarded or recognized for their efforts.

As an example, in redesigning its technical center, a tire manufacturer eliminated cubby-hole offices in favor of modular, half-wall open space; but even more importantly, space was provided for groups to meet. Lots of space. The new conference rooms were full almost immediately, the level of teamwork increased dramatically, and the cycle time for new product development decreased. No one told the engineers that they had to make use of the new space; they just did.

Tom Allen of MIT has done years of research on communication patterns that indicates that if you can't see another person you aren't nearly as likely to talk to them. Since communication is essential to the integration of ideas in product development, Allen helps organizations design R&D facilities to enable more people to see each other. Sometimes, effective communication is helpful in other settings as well, since R&D isn't the only place where thinking and communicating are important elements of work.

Think for a moment about the people you see on a regular basis at work, and then think about the people you don't see. Should any of the people you don't see know more about what you are doing? What kind of effort would it take for you to find them and tell them about your work? Would they be willing to listen if you did? Physical space arrangements influence not only who we talk to, but who we really know; who we feel close to, and who we are afraid of or avoid. It's a very simple, well understood phenomenon; yet we continue to work in offices or factories that are carved up into tiny bits of territory and surrounded by walls with guards to prevent errant communication from reaching where it shouldn't and bringing the whole house down. What would happen if manufacturing caught wind of what R&D was working on? Or if accounting overheard manufacturing talk about the capital budget? Or if customers could just walk in and talk directly to production workers? These are the nightmares that keep narrow-minded building designers and security people awake at night. The effect of these restrictions on communication is to limit communication precisely where it shouldn't be limited: among people with a shared goal and interdependent tasks.

As the task changes, the physical space should change as well. For example, different people need to work together during different phases of a project; yet it's common to find people traveling great distances on a regular basis in order to spend a day a week together. In at least some cases, it would make more sense to relocate people temporarily until the interdependent work was done. The inconvenience of being away from home for a longer stretch might counterbalance the hassle of weekly travel. Even within the same facility, people find it hard to move into common space with others in order to work together intensively for a period of time. The physical space of our offices reflects the prevailing mode of organizing: one person, one job. The space gets in the way of people working together, flexibly.

And the space is just one aspect of the system that makes work less flexible than it should be. People who work together intensively, each contributing the same amount of effort and often the same input into the final product, raise appropriate questions concerning the inequity of rewards they receive. Why should the senior manager, who nods wisely on occasion, receive four to six times the pay earned by the junior fellow in the meeting who is doing all the legwork and coming up with all the ideas? One could say that the manager is being rewarded for past effort, or for his or her knowledge of the bigger picture into which the current project fits, or for his or her wisdom in steering the group toward its solution; but, to the junior person, it still doesn't seem fair. Eventually, if it still feels unfair, the junior person will begin to reduce the effort he or she puts forth, and may start to entertain thoughts about working elsewhere. Search firms make a fortune each year by helping people discover that they are worth more than their current employer is paying them. It's much easier to hire in to a company at a higher wage than it is to receive a similar pay increase within the system. So the pay system limits what people can expect to receive in terms of rewards for their efforts; but it also defines what kinds of work they can do, what kinds of decisions they are allowed to make, who they spend time with, and whether or not they receive invitations to the boss's Christmas party. In the end, rigid pay systems define a person's status, and along with it, her future. They make work inflexible.

And so do the company's policies, and hiring procedures, and accounting systems, and security systems, and dining arrangements, and performance appraisal systems, and on and on. Each of these aspects of the system has been designed to make work less flexible than it should be. You hear stories about it almost every day: people who aren't allowed to see other people, who can't make even the tiniest of decisions, who didn't know that so and so had already done that work, who can't understand why those jerks in (you fill in your favorite function) can't get their act together. Anyone who says the system doesn't affect what people can or can't do is living in their own world—probably, their own system.

To design systems that support flexible work, we need to think differently about space and control. Instead of minimizing the expenditure on space in order to save a dollar on rent or heat, we need to consider the value space can provide in facilitating communication, cooperation, and teamwork. The hidden costs of limited space on performance are much greater than most people imagine. And so are the hidden costs of control systems, which are designed to prevent the loss of a dollar or the breaking of a rule but which cost much more than that in the effect they have on reducing flexibility. As long as nothing we are doing needs to be changed, and the system is designed and functioning perfectly, we can live with minimum space and tight controls; but if change is for real, and people need to work flexibly with others to get the job done, space and controls get in the way.

So, at a minimum, flexible work is work that requires that people adjust what they do to meet the demands of the situation. But more than that, flexible work is work that requires that people develop new skills, work with many different people over time, develop new methods and technologies to perform the work, move about from place to place in order to work with others to do it, receive rewards for innovation and for success in task completion, take responsibility for decision-making based on their expertise, and operate with a minimum of organizational restrictions on their actions. Kind of like professors.

THE BIGGER PICTURE

Achieving flexibility in working arrangements isn't easy for many organizations. The investment of time and money in training, coordination, and change required to make work flexible is often prohibitive in an already tight economy. So some organizations are finding other ways to make work flexible, and people are finding ways to move on or move up on their own. The last decade of corporate downsizing in the United States has broken the loyalty contract between companies and employees. When GM has layoffs, that's one thing; but when IBM has layoffs, that's another. GM never promised people a rose garden; but IBM, for a long time, hinted that it was immune to the ups and downs of poorly managed companies and that its people could expect to work for Big Blue for life. Life at IBM, for some people, is a lot shorter than it used to be.

Despite the gut-wrenching agony of letting long-service employees go, organizations discovered that there were some beneficial side effects of downsizing in addition to cutting costs. Some employees who had "retired on the job" got to retire for real. They got out of other people's way, and created opportunities for advancement that didn't exist previously. Some really terrible managers were moved out or around, giving employees who worked for them a new lease on life, a chance to be creative, more hope for change. Often, the span of control of remaining managers became so large that decision-making authority was forced down in the organization closer to where it should have been all along. And, faced with more work than they could possibly accomplish after the departure of their peers, some employees began to look for ways to eliminate unnecessary work or to streamline work processes. So in some cases, after the period of mourning was over, those who remained eventually found work to be better: a bit more meaningful, a bit less frustrating, a bit more flexible.

But what about those who were forced to leave? Many suffered severe depression and disorientation. Some never recovered. But others found new work for themselves, and the most creative and resourceful people found even better work for themselves. If downsizing is handled properly, people receive the assistance they need to get on with their lives. They go back to school, learn new skills, and find new careers. Or, if they are fortunate enough to receive a healthy severance package and have the drive, they try their hand at entrepreneurship. We are still in love with the American dream, and we are spellbound by stories of employees who were laid off by some huge corporation, started their own business, and then bought the huge corporation a few years later. The resourcefulness was there all along; the huge corporation just didn't know how to utilize it.

Life is full of uprootings, replantings, new growth, and harvests. When we let go of the false idols of security that entrap us and restrict our flexibility, we discover again that the same spirit that drove the Pilgrims, the pioneers and the voyagers lives in us all. We reawaken our long-dormant ability to dream, and reconnect with the excitement of moving on, in the pursuit of a world of our own making. We reclaim the meaning of life.

Here in Maine, there are examples of new pioneers everywhere. My neighbor is a graphic artist who gave up corporate life in Ohio for a chance to live free. Working out of his home, he runs a successful business with clients all over the country. When the Federal Express truck rumbles by on our sandy road, it's usually delivering proofs to my neighbor. Soon, he hopes that even more of his work can be computerized, so that even on the days that the Federal Express truck can't get through the snow, work can go on. The builder who works on our house gave up the rat race in Massachusetts and does just fine in completing a home every other year or so. People in our little town are lawyers and businessmen and factory workers who have started very small businesses that bring in a lot less money than they used to make; in exchange, they have a higher quality of life. All of them seem happier than most of the people I meet when I visit corporate America.

I'm not advocating that everyone should drop what they're doing and move to Maine, only that the transition that our economy is going through isn't all bad. In the end, I think we may be better off than before. Our passion for bigger cars and bigger companies is giving way to Schumacher's "small is beautiful" thinking. Less is more; smaller is more flexible. In the large companies that remain strong, there are clearer objectives and more attention is being paid to staying in tune with the environment and flexible enough to respond to change. There are more investments in people, in work system redesign, in quality, in reengineering, in making technology more flexible, in cutting the corporate red tape. And more real understanding of what it means to compete globally and do business globally. Work has become incredibly flexible for people who are working across borders.

How do you write the job description for a brand manager at Procter & Gamble who needs to work on a "world team" to make Tide or Camay or Pampers truly global products? How do you do career planning for a young engineer in a multinational corporation that designs its products in one country, assembles them in another, and markets them in a third? How do you explain to a factory worker with 30 years of experience that global competition has forced consideration of changes in the design of his job that will require him to learn to operate computers and interface directly with customers? None of these things is easy, but they are all becoming increasingly common challenges. Work is shifting in location as well as content, in culture as well as technology. The phrase "Made in the USA" is undergoing redefinition. Does it mean that 100 percent of the materials used in its construction are produced in the United States or only that its components are assembled here? Does it mean made by an organization that is based in the United States or does it include products made in the United States by foreign multinationals employing a U.S. labor force? Or by U.S. multinational with plants overseas? As the definition of "Made in the USA" expands, so does the nature of work and the meaning of work in society. Decisions about where work will be done and by whom were made in the recent past on the basis of simple economics. As the economics have dictated movements of factories from the North to the South, and then offshore, we have stood by our faith that capitalism will drive decisions that are the best for the most people in the long run. Even in the short run, there is certainly an argument to support giving work to those most in need, as evidenced by their willingness to work for less. But as our welfare ranks swell, and the average standard of living and quality of life in the United States begins to decline, one must also ask what the continued acceptance of these shifts in work location will be. If the trends continue unabated for a few decades, we might begin to see scenes reminiscent of Steinbeck's *Grapes of Wrath*, but this time with Americans reversing the flow of immigration to this country for the first time in its history as they leave to seek their fortunes elsewhere. But where would they go? Perhaps, as did the families in Steinbeck's novels, they would find only greater misery in their new homes; or perhaps a few bold visionaries would start yet another experiment like that which gave birth to the United States in the first place. It's difficult to say.

In the short run, before very much international movement takes place, I think we are much more likely to see more of what we see today—only intensified. More people out of work, retraining themselves to be gainfully employed again. More people working for organizations that ignore traditional boundaries, and expect their employees to do the same. More of us will have multiple careers that last for shorter and shorter durations. Some of us will settle for less in order to stay close to home or live where we want to live. And some of us will attempt to get out of the whole rat race by not depending on others to provide us with security. If you're looking for a good investment, my advice is to buy stock in moving companies and fast food restaurants; they will be busy for a while longer.

But we will also see more people stepping up to the challenge of flexible work: learning to speak multiple languages, to read international newspapers, to understand global economics. There will be a lot of work for people who can help their organizations cross borders: jobs for people who can establish the necessary relationships, help design the right products, negotiate the new deals, close the big sales.

None of this work is routine in nature, so it's likely that learning and flexibility will become more important qualifications for hiring. The question, "Are you willing to travel?" used to conjure up images of long trips on the road behind the wheel of the company car and night after night at Motel 6; now, the question often references travel across borders and for extended periods of time, and the willingness to be a student of language and culture. This can't be a simple life, or an easy way to raise a family. But the choice, as always, is between staying in the game and getting somewhere or opting out and falling ever further behind. Flexible work, even with its glamor and appeal, isn't always easier or more desirable work. But it is work, and we will learn to adapt to it, much as did our forefathers who left the fields to move into the factories. In the end, we may feel very much as we do today about the industrial revolution: that it had its good and bad points. If we had it to do all over again, we certainly would have done it differently; but there are other parts of it we would repeat. We are once again being thrust into a gigantic experiment in human existence before we know very clearly what the experiment is about or how it will turn out. We can take some comfort in knowing that we are a species that is capable of learning from our achievements and our mistakes and that we will probably learn from this, too. The brave among us will go first so that the masses may follow. The traditionalists will never admit that any of it has a lick of sense. Some of them will still be living on the farm or running the corner Seven-Eleven store or the neighborhood McDonald's. And for them, it *doesn't* make sense, and it needn't. The industrial revolution wasn't for everybody; flexible work isn't for everyone either. But it is happening for many people, and it will happen for many more.

THE LEARNING AGENDA FOR
FLEXIBLE WORKPLACES

Flexible work involves learning of many kinds. Learning new languages and cultures will be part of becoming more flexible for some. For others, it will be learning about new technology. And for still others, it will be learning about entirely new professions. The pace of learning and the degree of flexibility achieved are closely tied. The learning agenda for flexible workplaces, as I see it, should include curricula in human skills, technical skills, and business skills.

Human Skills

As discussed in Chapter 3, flexible work requires flexible people. People need to know how to participate, how to manage conflict, how to work in groups, how to solve problems, how to reach consensus, how to listen, how to value diversity, how to give and receive feedback, how to communicate effectively, and how to talk to customers. But truly flexible work requires more than basic interpersonal skills; it requires that people develop the capacity to learn how to learn. Given that flexible work is always changing, no set of skills or qualifications for a particular job can be set out in advance. Certainly, there are fundamental skills that we all should possess, but which, unfortunately, many of us don't. Giving and receiving feedback should be as natural for people working in organizations as tying our shoes. For most of us, it's not. But after we learn how to tie our shoes, we need to get on with learning more advanced material—such as understanding other cultures, or really understanding motivation and work design, or finding new ways to work together that aren't so dependent on hierarchy. We need to learn new ways to explore the world together and create the kind of world in which we would genuinely like to live. We need to learn about new forms of governance, which take the best from everything we know and make it better, both within our organizations and outside of them. We need to explore ways to bring our values about peace and equity and justice and the environment to life in our working lives and in what our organizations stand for.

A few people already know how to make this happen. In our project on social innovations in global management (SIGMA), we have studied individuals and organizations that are devoted to preserving what is already good about this planet and making the rest of it better. What we find is often amazing and, to tell the truth, a little humbling. After all, we are supposed to be the experts on effective organizing; but some of these people and organizations, with no formal training in the disciplines of organizational design or organization development, have put in place some incredibly innovative structures and practices. Some are far ahead of most corporations in learning to cross borders and manage diversity. All are incredible examples of people living in tune with their values and constantly finding new ways to get their work done with a minimum of resources and bureaucracy.

Some examples? Take the International Physicians for the Prevention of Nuclear War. Bernard Lown, its founder, is a world-famous cardiovascular surgeon and, among other credits, the inventor of the defibrillation process for zapping heart attack victims back to life. He has saved the lives of thousands of patients with his invention, but he may have saved millions through his leadership of the IPPNW. When a few of his colleagues gathered in Boston at the height of the Cold War, they, like many others, discussed the perils of nuclear war. Unlike other groups, however, this one decided to do something about it: Lown and his colleagues authored a paper in the *New England Journal of Medicine* that outlined their expert opinion of the medical community's ability to respond to an atomic explosion in the city of Boston. In a nutshell, the article said that your health insurance wouldn't do you much good. The article attracted widespread attention, and the Physicians for Social Responsibility was formed as a national organization to use the influence of the medical profession to lobby against nuclear arms proliferation. The organization grew in size and stature, but was unsuccessful in turning the tide of American opinion.

The Cold War raged on, and the organization labored on. Always, there was the question, "What will happen if we disarm first?" It became clear to Lown that the answer was not to change American *or* Soviet opinion, but rather to change *both* at the same time. He journeyed to Moscow to meet with the Kremlin's leading physician, Dr. Chazov, to propose creating a new international physicians' organization opposing nuclear war, the IPPNW. After some initial hesitation, his Soviet counterpart agreed, and just five years later, the IPPNW won the Nobel Peace prize. Many who know about the details of the situation credit Lown with beginning the thaw in relations that eventually led to talks between government leaders, then to arms reductions, and finally to the end of the Cold War. Until Lown stepped forward, no one knew how to break the vicious circle of the arms race; Lown and the IPPNW *invented* ways to end the cold war. They were inventors of truly flexible work.

The IPPNW grew to international proportions rapidly, with 200,000 physician members in 63 countries by the end of the 1980s. With the increase in diversity of the nations represented came new demands and new agendas. It wasn't enough simply to end the Cold War; physicians from less developed countries wanted the superpowers to end arms spending altogether and redirect funds to health concerns around the planet. Others insisted on a bigger stake in the governance of the IPPNW, so an international governing board from all 63 countries was created and convened every other year at the IPPNW international meetings. Staff members working in the IPPNW offices in Boston and Moscow constantly invent new ways of raising money to support the organization's work. Most staff members work for half the money they could make in a for-profit organization, but they do it out of the love they have for the organization and its mission. Despite the low pay and long hours, few workforces are more highly motivated.

The IPPNW organizes its staff into pods of people who deal with regional concerns or functions, such as planning the biannual meetings. The term "pod" came from pods of whales, the idea being that people would swim together cooperatively rather than work in a hierarchical structure whose members had fixed responsibilities. Ideas for getting the job done better are welcomed from all pod members, and staffers from all parts of the organization spend time together socially. Their strong common values make them natural companions, and the caring that grows from this social contact reinforces their respect for one another on the job. While the pay isn't great and the quarters are a bit cramped, the pride in their work shows on their faces. It's a very satisfying job, and one that is always changing as the world changes.

One of the parts of the job that the staffers value the most is the opportunity to meet and learn about people from other parts of the world. Staffers raise money to support their own travel to the international congresses, just as they do to support the travel of many physician members who can't afford to pay their own way. The international congresses are the tangible rewards for two years of hard work. Meeting the physicians who they helped to attend and hearing their concerns and action proposals is what makes the staff's jobs seem even more meaningful. And, as time goes on, the ties among physicians around the world strengthen as does their ability to make a difference through concerted cooperative action.

Another physician-led group was that headed by Dr. Henderson of John Hopkins University, who marshaled medical resources in every country in the world to eradicate smallpox from the face of the Earth. To date, it is the only disease to be completely eradicated; but through Dr. Henderson's efforts, we now know that what used to be unimaginable is indeed possible. What was required to eradicate smallpox wasn't as much the vaccine, which had existed for over one hundred years, as it was the invention of an organization that could cross both geographical and religious borders to get the job done. The eradication of smallpox is a twentieth century miracle that should give us hope for the twenty-first century. Human beings can learn to get their act together, after all.

Some are learning how to work together to save the environment. The Nature Conservancy, as just one example, has pioneered innovative ways to help less developed countries reduce their foreign debt by agreeing to protect sensitive habitats, such as the rain forests. In 40 years, the Nature Conservancy has grown to over 500,000 members, acquired over $565 million in assets, and protected more than 3.5 million acres of land from development or misuse. The Nature Conservancy began by protecting the habitats of animals in the United States but quickly discovered that, due to migratory patterns, protecting habitats in Latin America was equally important to the preservation of many species of birds. This led to a period of learning and expansion that is still continuing, as the Nature Conservancy tries to deal with cultural and economic differences between North and South Americans. The policies and programs that worked well in the United States did not work nearly as well elsewhere, and the organization was perceived initially as "more of the North deciding what should be important to the South." A great deal of human learning was required to overcome barriers to cooperation. New relationships and organizational arrangements were formed to create radically different programs, such as the exchanging of debt for a commitment to protect land, which fit the Latin American context. When the goal demands it, people can learn to invent new ways of doing things; and with these new ways of doing things, they can invent flexible work.

Flexible work requires human invention, human skills in learning how to cope and adapt to the most challenging of circumstances. As the hurdles become higher, the competition tougher, the distances greater, we need to be even better in discovering and utilizing our human capacity for change. When you get right down to it, we are a remarkably creative and adaptable species. When you think of what is going on around us on a global scale—what the Hendersons and the Lowns and the Nature Conservancy are accomplishing—it doesn't seem like it should be that difficult to discover more flexible ways of organizing ourselves to get our work done. We make it harder than it needs to be by talking ourselves out of trying new ways of organizing before we give them a try. Eliminating smallpox was something that could have been done a hundred years ago; it just took people willing to work together in new ways to get the job done. Maybe if people in other organizations try working together in new ways, they could get something done too.

Technical Skills

In her book, *In the Age of the Smart Machine*, Shoshana Zuboff urges us to *informate* rather than just automate our organizations.[2] Replacing human beings with machines by itself won't guarantee long term success; organizations that use information to improve their decision-making will be the evolutionary survivors.

Learning how to use technology smartly is another important learning agenda in creating flexible work. Flexible work that allows adaptation depends on technology that is adaptable, too, and upon people that are able to understand and utilize technology flexibly. Even if you aren't a "Star Trek" fan, you probably know that one of the enduring plots within the series is the creation of a problem that requires some kind of technical modification in the *Enterprise* to allow the crew to escape. While Kirk or Picard are the captains, when it comes to dealing with technological innovation, they are left biting their nails. Someone else knows how the ship is put together and how to take it apart and put it back together again in order to make it do something it wasn't designed to do. The fewer of these people there are around, the less likely it is that an organization's technology will be as flexible as it needs to be to support flexible work. *Lots* of people who know what the technology is designed to do and not to do, what alternative technologies are available, and how to informate instead of just automate create the technical preconditions for flexible work.

Companies with strong commitments to developing technical expertise are more adaptable to change than companies that train people in the minimum they need to know. At Exxon's Baytown Refinery and Gaines' Topeka plant, operators rotate through maintenance positions so that they learn what the technical system is all about. When it comes time for improving the technical system, these organizations receive better suggestions from more people than in plants with separate maintenance departments. And when there are problems that require attention, lots of people get into the act until the problem gets fixed. It's quite a different story than that in the factory where the machine operator says, "Thank God, I finally get to take a break now that this stupid machine is broken."

Larry Hirschhorn, in *Beyond Mechanization*, writes about the learning that accompanies the introduction of more flexible technology and how it supports continued improvement:[3]

> The new technologies thus provide a more receptive framework than do traditional technology settings for the development of socio-technical designs. Moreover, such designs are reinforced by subsequent developments. The flexibility of the technology encourages managers to make changes when it seems profitable to do so, while the workers themselves, used to learning, more readily accept such changes. Thus advanced technology, changing technology, and job design based on learning reinforce one another. (p. 123)

When organizations train their people to operate equipment but not to understand how the equipment operates, the time bomb of obsolescence starts ticking. When it comes time to change the technical system, a quantum leap is required to retrain people to learn what is necessary to keep new equipment running properly. New technical systems may not match the needs of the organization for quality or capacity or reliability, or the human abilities of the people being asked to operate them. But people who care about keeping their jobs care about their technology, and will gladly learn how to maintain it and even improve it if given the chance. Providing in-depth technical training improves organizational health, just as exercise and eating right improve personal health. Technical training prevents premature organizational death due to heart attacks caused by the clogged arteries of inflexible work.

Business Skills

Creating opportunities for flexible work without helping people understand the organization's business is like my giving my car keys to my five year old. We'll get somewhere, and we'll get there *fast*; but it won't be a fun ride, at least for me. The more people understand the business they are in, the more they know how to steer, when to go fast, and when to hit the brakes. In organizations where only a few people understand the strategies, directions, and criteria for making business decisions, it's like having one adult in the back of a *bus* full of five-year-old drivers. The adult can shout out directions, but the kids have a hard time understanding and doing what they are told.

Explaining business strategies and complicated financial statements to people who have never been in management positions can be difficult at first. It's a new language, and one that seems especially hard to learn. All the words in the language that meant something last year mean something else this year, or are replaced by other words or abbreviations altogether. Two people speaking the same language seem to be saying different things, even though they nod their heads in agreement with one another. The truth is, no one really knows how to speak the language because it's constantly changing; and that makes it hard to teach to others.

Still, it's important for people to learn the language as best they can, especially for the people with their hands on the wheel. These are the people who can help to invent new strategies and new business opportunities or find ways to cut costs or improve quality if they just understand what is going on; who know a good product when they go into a store to buy it, and know when they are making a product they wouldn't buy themselves; who manage their household budget better than some cities manage theirs; who know how to set plans in their lives and achieve them instead of just putting them away in file drawers until it's time to do the exercise again next year; who aren't trained in business, but who *are* the business.

It always surprises me to learn how much time executives

spend planning in isolation—locked away from the people who will need to understand the plan to implement it, from the customers who know what they really want, from the shareholders who will decide whether to support the plan or not with their pocketbooks. The planning goes on almost in self-defense, as if to protect the planners from being accused of not having a plan. When it comes time to implement the plan, all the people on the bus have been left out; and the bus stalls.

Helping people learn *about* the business takes involving them *in* the business. It takes letting them in on what's going on, good and bad; trusting them with sensitive information, sharing how uncertain the future is, helping them understand the risks that are being taken and why. A lot of this is hard to explain, to *anyone*.

But just because it's hard doesn't mean it's not worth doing. Employees learn quickly; they ask perceptive questions; often, even have something worthwhile to add. I sat in a meeting made up of a mix of managers and union people in an organization in Texas recently when one of the union employees pulled out a copy of Lester Thurow's latest book on global competition and asked me what I thought of it. I confessed that I hadn't read it yet, but that I had heard that it was good. None of the managers had read it either. If anyone was going to bring a global perspective to the table that day, it was going to be that hourly worker. The rest of us felt ashamed, even though it's impossible for any of us to read everything in print. Feeling ashamed is old-school thinking; we should be glad that in a group people are reading different things, teaching the rest of us what they contain. We can't all keep up with everything; in fact, *all* of us can't even keep up with everything. So we should be pleased whenever one of us reads something on behalf of the rest of us. We're all smarter if we divide the duty. But the point is that each person in the organization is a potential *business* resource.

What if we looked at people as strategists, as planners, as financiers, as resources to help us find ways to *grow* the business, in the face of internal and external change? What if we considered people as partners who could help us manage better, plan better, and devise ways to make plans actually happen? What would it be worth to the average organization to be able to implement even 50 percent of its strategies into action instead of 10 percent or none? Certainly, it would be worth more than the investment needed to share information with people that would allow them to behave as partners.

As a professor in a business school, and as a graduate of business programs myself, I know that the majority of people are capable of learning the basics of managing a business. The real basics of business are pretty easy to pick up; they may not even require a degree. The difficult material—regression analysis, linear programming, net present value computations, the intricacies of labor law, and the specifics of designing an MIS program or system—can be left to the specialists.

Once the basics are mastered, it's easy to go on learning on the job. Most of what it takes to be a truly great manager rather than a mediocre one is learned on the job, by hanging around other managers who teach the craft. By exposure, trial and error, and simply being included in the right conversations, managers learn what they need to know to manage effectively. The same could happen for others. There really aren't two kinds of people in the world: managers and nonmanagers. But we have led managers to believe that they are somehow different, and that they are capable of understanding what is going on and deciding what to do when others are completely lost. Of course, this isn't true; no one really knows what is going on. But managers learn how to *act* like they know what is going on; and, since others know even less, it's pretty easy to maintain the illusion.

I don't see any problem with this until managers begin to believe that they really *do* know what is going on, or that they know *more* about what is going on than anyone else knows or could ever know. That's dangerous. That takes ignoring the evidence, and I'm not a believer in managing by intentional ignorance. It's hard enough to know what's going on when you're trying to find out; it's even harder when you're refusing to admit anything is happening that you don't already know. Woody Allen says he's amazed at the people who want to understand the universe when he can't even find his way around Chinatown; I'm amazed at people who think they *do* understand the universe when they don't *know* they're in Chinatown.

Teaching people about the business is a lot easier than it seems at first. *Listening* to what they say after they understand the business is what's hard. The trouble is, most of the time, they're right.

Work is becoming more flexible and, as I said, "You ain't seen nothin' yet!" Some work is becoming more flexible because the job or the competitive environment is demanding that it becomes more flexible. Organizations trying to save our planet need to invent new ways of working with people around the planet to accomplish their mission. As Russ Ackoff, the systems theorist says, "You can't solve a problem using the same thinking that created it." New challenges require new ways of working. People forced to seek alternative employment are pushed to discover skills and talents they may not have known they had. Corporations trying to do business globally are discovering what managing diversity really means.

Other work is becoming more flexible because flexibility helps people and organizations adapt to change. Multiskilling, technical training, learning how to learn, learning how to work with other human beings—all of these things help organizations be more ready, willing, and able to take the next step to remain competitive, as learning and change become more familiar ways of life.

While work will remain simple and routine for some, many more will hear the call for flexibility. Some will respond, and they will be the ones who lead the way.

CHAPTER

6

Flexible Thinking
A New Type of Organization

Spring has come to Maine. The light dances off the lake, where ice and snow have been replaced by open water. During the winter months, we rarely heard a sound; now, birds have returned in profusion, and an occasional early spring fisherman drones by, making the haunting coming and going sound that only a small outboard engine on a large empty lake can make. The air is so fresh after each rain, and full of the smell of the woods, that I make myself dizzy taking deep breaths of it. It clears out my head and helps me to think more lucidly. In this moment, I'm thinking about thinking.

I'm aware as I reflect of how important thinking has become to our society; that our thoughts about business and technology and international relations are broadcast and translated into actions with tangible impacts on all of our lives much more quickly than they ever have been before. Thinking has always been important to the evolution of our species and planet; the invention of the wheel, the taming of fire, the steam engine, the light bulb, the airplane, the telephone; there can be no doubt that we are descendants of a great line of thinkers, and that we possess the proper combination of genes and cells to allow us to continue the tradition. We may not think any faster or smarter than our forebears; but these days, we get to see the results of our thinking much more quickly, and to see its impacts come back around in time for us to realize what we have done. Whoever invented the wheel would be amazed to see its uses today, a million years later; but the inventor of the hula hoop got to watch his idea be born, mature, and die in a matter of a few years. Mostly, this faster translation of thinking into reality is good; even the 14 years it takes the average new drug to work its way through its serpentine path in laboratories both in companies and at the Food and Drug Administration is a relatively short period of time for major health-improving substances to be invented, tested, and made available to the public.

Sometimes, faster thinking is our downfall: We invent automobiles that pollute before we know what the effects of the pollution will be or how to deal with them; we invent nuclear reactors before we know how to operate them safely or dispose of their waste; we send shuttles into space before we understand how the O-rings in them work; we intervene with military force before we fully understand what we are committing ourselves to or what other options might be available.

You would think that, with all this thinking going on, we would be more concerned about improving our thinking; that we would be thinking about ways to think faster and better, particularly when it counts—in organizations, where the difference between good thinking and bad thinking or fast thinking and slow thinking can mean the difference between success and failure. Some attention has been paid to thinking more creatively, but I'm not certain that more creative thinking alone is the answer. My observation is that organizations are full of people with creative ideas that never get implemented; and even ideas that everyone would agree are great ones go untested because of

individual and organizational inertia. Despite our love of thinking individually, we are terrible thinkers when we get together
in groups larger than about two or three. Once we decide we
need an organizational chart, we can almost forget about free
thinking. Our capacity to do free thinking far outstrips the capacity of our organizations to process and act on what we imagine,
to deal with our innocent questions and wild dreams.

Innocent questions and wild dreams are the engines of innovation. Organizations aren't usually designed to help people ask
innocent questions, and most are definitely opposed to wild
dreams. Organizations are designed to tell people what to do,
not to answer their questions. They are designed for conformity,
even in areas where everyone agrees that innovation is really
more important. I have come to believe that our current definition of organizing itself is antithetical to human creativity and
expressiveness. We need not only to learn to *think* more flexibly;
we need to learn to *organize* to think more flexibly.

For a few organizations that exist in stable environments,
inflexible thinking isn't a problem; but for most, the ability to
change and adapt is critical to success. Flexible thinking is especially important in R&D, marketing, and management. In fact,
flexible thinking is a good thing in any part of an organization in
which creating or applying knowledge is an important element
in task completion. In these parts of the organization, work is
nonroutine in nature. That is, tasks are frequently changing and
rarely performed in exactly the same way twice. Routine tasks
are repetitive, requiring little learning or creativity once they
have been mastered. Nonroutine tasks demand some degree of
both creativity and expertise; people may be professionally prepared to undertake nonroutine tasks, but still find their completion challenging or impossible. Medical researchers may be trained
to look for a cure for the AIDS virus, for example, but still
experience difficulty in finding one.

The fact that nonroutine work involves human thinking rather
than machine performance makes it fascinatingly unpredictable
and subject to all sorts of human foibles. In the wonderful and
wacky world of nonroutine work, whether you like the person
you are working with can make the difference between succeed-

ing at a task or failing; doubling the number of people working on a project may just slow things down; and relying on what you think you know may only get in the way. It's as if nonroutine work takes place in some science fiction-inspired other dimension in which the laws of normal work don't hold. "Do it right the first time" and "zero defects" make no sense at all; goals can change in midstream; productivity is virtually immeasurable until the task is finished, and even then people argue about what has been accomplished. The history of product development is replete with examples of failures turned into successes and accidental inventions that appear brilliant only in retrospect. More than a few ulcers have resulted from people betting their careers on the outcomes of work that at its very core is inherently unpredictable and nonroutine.

Despite its silly-putty character, nonroutine work is of extreme importance in any organization facing change. The task of understanding how the world around the organization is changing is nonroutine in nature. So is deciding what to do once the environment is understood. And then there's figuring out how to do it; and deciding how much doing it will cost; and whether the results of doing it will be worthwhile; and whether having done whatever it was produced the results intended.

Because nonroutine work is both important and difficult to do, it makes for great consulting opportunities. There are consultants in strategic planning, financial analysis, information systems design, marketing, scientific specialties, investment planning, product development, compensation, and, yes, even in organization design. All of them have tools they apply to make it appear that they have found ways to remove some of the basic unpredictability from thinking tasks; but the truth be told, they do more to provide comfort to nervous decision-makers than to overcome the whimsical nature of nonroutine work.

We have resisted analyzing nonroutine work using methods developed for understanding routine work because the models underlying the analysis of routine work are based on predictability and measurability. Time and motion studies don't make much sense in the R&D laboratory. Running experiments a little bit faster probably won't save much time in finding a cure for AIDS or the secret of teleportation. Telling people to "think better" is also difficult. Courses on creativity may help, but there are still no guarantees. Dreaming about invisibility or doubling the value of a company's stock is easy; achieving it is hard.

We desperately need new ways of thinking about thinking, and of organizing to think. I'm convinced that this is the next frontier for achieving megaimprovements in organizational effectiveness. In fact, when I get just a little carried away, I think that organizing for flexible thinking may produce improvements in organizational performance that are greater than anything else we have ever done, socially or technically. If learning how to organize to build the pyramids was step 1, everything we have done since has been step 1a, step 1b, and so forth. Learning how to organize for flexible thinking is a whole new step, a whole new way of thinking about organizing. Given the challenges we have created for ourselves as inhabitants of this planet, discovering how to organize ourselves to think comes none too soon. We can't solve the organizational problems we have created for ourselves by using the same form of organization that got us here; we have to reorganize in order to think ourselves out of our restrictive boxes and borders.

If we are going to reorganize ourselves to think more flexibly, it would be useful to understand what it is that we are trying to accomplish, and then invent an organization to help us do it. Then, we might imagine some more specific details about making such an organization work. There aren't very many organizations that have completed this exercise, so there are few examples we can look to for guidance—you're going to have to trust me on this one. In the end, I think you will find that what emerges is familiar, almost common sense, but certainly quite different from what most of us think about when we think of organizations.

THE NATURE OF KNOWLEDGE WORK

On the surface, it doesn't seem like it should be so difficult to understand: We think about something, we tell other people about our ideas, we work together to implement them, and, finally, we evaluate what we have accomplished. Knowledge work is simply thinking, and then translating thoughts into actions. But beneath the surface, in actual practice, it's much more than that. Why do we have to make simple things so complicated? Why can't we just design an organization to help us think?

The answer lies in our fear of uncertainty and our desire to avoid wasting precious scarce resources on "bad" ideas. To prevent us from wandering from one aimless idea to the next, and from throwing good money after bad, we invent ways of censoring our thoughts. Not every idea is a "good" idea; in fact, we are led quickly to believe by our families, friends, teachers, and other "expert" authorities in our lives that there are actually very few really good ideas, and that it is unlikely that we will ever have one. The history books are full of people with great ideas, but they are also full of people who thought their ideas were good ideas and who did some really foolish things in pursuing them. So even before an idea can be uttered, we are already at work censoring our thoughts, anticipating the reactions that others will have to them even before we speak. Social scientists, led by Victor Vroom, describe this phenomenon as "expectancy theory."[1] Expectancy theory suggests that not only in our thinking, but in a wide range of behaviors, we choose how to act based upon our best guesses of what reactions our thoughts and behaviors will produce in others. The more important the others are to us, and the more important the rewards at stake, the less likely it is that we will allow ourselves to act in ways of which others might not approve. We search for clues regarding their preferences, and then try to do what we think they want us to do in order to receive their approval.

If expectancy theory holds (and there is good reason to believe that it does much of the time), it makes flexible thinking extremely difficult. Very little of what we possess is as valuable to us as our egos, and the best part of our egos is represented to the outside world by our verbalized thoughts. At least to others, we are what we say we think. We may see ourselves differently, as thinking and knowing much more than the thoughts we offer publicly; but, to the public, we are what they hear. Realizing this, according to expectancy theory, we have an ideal situation for self-censoring: One of our most cherished possessions, our ego, is on the line. Being social creatures, we find it difficult to make judgments about the relative worth of our egos in isolation; we search for feedback from the rest of the world to confirm or deny our own self-evaluations. Knowing that our ego is on the line, we think before we speak (as we often have been told to do). What we edit out of our speech is everything that we think might raise eyebrows, set off titters of laughter, or cause others to think us stupid. We put our best foot forward; that is, the foot we think others want to see. The result is that our thoughts "fit in"; they conform to what others are likely to think and believe.

Organizations add to the difficulty by making the source of evaluation of our thoughts powerful in its control over our destiny. While we might risk throwing out a controversial idea, asking a stupid question, or putting forth a half-baked idea in front of our friends at a cocktail party, we would be much less inclined to do so in front of the *boss*. The boss controls our present and our future; who we are to the boss is how we will be interpreted to the entire organization through the boss's eyes. If thought editing was important before, it's more important now than ever. Every time we speak, we are at risk of committing a *faux pas*, a breech of the secret code the boss uses to make evaluations of a person's true worth. So rather than simply think out loud, we think quietly, to ourselves, and for a long time before we speak. We test out parts of our ideas in safe contexts and then let out a little at a time if we receive positive feedback. Along the way, we alter, edit, or even change our ideas to make them fit better with the receiving audience, until they are hardly our ideas at all. By the time we tell the boss, the idea is honed, ready, and calculated to produce a certain effect; usually, the effect of producing interest in our idea. To create this effect, the idea can't be too radical; and it must help produce outcomes that we know the boss desires; and it must be presented in a way that the boss can hear it; and it should contain just enough of something new that it sounds different from everything else the boss has heard. In short, it should be presented in an acceptable form and fashion. It should fit in.

This basic process of learning how to fashion our ideas to fit in is important to understand, because it is the cause of inflexible thinking and inflexible organizing. All of us who work in organizations and desire to continue to do so have learned the skill of making our ideas fit in. It's part of working in a system in which the activities of people must be coordinated and directed toward consensual goals. Imagine an organization in which we each pursued our own ideas about what the organization should be doing; when every time we came up with an idea, we just acted upon it, and expected others to support it. In no time, we would become "disorganized"; people would be moving in different directions, pursuing different objectives in different priorities. Lots of things would get done by individuals, but they wouldn't add up to much; and the ideas that took coordinated effort would never be implemented. So we look for ways to "get organized"; we appoint leaders, and then the leaders listen to our ideas, evaluate them, and decide which ones we will pursue. We want to believe that the leaders are wise, and that the best ideas are the ones chosen for implementation. But are the leaders really that wise? Do they really know the good ideas from the bad ones? What criteria are they using to judge ideas? Most of the time, we don't know the answers to these questions; but to the extent that we do know, we begin to learn the code that tells us how to present our ideas so that they will be selected for action. We fall into the trap of editing our thinking to fit the rigid tests of what makes an idea good or bad in our organization.

We become inflexible in our thinking, and the organization becomes inflexible because our ideas can't challenge the status quo without being rejected. We create a self-sealing system designed to eliminate flexible thinking.

Unfortunately, it doesn't stop there. James March and Herbert Simon's classic book, *Organizations*, reveals how inflexible thinking affects the processes by which organizations learn and change.[2]

As decision-makers rise in the hierarchy and accumulate more and more power, they take their thinking patterns with them. Then, when they are able, both consciously and unconsciously, they use their power to shape what others think and believe. They make it legitimate to listen to some sources of information and they discredit others; they appoint as investigators subordinates who are indebted to them and anxious to find answers that fit their preferred courses of action. Policies and rules are written to codify the present ways of acting and thinking; fewer and fewer significant challenges to the status quo reach the top, as more and more levels screen out information that doesn't fit that which top level people are believed to want to hear. Nonconformists are denied promotions, screened out of the system, or banished to distant corners of the empire where they are unlikely to cause trouble. Others learn from watching what to do and not to do, what to say and not to say, even what to think and not to think. Chris Argyris, in his many books and articles on individual and organizational learning, explains how we form defensive routines that prevent us from hearing ourselves think.[3] We deny our emotions, bury them, and learn to act like we're best friends with people we despise. It's all in a day's work. If organizations were really designed to support knowledge work, they wouldn't work this way.

I hope this all sounds depressingly Orwellian. It should. We are trapped in organizational structures that make thinking flexibly nearly impossible. Those who insist on thinking flexibly in spite of all this do so at incredible risk to their careers and egos. Too many of these people simply give up, opting for a life of sanity outside organizations. Our organizations shouldn't make flexible thinking so difficult; if we want our organizations to be places that produce creative new products and services, are responsive to change, and utilize the best thinking that human beings have to offer, a lot has to change.

Knowledge work involves thinking. It involves discovering, formulating ideas, communicating thoughts, mustering support, and committing resources to action. None of these things is easy to do. But the belief that our present organizational structures will make this process easier is mistaken. Organizational structures that were designed to build pyramids and fight wars are not well suited to knowledge work. Why not? Here are some illustrations of the kinds of problems our traditional organizational structures create for knowledge work and knowledge workers.

ORGANIZATIONAL LEARNING DISABILITIES

Peter Wensberg's book, *Land's Polaroid*, tells the fascinating history of Edwin Land's creation, growth, and eventual parting from one of this country's most innovative, daring, knowledge-intensive organizations.[4] Wensberg details Land's many inventions (he holds more patents than anyone except Thomas Edison), which include processes for light polarization, missile guidance systems, and various aspects of instant photography. By any measure, Land was a true genius; even today, few people within Polaroid possess a complete understanding of the concepts behind some of Land's inventions.

According to Wensberg, Land was a benevolent but slightly paranoid autocrat who disdained market research because he felt that his products would create demand, and who let very few people in on his ideas before they were ready to go to the market. He personally selected and educated his closest confidants in the secrets of instant photography so that they would be intensely loyal to him. Then, he gave them instructions to conduct certain experiments or create new processes, the purpose of which only he understood. He also gave his subordinates strict orders to tell no one, including their peers, what they were working on, and to report results directly to him.

Despite the complexity of the knowledge work involved in inventions like instant photography, Land was able to integrate the knowledge produced by a multitude of researchers conducting myriads of experiments. He proved over and over again that his ideas, at first seeming impossible or unmarketable, had merit. The company grew from a basement room in New York City to the *Fortune* 500 company with $2 billion in annual sales that it is today largely under his paternal guidance.

By any measure of success, Polaroid under Ed Land was a winner; a true, shining example of the American dream combining with Yankee ingenuity to create spectacular business results. But, unfortunately, the dream took a nightmarish turn.

In the late 1960s and early 1970s, Land put his researchers to work on two important projects. The first was to create an integral film format for instant still photos (the picture that develops in front of your eyes); the second was instant movies. The integral film product development effort turned out to be more difficult and expensive than even Land had imagined, but it remained the higher priority of the two; instant movies had to wait.

By the time Polaroid's instant movie product, named Polavision, appeared in April of 1977, the market had changed. Commercial videotape had been introduced in 1965; home versions began to appear in the early '70s, although they were much too expensive at the time to compete with super-eight movie film, which by 1977 carried features such as zoom and sound. Polavision used a chemically-based additive film rather than an electronic medium; the film cassette held only enough film for 2-1/2 minutes of viewing; there was no sound; an expensive developing/playback unit was required; the images were murky; and, since the film had an extremely low ASA, blinding lights were required to take pictures of subjects. In the 1960s, there may have been a market for the product; but, by the 1970s, the specter of videotape loomed on the horizon.

When Bill McCune, then president, balked at bringing Polavision to market, Land, chairman and director of research, marched into the board of directors and demanded that he be put in charge of the program personally. The board had assumed that he already was, and rubber stamped his request.

Although the accurate numbers are difficult to obtain, it is estimated that Polaroid spent over a billion dollars creating, manufacturing, and marketing Polavision before the decision to kill the project was made. In the end, Polaroid stock tumbled, Land lost a large share of his personal fortune, and, more importantly to him, he lost control of the company he had created.

The moral of the story, from a knowledge work perspective, is that in a company run by a genius, there are a lot of stupid people. Not stupid in reality, of course; the scientists, researchers, marketing people, and others at Polaroid were among the brightest and best in the world. But in the face of Land, they acquiesced. How could they not have? Land created the company. He invented the products. He had proven himself right in the face of detractors time and time again. At the zenith of his career, it was difficult for anyone, including his closest friends and associates, to tell the emperor that he had no clothes. Who was at fault for Polaroid's difficulties, Land or the people who worked for him? Does it matter? Both were present, and neither was able to help the other overcome the hierarchical dynamics that led to the Polavision decision.

In the 1960s, Solomon Asch conducted a number of experiments on conformity that shed further light on the dynamics that plagued Polaroid during the 1970s and still plague any organization attempting to conduct knowledge work within a hierarchical structure.[5] Asch's experiments were simple but powerful. On a blackboard, he would draw three lines; he labeled them A, B, and C. Line C was half the length of the other two. He would then ask the four people sitting in the room to tell him which line was the shortest. Unknown to the experimental subject, the first three people to speak were experimental confederates Asch had instructed to answer, "B." When it came time for the real subject to answer, the reply, by over 60 percent of the subjects, was "B"! Why? Some subjects really didn't believe their own eyes; they were convinced that their vision must be faulty. Others didn't want to embarrass the other three poor fools by pointing out their obvious ignorance. Some just wanted to get out of the situation as quickly and quietly as possible. One or two may actually have thought "B" *was* the correct answer. Regardless of the reason, the point is that most of us feel tremendous pressures to fit in, to conform. Asch was interested in explaining why so many people willingly participated in the Nazi genocide of Jews during the Second World War. But his experiment has implications for any organization in which conformity is valued and rewarded.

In Asch's experiment, the "subjects" were all peers, supposedly strangers, and did not expect to see each other again. Still, conformity was evident among a majority of subjects. Imagine the effect of changing the experimental design so that the three people saying "B" before you were your boss, your boss's boss, and the your boss's boss's boss, the director of research . Now what do you say? Further, add to this that the decision you are being asked to make is one that will make or break the company, and that the difference between C and A and B is clear to you but almost imperceptible to others. What do you say now? Add to this further that you know the track record of the director of research, who is personally responsible for inventing the products that built the company and made it possible for you to be employed in it in the first place. And perhaps that you are young, or new to the company, or female, or a person of color, or from a different culture, or that your last project hadn't turned out as well as you had hoped that it would, or you knew you were being evaluated for an up or out decision. Which line looks shorter now?

On January 28, 1986, the space shuttle *Challenger* exploded 73 seconds after liftoff, killing the six astronauts and one school teacher on board. The launch order was given over the objections of Roger Boisjoly, an engineer at Morton Thiokol who had been studying problems with the O-rings in the solid rocket booster for over a year at the time of the tragedy. Despite Boisjoly's acknowledged expertise in his field, his verbal and even written warnings were ignored. Both Morton Thiokol and NASA were well aware of problems with the O-rings; they were listed as a "criticality 1" item in NASA's list of shuttle problems, meaning that the shuttle should not have been allowed to fly until the problem was corrected. But since the shuttle had flown successfully even with O-ring problems, waivers were signed for each flight allowing the program to proceed.

When it became obvious the day before *Challenger's* scheduled liftoff that the temperature at launch time would be far below any temperatures experienced previously, a teleconference was called to discuss what additional problems the cold weather might cause, specifically concerning the O-rings in the booster rockets. Boisjoly participated in the teleconference and strenuously objected to the launch. His superiors at Morton Thiokol backed him up initially, but then caved in to perceived pressure from NASA to reverse their decision. The program was on the line; Thiokol's contract was on the line; the shuttle had repeatedly flown successfully despite O-ring problems; Boisjoly was known to be emotional in his dealings with others about the problem; in the end, all agreed that line "B" really was shorter than line "C". The astronauts and Christa McAuliffe were not party to the discussion.

These examples illustrate a fundamental problem associated with knowledge work in hierarchical organizations: *The people with the most knowledge about something are often the least empowered to make decisions.* Even when they are invited to be part of the discussion, as in the case of Roger Boisjoly and the *Challenger* tragedy, their testimony is often discounted. More often, as in the case of Polavision, their opinion isn't even asked. Why do we manage knowledge workers this way?

When I ask managers this question, their most frequent answer is, "There's too much at stake." But what's the logic here? That the more important the decision is, the less important it is to have knowledgeable people making it? When managers say, "There's too much at stake," what are they really saying? There's too much at stake for the company? Or there's too much at stake in their own careers? Or is it that they just don't trust others to make the same decisions they would make themselves? Don't knowledge workers also have a lot at stake? Don't their continued employment and well-being depend on the organization's finding the right answers to the tough questions?

Personally, I think that the reason we don't align knowledge with authority in organizations is that we are affected by the many diseases of hierarchy, which destroy our common sense.

Here are some quotes from members of a first-rate research and development group in a well respected company:

> "Product development teams don't like to report bad news upward, sometimes they will even hide unfavorable data. When you raise issues, you get an arrow through the heart. Upper management doesn't want to hear the truth."

Does that affect the speed of product development when it happens? You bet!

> "Managers are aligned with their *functional* accountabilities. They can go away from a meeting and have very different perspectives on what was agreed upon."

Does that affect cooperation among their people on projects later on? You bet!

> "We need to find ways to pass on decisions and earlier work. Usually, when a new person representing a new function comes onto the team, they want to challenge the work done previously."

Does it slow things down when you hand off work between departments? You bet!

> " People we hire think that working in industry is going to be just like graduate school. It isn't. It takes us years to teach them to work in teams instead of as individuals and to learn to ask the right questions instead of just answering a question raised by the professor."

Does socializing people to fit into the organizational culture take time? You bet!

> "There's a great deal of uncertainty associated with early test data. Market research often tries to make it look like science— almost to fool people."

Do departmental boundaries create mistrust? You bet!

"Turning over our ideas to marketing is like giving the keys to a race car to a three-year-old."

Do departmental boundaries get in the way of communication and teamwork? You bet!

"A problem in the organization is that everybody can say 'no' and nobody can say 'yes.'"

Does the hierarchy sometimes slow things down?
YOU BET!!
Hierarchies exist to control things. It would be good if they existed to help people get what they needed, support their creativity, or protect people from unnecessary interruptions; but they rarely serve such benign purposes. The fundamental idea underlying hierarchy is that those at the top are better than those at the bottom. And not just better at one thing, better at *everything*. I've listened to directors of R&D tell PhDs who are experts in their disciplines and who have been working on projects for months that their data are incorrect and their conclusions flawed. In some cases, the directors were probably right; research is an inexact undertaking, and the perfect experiment has yet to be performed. A good critic can always poke holes in another person's work. Just try submitting an article to a good research journal sometime; it's like throwing meat to the dogs. I know, because I serve as a reviewer; and I'm sure I've caused my share of pain to struggling, young, hoping-to-be-tenured academics. In the final analysis, unless the work is fatally flawed (which it usually isn't) what we end up doing is forcing people to fit their ideas to ours because, as reviewers, we know what good ideas really are. Or so we think. And so the R&D director thinks. After all, they think to themselves, "I wouldn't be the manager unless I was smarter than the people who work for me!"

In knowledge work organizations especially, the brightest people often do get promoted. Even so, being promoted doesn't make them the brightest person in everything, in every specialty, in every situation. But the pressure is on to demonstrate leadership and that means making decisions. Or, more precisely, making certain the right decisions are made. There's a big difference. I asked the project manager in charge of a 200-person team working on an extremely critical project how the objectives for his team's efforts were set. He replied proudly, "I stayed up until 1 A.M. for a week after I got the job and wrote them."

David Bradford and Allen Cohen, in their book *Managing for Excellence*, call this the myth of heroic management.[6] Bradford and Cohen (pp. 10–11) state that in order to feel competent, managers must live up to the following myths:

- A good manager knows at all times what is going on in the department.
- A good manager should have more technical expertise than any subordinate.
- A good manager should be able to solve any problem that comes up.
- A good manager should be the primary person responsible for how the department is working.

It's not just that managers have inflated egos; managers *learn* to expect these things of themselves from other managers and from other role models, such as great leaders in history. To add to the problem, other people, including both their higher level managers *and their subordinates* expect them to be heroic as well. To be otherwise in our culture would be to abdicate the position or invite a poor performance appraisal. The trouble with this state of affairs is the Edwin Land problem at Polaroid; the more the leader tries to do himself, the more others *let* him and, in fact, the more they *expect* him to do in the future. Everyone learns their roles in the system: Some are to lead and to think, others are to follow directions. When there comes a time to change the roles or reverse the direction of leadership, it is nearly impossible to do so. The design of the organization, combined with our hierarchical culture, does us in.

A fixed hierarchy is antithetical to knowledge work. When permanent levels of an organization come into contact with one another concerning a task that requires clear thinking, more times than not instead of clarity you get mud. People aren't sure what to say and what not to say, what they have heard or what they haven't heard, what to believe and what not to believe. How many times, after hours of listening to subordinates make presentations, do top managers close the door in order to ask each other, "Well, what do you really think?"

The only cure for this disease is to remove the permanent hierarchy. Hierarchies are useful as coordinating mechanisms. But the same hierarchy doesn't need to coordinate everything; and, certainly, the same people don't need to try to coordinate everything. If they do, they quickly find themselves overwhelmed with the details, asking for shorter and shorter reports, less and less input into their decisions. It's the only way possible to manage it all. The logic here is, "If you can't manage everything well, at least manage everything poorly." Instead, the answer should be, "Get help!" Involve more people in the decisions, and allow them to do an excellent job of managing what they are responsible for managing. Integrate, yes; coordinate, yes; share learnings, yes; all of this can be done without the presence of a single permanent hierarchy. Sometimes, as in the case of EDS Corporation, smaller project teams are given authority to run their own show. In other organizations, such as McKinsey & Company, project teams *are* the show.[7] Once management understands that people really do want the organization to be successful and will do amazing things to help it succeed if they are allowed, miracles start to happen. People naturally and spontaneously do all the things that the old hierarchy strained to force them to do. People communicate, cooperate, change their roles, integrate, provide leadership, listen to the customer, watch their quality closely, help others develop, manage the expense budget frugally, come up with ideas for making things more efficient, raise their standards, cut out unnecessary tasks, and even reduce staffing levels when necessary. We have only begun to see what is possible—and to fully understand how terribly wrong we have been about the value of hierarchy—particularly in knowledge work organizations.

Hierarchies were invented to direct slaves and privates and sinners; in short, people who management really didn't want to know very much. If you are a manager who still doesn't want your people to know very much, shame on you. It's time to start learning what they know and teaching them what they need to know. Chances are, after 10, 20, or 30 years on the job, they know more than they're letting on. In professional organizations that exist to perform knowledge work, we know that the average employee knows a lot of important things, or she wouldn't be on the payroll. Yet we still manage our employees like slaves or privates or sinners. Knowledge work isn't like building pyramids or fighting wars or converting heathens. It's creative work that involves the development and application of human intellect to organizational opportunities. In an organization of 100 or 500 highly trained thinkers, it rarely makes sense for one person to do all the thinking. Land was successful for a time at Polaroid; but, ultimately, he failed. Even though he was successful, we must ask, how successful *might* he have been? Perhaps if Land had learned sooner the value of listening to others and allowing them to join in his thinking, Polaroid would be twice or 10 times the size it is today. We'll never know. The point is, we have to explode the myth that our hierarchical system of heroic management is working, has ever worked, or *could* ever work as well as other ways of organizing, particularly when it comes to knowledge work.

We must search instead for different modes of organizing that allow people with intelligence to influence decision-making. This doesn't mean simply replacing one tyrant with another; it means experimenting with ways that improve the overall contribution of learning to organizational decision making, regardless of who is involved or for how long. If changing the boss every day helps the learning process, maybe it's worth a try—especially if we can find a way to maintain continuity of purpose and direction in an atmosphere of regular leadership change out. Before you insist that this can't be done, reread Bradford and Cohen's *Managing for Excellence*. You will be forced to admit that the current system isn't providing realistic continuity and direction, either. Then read any one of Tom Peters' latest books for a whole shelf full of examples of people who have found better ways to manage; and Margaret Wheatly's book on leadership and chaos; and Chris Aygris' new book *Knowledge for Action*, and Ralph Stacey's *Managing the Unknowable*, and William Berquist's book on postmodern organizations; and Charles Handy's *The Age of Unreason*.[8,9,10,11,12,13,14] You'll be ready to throw away the organizational chart forever.

*　*　*

Eliminating the hierarchy is a good first step, but it's not enough. Knowledge workers are extremely sensitive to their environment and are affected by a number of other potentially dangerous social and physical forces. Interdepartmental or interproject competition, for example, can cause knowledge workers to interpret truth based on localized criteria and thereby lose their scientific objectivity: "If only one project is going to get funded, by damn it better be ours!" In the name of competition, people put forth inventions that aren't fully tested in order to be first out the gate, provide misinformation to internal competitors to throw them off the track, withhold negative information from decision-makers who might not understand, promise more than they can deliver and then find ways to forget what they promised, attempt to discredit others' work, plagiarize ideas, squirrel away budgets, neglect to promote key people, submit false data, sabotage others' tests, chum up with important people, get the customer to fight their battles, overstate the benefits of their case, call in expert witnesses, threaten to quit if they aren't supported. With all this going on, it's amazing that any work gets done. Yet we believe in the benefits of good, healthy competition because it *motivates* people. Yes, it does. But what does it motivate them to do?

And then there are the behaviors to which knowledge workers, as human beings, are susceptible. I know I am. Such as believing that my ideas are better than other ideas; that the people I know and like have better ideas than the people I don't know or don't like; looking more diligently for evidence that supports my point of view than evidence that refutes it; using knowledge I already possess to solve a problem rather than learning something new and more appropriate; being afraid to expose my ignorance about things I don't fully understand but think I should; being attracted to people who think the way I do; finding it easy to learn in the way I like to learn and difficult to learn if information is presented in some other way; skipping steps I think are obvious; avoiding negative feedback; relying on gossip to form opinions of other people's abilities; equating people's ability with their rank or status; interacting with people who are close to me but not those further removed; continuing too long to try to make one solution to a problem work before shifting to another solution; feeling more motivated by work that is new or important than work that seems old or routine; enjoying doing the work more than telling others what I have done; failing to catalogue my learnings so that they are available to me or others when I need them; saying more or less about my work than others want to hear; not spending enough time reflecting before acting; taking a long time to get to know people before I can trust them and work with them productively; being affected by events outside of work; or maybe just having a bad day.

With all these human foibles, it's amazing that we are able to learn anything at all; but clearly we do. We find a way to overcome our deficiencies in order to keep knowledge moving forward, sometimes in great bursts of energy and insight, and at other times in small fits and spurts. But until recently, we have taken these foibles as givens that we must tolerate or work around in order to succeed in learning. We haven't asked the question, "Is there a way our organizations can help us to make the task of learning easier?" In the realm of knowledge work, we are still crossing the plains in covered wagons to mine our gold by pick and shovel. Perhaps technology will assist the human condition with further developments in artificial intelligence, but I think there's a lot to appreciate about the human condition that I hope machines don't ever cause us to forget. Rather than viewing our foibles as threats to knowledge work, we should view them as challenges to be understood and mastered, and then turned to our advantage. It may be possible in the future for machines to create Mona Lisas and symphonies to rival those of Brahms or Beethoven, but I like knowing that these masterpieces were created by people, and that there is still room for human creativity in the world.

Given these individual, group, and organizational barriers to developing and applying knowledge, what can be done to enhance organizational learning? How can we help people do a better job of making themselves more knowledgeable and using what they know to help our organizations succeed? The answer to this question is not a simple, single recommendation but rather a *system* of interventions into how we think and work. These interventions involve *preparing* to do flexible thinking, *framing* opportunities or problems, *organizing* to think collectively, and *empowering* thoughtful action.

PREPARING TO THINK FLEXIBLY

Think about any important new endeavor in your life: a trip to a new country, learning a new skill or sport, having your first child. Rarely would you consider doing something new or important without preparing yourself for the adventure. You might read a bit about other's experiences, get some advice from knowledgeable friends, sit down and plan things out, and pack accordingly. Too often, however, when we approach knowledge work tasks we mistakenly believe that we need no further preparation, that whatever qualified us to be given this piece of work to think about also qualifies us as experts in it, with no need for further practice, information, or input. We simply set to work.

Likewise, too often when we begin a piece of knowledge work with a team, we assume that all the members of the team are comfortable working together, that we all know how to behave appropriately in team meetings, that we understand each other's point of view, that we care more about the success of the team than our individual accomplishments, that we understand and agree upon the role the team leader is to play, how we are going to make decisions, what information we need to collect or develop to answer the questions we are asking, how we will get that information, and what we will know when we have finished our work.

Finally, at the organizational level, we assign people to R&D work or other knowledge-intensive activities with the often mistaken belief that they understand what we want them to do, what the customer wants them to do, how they should go about doing it, how they should integrate their work with that of people in other parts of the organization, how they should organize internally to get the work done, how they should manage and motivate knowledge workers, and what to do when things don't turn out as planned.

On the one hand, it makes sense not to overprepare, because overpreparation reduces flexibility. A lack of preparation leaves us open to experiences as they happen and free to adjust our plans without feeling that we are breaking our own promises to ourselves. But preparing too little is a much more frequent problem than overpreparing, and underpreparation leads to wasted effort, not flexibility. Although accidents do sometimes produce breakthroughs, it doesn't make sense to count on accidents as the primary engine to drive productive knowledge work. What *does* make sense?

At the individual level, preparation requires learning. As professionals in our fields, we too often feel that our period of learning in life is over; we finished our formal education in college or graduate school, and the rest has come through on-the-job experience. We will continue to learn, of course, but only as we perform our work. Isn't that what the organization expects? Whoever heard of returning to school to learn *after* finally finishing that MBA? Yet that is precisely what needs to happen, each time we undertake a significant, new knowledge work challenge. We may not need to return to the university for a two- or four-year program; we may not need to return to the university at all. If the task is new and significant, however, we do need a way to learn, to push ourselves out of our comfort zone, to become world-class experts in what we are about to do. If the task is either familiar or insignificant, the need for learning is less; but beware the trap of forcing new work and new opportunities to fit into old routines.

If we are about to work on a task with new people, or with people from functions other than our own, or with customers from outside of our own organization, we also need to learn, in this case about them and what they do and what they expect from us in performing this task. We need to spend enough time to understand their point of view, to know enough about their area of expertise to begin to blend it with our own. We can wait to discover this as we work together over time, but if we do, precious effort will be lost retracing our steps once we finally understand what we should have been thinking about all along.

Even in our own specialty, periodic renewal of our knowledge base should become a legitimate activity. How else can we help our organizations compete in a global marketplace with people who are using the latest knowledge available in our field? If we aren't on the cutting edge, we're about to be cut. It's as simple as that. Sabbaticals, intensive in-house workshops, cross-functional internships, keeping up with the literature, going to school part time; somehow, some way, we need to find the knowledge that is relevant to our work, make sure we get it, and understand what we have. Once we have it, we are ready to begin work on the task. Does getting it take time? Yes, but usually not as much as we think. Does taking time to get prepared delay getting started on the task? It depends on how you define "getting started." If getting started means setting up the experimental equipment and starting to run experiments that we *hope* will teach us something about what we need to know, the answer is yes. But if getting started means beginning the process of quality thinking about the challenge on our plate, then preparation *is* getting started, even if we have to leave the organization to do it.

In many organizations, travel away from work or time off-premises is reserved for management, except for an occasional conference or two. But does it make sense for managers to be the only ones who have new knowledge when they are not even doing the crucial knowledge work themselves? The idea that one person can learn on behalf of another, distill what is important from that learning, and then effectively transfer that learning to them in a useful form is baseless. It makes more sense for people who are trying to think their way through a problem to acquire the knowledge for themselves. They know what they need to know; they understand how to apply what they have learned; they don't need to get on someone else's calendar or depend on someone else to get the facts straight. Individual knowledge workers need to view preparation as a necessary part of the job, and organizations should support them in preparing. Each knowledge worker should have a strategy and operational plan to prepare for each significant new piece of work she is asked to do. The time and resources spent preparing may save months or even years of effort later on. Preparing and the next step, framing, are like controlling variances at their source in routine work. Get the people actually doing the work involved in solving the problem early to avoid rework and wasted effort later in the project.

At the team level, many options for team building are available. Some of them are worthless and make matters worse instead of better. The best ones help team members focus precisely on the most critical questions and leave the rest up to people to work out for themselves over time. The key issues to be clarified in the beginning are the objectives the group is to accomplish, the time and resources available, the outside influences on the project, the roles group members are expected to play, the way the group will reach decisions, and the basis for the team's and individual's evaluation of performance. Subsequent issues should be addressed as the need arises. Since groups have natural development phases, team building can accelerate but not eliminate the need for time to work through them. Therefore, team building works best when it's not an up-front, one-shot activity, but an anticipated series of steps in a process of developing an effective working team. Unfortunately, I talk to many brilliant people who detest the team they are on and in fact detest the whole idea of working in teams. Most of these people have never had the luxury of working on an effective team, or at least one in which they could select their peers. Far too often, people are forced to work together on teams where autocratic leaders tell people that if they have trouble working on a team they just aren't mature or company-minded enough: "Put aside your personal concerns and pull for the team, even if you think the other members of the team are idiots and the way we're going about solving the problem is ridiculous. That's what being a good team player is all about." The message is to conform, to be quiet about it, and to stop thinking altogether if your thoughts differ from those of the team or the team leader. Good advice for privates, sinners, or slaves, but a recipe for disaster in knowledge work.

Organizations add to the problem by exerting pressure on thinkers to act rather than think. Despite hiring the best and brightest and superbly well trained people, once in the door, the basis for all evaluation is performance as in, "what have you done for us lately?" We've all heard how the pressure from Wall Street for quarterly profits provokes short-term thinking that undercuts the long-term well being of the firm. Realizing that this pressure can be detrimental to basic research, some organizations attempt to remove research from the corporate headquarters environment, allocate fixed special budgets to R&D activities, and shield R&D managers from regular reporting requirements. But even these steps may not be enough to create the proper climate for the preparation phase. R&D managers are still under tremendous pressures to demonstrate results through return on investment, and the way to do this, they sometimes believe, is to make certain that each person is assigned to a project and *working*. The fundamental problem here is that even among knowledge workers, *thinking is not regarded as legitimate work*. Only results count; and the sooner you are doing something that produces some kind of results, even a laboratory report on a failed experiment, the better.

One R&D manager I worked with wanted all of his scientists to *begin* their work by answering the most critical questions in their projects first. In that way, he felt that they could avoid doing the detailed preparation work that eventually allowed them to feel comfortable in testing their hypotheses. His perception was that all the detailed preparation work was simply the product of university schooling by anal-retentive professors who forbade their students to ask questions they hadn't laid the proper groundwork to answer. He wanted his scientists to think outside of the rules, to leap to the final question, "If this really worked, what would it do and how would it do it?" His scientists would have gladly complied if they could, but they realized that the preparation work was what enabled them to see opportunities they could pursue that would eventually lead to insights about what might work and how. Leaping to the final question was like finding a cure to the common cold: Seeing the objective was easy, but it still didn't make finding the answer any faster. If the R&D director had helped people prepare their knowledge base instead of pressuring them to run the critical experiment, more would have been accomplished faster. The only way to run the critical experiment was to already know the cure; and if the cure was known, the experiment wouldn't have been necessary. Other than blind luck, there's no substitute for learning.

A great deal of knowledge work occurs outside of R&D, as well. It is even less likely that knowledge workers in marketing, planning, information systems, manufacturing, or finance will be allowed the luxury of preparing for significant, new tasks; yet each of these areas presents an opportunity for improvements in organizational performance and competitive advantage that could benefit from enhancements in how knowledge work is performed. How much is an effective information system worth to an organization compared to an ineffective one? How much is a critical investment decision worth if made correctly versus incorrectly? Why is it that only about 10 percent of all mergers and acquisitions result in the organization being better off afterwards than before? What would it have been worth to the U.S. auto or steel industry to respond to off-shore competition 10 years sooner than they did? Knowledge work improvement has enormous potential for having a positive impact on the corporate bottom line; but when it is treated like routine work for which people need no preparation, the result is not flexible thinking, but the same old answers that we used last year.

FRAMING THE OPPORTUNITY

Pareto analysis tells us that 20 percent of the problems cause 80 percent of our wasted effort. If we can identify and eliminate the critical 20 percent we get a much larger return on our investment than fooling around with the 80 percent of problems that are less important. In knowledge work, framing the opportunity is one of the critical problems. Because opportunity framing is inherently difficult, it is one of those things that we want to avoid mucking around in; we tell ourselves that it is better to throw a dart at the wall and start doing *something* than to keep asking the question, "What should we be doing?" But if we want to avoid being on Pareto's most wanted list, we have to learn to live with the uncertainty, as uncomfortable as it can be.

The highest hurdle to overcome in problem framing is to get outside of ourselves, to listen to other stakeholders, and especially to hear the voice of the customer. In this age of customer awareness, there should be no excuse for beginning work on a knowledge-intensive task without first clarifying the desired outcomes of the work with the recipient, internal or external to the organization. As mentioned earlier, RR Donnelly and others are inviting customers to become part of knowledge work teams, to have continuous input rather than one-time, secondhand input after they receive the finished product. So, gaining customer clarity, if it exists, is step one in opportunity framing.

The next step is to frame the opportunity technically, and it is here that the preparation phase begins to pay off. Is this an opportunity that we or others have encountered previously? What is known about this kind of opportunity? What approaches have been taken by others? Can we benchmark competitors' products or services? What other approaches are available? Before selecting one approach and committing to it, are there ways to quickly and relatively inexpensively test out alternative approaches? Which approach is most likely to fulfill the opportunity? Which approach will be easier to sell? What are the implications for manufacturing? For the regulatory area? For existing products or services? Who can work with us to help frame this opportunity more precisely? Who can we use as a devil's advocate to critique our approach? What are the major questions that need to be answered? Where in the world does expertise related to these questions exist and how can we get our hands on it? What are the critical go–no go points? What are the limits we are working under in terms of cost, effectiveness, safety, timeliness, maintainability, and so forth? Answering these questions may require that a much larger team be involved in the framing process than in later project work. Representatives from other functions, from suppliers, from customers, expert consultants, people working on other projects, market analysts, and others with pertinent knowledge may be called together to help with the framing process. Again, if the opportunity is both new and significant, an all-out effort in framing is well worth the time and expense incurred in preventing problems downstream. Once the problem is framed, it's time to get organized to do knowledge work.

ORGANIZING FOR KNOWLEDGE WORK

It used to be that the way to manage knowledge work was a combination of brute force and wishful thinking. The best people were hired or recruited to a large team. They were given space, equipment and resources; told to go to work; and then flogged regularly for not producing results fast enough. The nature of knowledge work, being inherently nonroutine, made for lots of floggings. As Albert Einstein said, "Science is a wonderful thing as long as one doesn't have to make a living at it."

But what other choice did the manager of knowledge workers have? He or she could get involved directly, but since the subordinates know more than the manager, the result of direct involvement was a lot of time spent in educating the boss just enough to screw up the decision-making on the project. Leaving people alone didn't feel very comfortable either, particularly with someone higher up the chain of command breathing down the manager's neck. Something must be done, action must be taken, people need leadership! They need management! So lead! The manager would lead, if he could just figure out how, when neither he nor others know exactly what is supposed to be done or how to do it.

The answer, it turns out, is neither to jump in nor to stand back. It's to make certain that people and teams are adequately prepared for the tasks they have been given, that the problem has been framed properly, and to help people organize themselves to answer the critical questions they have identified. What does organizing for knowledge work entail?

It's here that Calvin Pava's breakthrough in perceiving knowledge work as a series of deliberations, rather than discrete decisions, provides important clues.[15] Pava's argument, essentially, is that by the time people are ready to decide something, the knowledge work is over. Therefore, all of the attention that has been placed on organizational decision-making is in fact *misplaced*. The real knowledge work goes on long before the meeting at which the decision is made; and it tends to be a very messy, disorganized process, open to the full negative force of all the human foibles and social dynamics described earlier. By the time the decision is framed, the battle is lost; it's classic garbage in–garbage out.

Instead, Pava suggests that we trace the process of developing knowledge concerning key decisions over time, in all the various forums in which learning and discussion take place. Some of this work is individual in nature, some of it is collective. Some work is open for all to see, other work goes on in the minds of one or two people or behind closed doors in private sessions. To understand how knowledge is invented, processed, and eventually made available for decisions, we need to trace the evolution of knowledge about a topic through what Pava labeled *deliberations* to distinguish them from what we typically think of as meetings or decisions. Deliberations are times when people think about a topic, when they learn what they think they know, when they share their learnings with others, and when, ultimately, sense is made of that knowledge and concretized into a decision. If the quality of decisions can't be affected much once the knowledge work that goes into the decision is over, it follows that the point of optimal intervention in knowledge work is *while the knowledge is still being developed*. Organizing for knowledge work and *managing knowledge workers* means making the process by which people in the organization learn and influence each other much more explicit, and then working to improve that process over time, as its mechanisms are better understood and experiments with new ways of approaching knowledge tasks are conducted.

Typically, deliberations are spontaneous, unplanned events that we regard as practically inconsequential, yet they are the essence of knowledge work. Deliberately planning and managing them allows us to enhance the quality of knowledge work; it's almost like putting a power tool in the hands of someone who has been doing a task manually. Since knowledge work is made up of a series of deliberations, if we improve individual deliberations, we eventually improve the overall knowledge output and application. The secret is in recognizing what knowledge work is, and how to improve it at the microlevel. Here are some interesting examples of organizations deliberating.

Jean Francois Lyotard, in *Le Condition Postmodern*, writes about the Cashinaua Indians of South America. These Indians are interesting because they live in a very remote region and exist much as they have for thousands of years, so the ritualistic customs they have developed to protect them from all kinds of threats to their existence must work; and we can look at these rituals, unchanged for thousands of years, to see how members of the tribe make decisions about what to do in the face of dangerous uncertainty. As with most tribes, decisions are made by a group of elders, in this case all male. And, also as in most ancient cultures, there is an implicit assumption that those who have lived the longest are the best qualified to decide what to do. But the Cashinaua take this a step further: Each time the elders meet about a new topic (and remember, this has been going on for generations) each member introduces himself to the others, telling his story of his life and what it is that qualifies him to speak at this meeting on this topic. Depending on the topic and the speaker's introduction of himself in relation to it, a person may gain or lose influence in the discussion that day. Thus, every decision is influenced most by those who establish themselves as the most expert on a particular topic.

What is interesting about the Cashinaua is that they recognize that authority should be equated with knowledge in the decisions that are most important to the future of the tribe, and they don't presume that one person—a chief (or CEO)—is necessarily the most qualified to speak on any topic that comes before the tribe. It's quite a different way of deliberating than most of our organizations use. If an anthropologist were to study our tribal corporate culture in regard to its deliberations, she might find that there are all kinds of rituals and customs that exist to determine ultimately who has the authority to make decisions on behalf of the firm. Think for a moment about how people gain credibility in your organization, and how they lose it, and how your organization's customs make some types of experiments in learning legitimate and others illegitimate. What are examples of some "type I" errors (the right person is listened to but makes the wrong decision) and "type II" errors (the wrong person is listened to in the first place and makes the wrong decision)? If we want to improve the effectiveness of our teams and organizations, we have to challenge some of these existing deliberation customs. Perhaps we can learn something from an ancient Indian culture.

Now, another story. This time, a modern tribal culture: Xerox Corporation.

We all know the story of Xerox: 20-year-old Chester Carlson approached 21 companies with his ideas about electrophotography until he found one that would listen to him. The first model he developed weighed 654 pounds, cost $29,750, and could copy about one page a minute. Xerography wasn't an immediate success. Despite the tough beginning, by 1970 Xerox Corporation was on the *Fortune* 500 list and owned 95 percent of the world market share in copying. Then, something happened. In the next 10 years, Xerox's market share slipped from 95 percent to less than 50 percent; and none of its products were leaders in customer satisfaction in any market segment.

The Japanese market share during this period grew despite the fact that Xerox was spending twice as much to make its copiers as the Japanese, and employed twice as many design engineers. Still, Xerox's quality defects were 10 times greater, and it took them twice as long as it took the Japanese to get new products to market.

I sat in a meeting between Xerox engineering and Xerox marketing sometime around 1977. What I heard was unbelievable. Xerox marketing people were telling Xerox engineers that they couldn't sell Xerox copiers because the Japanese copiers were far superior in quality and features. The engineers insisted that the marketing people must have been mistaken, because Xerox was the leading copier engineering company in the world, and therefore that the quality and features of Xerox copiers simply must be the best. Sound familiar? Eventually, the marketing people bought some of the Japanese copiers and brought them to the engineers to see for themselves. This began a period of intensive benchmarking by the engineers, in which they tore down the competitors' products and evaluated every component to see if Xerox could design it better or cheaper. Benchmarking spread to other functions in Xerox as well, from manufacturing to order processing. Few organizations have ever undertaken benchmarking with such thoroughness. The good-news ending to the story is that, since 1983, Xerox has cut its manufacturing costs by 50 percent, improved quality tenfold, and has a product at the top of every market segment. They did it by *learning*. They stopped saying "We're the best" and started challenging their cultural belief that their own engineers were the best in the world. They opened themselves up to information from external sources and began to invite marketing people into deliberations regarding product design. Xerox's internal thinking process changed; and, because of this, the names Xerox and the Penn Central Railroad don't belong in the same category. Xerox responded to its crisis by learning how to learn; the Penn Central relied on its same deliberation processes until the very end.

Xerox was inspired to act by a crisis, but there are many other examples of good companies that undertake efforts to improve without the wolf at the door. Historically, however, improvements have happened faster in manufacturing than in other parts of companies. Quality programs, work redesign, innovative compensation, just in time inventory started in manufacturing and only later spread to other parts of the organization. Knowledge workers are frequently able to resist the pressure to change for longer than others because of the nature of their work and their highly developed expertise. It's easier to be sloppy in knowledge work, because the efficiency of knowledge work is hard to measure and experts are hard to challenge. While no one is intentionally *trying* to be sloppy, simply doing more of what has been done before in the same ways it has been done before, even if we are trying harder to do it, *is* sloppy. Unless there is learning and evolution taking place in how you go about doing knowledge work—in how you're organized to do it, how you handle knowledge, how you develop people, how you pay attention to the competitive environment—unless you're constantly getting better at all of these things and more, you're being sloppy, and there's a good chance that, eventually, you will find your organization falling behind.

What can we learn from these examples about effective and ineffective deliberations? Some characteristics of effective deliberations are listed in Figure 6-1.

The first characteristic, knowledge highly developed and available, is determined primarily by effective preparation. The next two, knowledge utilized fully and without bias and apolitical discussion, have more to do with the dynamics that occur during the deliberation process. Having the right people present is a matter of deliberation planning. Often, we forget to include people with knowledge relevant to a problem or, worse, actively exclude them because they are not from our department, not at the proper "level" to be part of the discussion, or have opinions contrary to our own. Disruptive people are those who use their

- Knowledge highly developed and available
- Knowledge utilized fully and without bias
- Apolitical discussion of facts and alternatives
- People with most knowledge present
- Disruptive/inappropriate people absent
- Discussion held at key choice points
- Goals clear and shared
- Challenging but realistic time frames
- Decision making procedures clear
- Appropriate attention to external environment
- Minimum bureaucracy

Figure 6.1 Characteristics of effective deliberations.

position power to influence deliberation outcomes even when they know nothing about the content being discussed. Planning and holding discussions at key choice points eliminates some of the problems associated with people who want to work alone and commit others to their decisions without the others' input. The next four items have to do with preparation and opportunity framing: goals clear and shared, challenging but realistic time frames, decision-making procedures clear, and appropriate attention to the external environment. The last item is a reminder that the purpose of planning deliberations is not to add bureaucracy or to slow things down, but rather to try to make certain that knowledge work is performed as effectively as it possibly can be.

Ineffective deliberations, by contrast, proceed without highly developed knowledge, resulting in the wrong decisions being made or decisions constantly being postponed. Knowledge that is available may be set aside, as in the *Challenger* incident, for a variety of social or political reasons. Parties to ineffective deliberations may enter dialogue with one another from an adversarial or defensive posture, leading to incomplete or misleading information in key decisions. Disruptive parties can undo months of careful work as powerful individuals inject opinions or push personal agendas. The avoidance of deliberations at key decision points makes it impossible for people with relevant knowledge to influence the course of knowledge work in a timely fashion. Goals not clearly set forth cause knowledge workers to diverge in their thinking and then to become set in the paths they have chosen. Unrealistic time frames cause people to forego adequate preparation, rush through deliberations, exclude important external parties, and settle for lower quality than desired. Unclear procedures for making decisions leave the door open for one-on-one lobbying, subgroup influence, majority voting, and a host of other threats to quality decision-making. Inadequate attention to the external environment, as in the case of Xerox, creates self-sealing truths, and an insistence on internal decisions being the only logical way to look at the world. Too much structure constrains flexible thinking and causes people to avoid the deliberation process altogether.

There are many ways to improve the quality of deliberations. Knowledge workers can form *learning action teams* which are the parallel of quality action teams in routine work settings. Learning action teams conduct regular brainstorming, analysis, and action planning about how to improve knowledge availability, knowledge utilization, and the flexibility of organizational thinking processes. Learning action teams can be formed within a single function, such as marketing, or across functions, such as marketing and R&D. Like quality action teams, learning action teams are authorized to try experiments to improve performance within limits imposed by a steering committee. Proposals from learning action teams can range from simple changes in data gathering procedures to changes in organizational design.

Deliberation quality also can be improved by studying past deliberations and performing a critical review of what went well and what went poorly. Particularly if outsiders are invited to join in the discussion and ask innocent questions regarding the culture of deliberations, the learnings can be eye opening.

Alternately, deliberations can be improved by planning them in advance, making certain that the right people are involved, that they come prepared with the right knowledge, and that rules are agreed upon before interaction begins. Planning important deliberations in advance makes sense, particularly in these days of impossibly busy calendars and multiple responsibilities.

Ultimately, however, the most important intervention to improve deliberation quality is to redesign the organization so that effective deliberations take place naturally, rather than fighting against improper structural influences. The organization design for effective deliberating takes into account the need to constantly realign knowledge with authority, yet integrate the outcomes of separate deliberations. What kind of organization design allows both flexibility and integration?

DESIGNING ORGANIZATIONS TO THINK: THE POLYNOETIC ORGANIZATION

Clearly, the design can't be based upon hierarchy. Hierarchy is one means of achieving integration, but it is not the only means; and hierarchy destroys flexibility and almost guarantees that knowledge will not be aligned with authority. So the first principle is that *the design must be nonhierarchical*.

The second principle is that people with knowledge must be capable of working with others who need that knowledge in order to complete their thinking about an interdependent task. Maximum freedom of movement is achieved by reducing role and boundary restrictions. So, the second principle is that *the organization should maximize freedom of movement*.

Third, because it is extremely important for everyone to know what knowledge exists in the system and how to access it, the organization must be holographic; that is, everyone needs to know a little about what is going on in the rest of the organization. So, the third principle is that *knowledge must be widely shared and easily accessible*.

Fourth, in order to provide integration and direction, there must be ways for people to agree on goals and strategies. Based on these goals and strategies, further choices regarding projects and teams can be made. Since it is important for people with

knowledge to be involved in setting direction, the fourth principle is that *the organization must involve people with knowledge in
goal setting and integration activities.*

Finally, because the development and utilization of knowledge requires the development of people who are knowledgeable and highly committed, *the organization must be designed to
encourage, support, and reward learning.* Together, these five principles point toward a form of organization which is quite different from the norm in use today. This new form of organization,
which I will call *polynoetic,* meaning many centers of knowledge,
is best depicted as a number of overlapping circles, as shown in
Figure 6-2.

The polynoetic organization is coordinated by a central group
of knowledge workers who are themselves representatives of the
various projects and activities undertaken by the organization.
In addition, the integrating group contains individuals who represent administrative support functions, such as financial analysis, which provide information crucial to decision-making *when
such information is appropriate.* In contrast to typical top management groups, the integration group has no stable membership or
roles. The membership of the group varies depending upon the

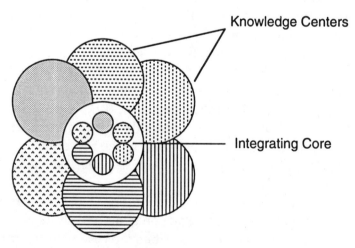

Figure 6.2   The polynoetic organization.

topics under discussion, the players heading up important projects, and suppliers of information relevant to the discourse. The integration group provides overall strategy guidance and allocates resources among competing demands. Leadership within the integration group rotates depending again on the knowledge demands of the ongoing and special deliberations on the agenda.

The remainder of the organization consists of teams that vary in duration and size. Each team is composed of a core of stable resources who maintain responsibility for the team's progress; members of the integration group are drawn from this core. Surrounding the core group of each project is a more transient pool of resources who join the project as it requires their expertise. Members of a core group may serve as resources to another project or even several projects as needed. In this way, both core members and support resources provide their project teams with holographic knowledge concerning other projects in the organization.

Centralized resource groups, such as market research, human resources, or information management appear as project teams as well, with cores of experts joined by support resources who vary depending on the task under completion. Since these centralized resource groups provide crucial information and conduct work that is important to organizational planning and maintenance, they must also develop holographic knowledge. Their direct involvement in projects at appropriate times provides some of the knowledge they need, and having others join them in their work adds another dimension of understanding.

The polynoetic organization also contains teams designated as *learning projects*. Learning projects provide opportunities for individuals from project teams or central resource groups to undertake activities that enhance their understanding either of their area of expertise or of the organization, its customers, or its environment. Unlike traditional organizations, in which a few people are designated as full-time learners and the rest are cast as doers, in the polynoetic organization every person has the option of being involved on a learning project. The integration group may ask for proposals for learning projects, which are then staffed and supported according to the goals of each project.

To support the fluidity of the polynoetic organization, information technology must be available that allows easy access to a database of knowledge resources internal and external to the organization. Combining this database with direct electronic communication eases the burden of getting knowledge from where it is located to where it is needed.

Reward systems in the polynoetic organization should reinforce both project performance and learning, since both are important to organizational success. Peer reviews make sense, since direct measurement of results is often difficult in nonroutine work. Increases in pay do not correspond to increases in formal authority, since a person's value in the polynoetic organization depends on the current utility of their knowledge and ability to contribute to the success of contemporary projects.

Issues such as governance, equity, and resource allocation are managed as participatively as possible, at times bringing representatives of all projects together for discussion. While participation is often perceived as a "nice thing to do" in routine work, in nonroutine work participation is essential. It builds the commitment necessary to undertake high-performance intellectual work.

Each member of the polynoetic organization has at least two primary responsibilities. The first is to the projects they are currently working on; the second is to the future. In the true polynoetic organization, the second responsibility carries as much weight as the first.

Polynoetic organizations must have the ability to expand or contract as their knowledge demands dictate. Since knowledge is an expensive commodity to develop, the polynoetic organization may form temporary alliances with other organizations to help acquire knowledge. Or, in the case where knowledge needs require a long-term effort of some magnitude, mergers or acquisitions involving other polynoetic organizations may be appropriate.

EMPOWERING FLEXIBLE THOUGHT

Presuming that organizations have succeeded in helping people to prepare themselves for flexible thinking, framed appropriate opportunities to pursue, and organized for polynoetic work, empowerment should follow naturally. The most serious barrier to empowerment, as noted in our earlier discussion of participation, is fear of loss of control by those in charge. In the polynoetic organization, *everyone is in charge*; and this works, not because everyone thinks alike, but because each person shares in the holographic knowledge of the whole. This is the fundamental paradigm shift that takes us out of our traditional thinking about organizing. Without holographic knowledge, people cannot manage themselves in a manner that produces an integrated outcome for the organization; with it, people can help the organization think, answer questions, develop solutions, and seize opportunities that are appropriate to pursue.

How do people gain holographic knowledge? In the traditional model, years of experience, exposure to many different functions, and living through a variety of situations was the way to learn about the whole organization. In a nonchanging world, this model of learning made sense. But in a world of rapid change, the old model of gaining holographic knowledge is no longer valid. The world is simply changing faster and in more significant ways than it did before, and this demands new ways of learning. Today and into the future, we need people to get up to speed quickly and begin to use their brains even before their hair turns grey. But we don't need the recklessness of youth; we need the brilliance of a creative fresh perspective from a well trained mind, dedicated to organizational success in the context of what others are trying to achieve.

The fastest way to produce holographic knowledge is through multiple points of contact with a system. In the polynoetic organization, each project team or learning team carries both an operational responsibility and an educational one. Further, the integration group must fulfill its obligation to provide information concerning its deliberations and decisions to everyone in the organization.

Again, information systems support is essential to effective learning and communication concerning holographic knowledge. E-mail, newsletters, and monthly meetings alone won't do the job. Instant, in-depth access is required so that people can figure out how to plug their activities in to what others are doing.

Once people have a sense of what is happening, they can begin to make decisions about where to assist, where to take responsibility, and when to let go of less important tasks. As project groups form around a nucleus of interest, members of the core group can begin to advertise their knowledge needs. Others with interest or ideas can answer the ads that are related to their areas of specialization. Others, who can assist by providing support or linkages with outside groups, also respond. Periodically, as the project team grows and progresses in defining knowledge needs, new ads can be placed and new talent added to the team. When they have done what they can, some members of the team drop off to pursue new opportunities.

Informal organizations have always behaved this way. Precisely because they were informal and outside of the chain of command, no one "empowered" them to act. People empowered themselves. Often, the informal organizations I have observed are as effective if not more effective than formal organizations at capturing energy and making progress in their thinking. People join informal organizations voluntarily and stay only as long as they feel that they are contributing something that is valued by others. Expectancy theory doesn't produce conformity in this case because there is nothing to conform to; the informal organization emerges from the inputs of its members and is transformed as their interests change. Informal organizations work wonderfully at developing and utilizing knowledge; but, typically, because they operate outside of the formal chain of command, they fail to support organizational objectives. I've witnessed the tragedy of a fired-up informal team present its wonderful new ideas to managers who had to tell them that the ideas just didn't fit into the big picture. It's not pretty, and the heartbreak really is not necessary. Why should only managers know what fits into the big picture? In traditional, hierarchical organizations, we have people with the know-how working on projects they aren't excited about; they lack commitment, or what we might call the "want-to." Informal organizations have the want-to but not the know-how. When we combine the enthusiasm of informal organizations with access to holographic knowledge to create the empowered polynoetic organization, we have the perfect combination of know-how and want-to. Everyone wins.

Do polynoetic organizations exist? Do they work? Yes, they do. Earlier, I mentioned McKinsey & Company, the consulting firm, and EDS, which Tom Peters described in detail in his recent book, *Liberation Management*. I also discussed the International Physicians for the Prevention of Nuclear War and other groups that are really networks of people sharing a common interest and acting together at times and separately at times to make things happen. Closer to home, community groups, professional service and consulting firms, and professional associations operate in much the same way as the polynoetic organizations described here. These organizations need to operate flexibly to take full advantage of the knowledge resources at their command, and to gain the full support of their members.

Other organizations have elements of the polynoetic organization incorporated in their design, even if they haven't adopted all five design principles. For example, I recall seeing a special on the Israeli Air Force done by "60 Minutes" that captured a few of the secrets behind the tremendous success achieved by that service in its last few wars. One segment that struck me concerned the flexibility of rank during combat; during missions, ability rather than rank determines who leads the mission. It is apparently not uncommon to have a lieutenant in command of a mission that also includes a captain, major, and colonel. The lieutenant is in command because his skills and knowledge are most up to date; and the rest allow him to lead because they are committed to the success of the mission, and having the lieutenant in charge simply makes the most sense. At least to the Israelis. Can you imagine a scene from the old-fashioned military in which the cigar chewing general turns to a private and says, "Son, you're the best at what we're about to do; you'd better take command!" The old military is more invested in maintaining the hierarchy than in winning. Otherwise, the scene would make sense, just as it does to the Israelis.

Matrix organizations grew up in the aerospace industry out of a need to bring a dual focus to project work and functional depth. Before they were invented, no one would have believed that a person could report to more than one supervisor without being in a constant state of role conflict. But now that they have been around for a while, matrix organizations are less scary and have spread to all kinds of organizations. In the near term, I expect polynoetic organizations to be confined to situations where they are most needed, such as research and development departments in firms in competitive industries, or professional service organizations and associations that can survive only as long as their members are satisfied and productive. But, slowly, the wisdom of more fully developing and utilizing knowledge resources will spread to other organizations as well. Eventually, we may see elements of polynoetic organizations in almost every organization in which knowledge is important to organizational success. Come to think of it, are there organizations that *don't* depend on knowledge for survival?

CHAPTER

7

Flexible Managers
What Happens to the Leaders?

Are leaders about to become extinct? Do they serve any useful purpose in the new paradigm, polynoetic organization, or do they simply block change rather than help to create it?

I hope not. I have a fondness for leaders, and an old-fashioned belief in the American dream; great leaders are truly exceptional people, and they help all of us to fulfill dreams we may never have had the bravery or wisdom to dream on our own. There have been many times in my life when I have benefited greatly from another's leadership, and I thank all of the people who were willing to take the risk of leading me for their courage. There is no doubt that leadership is under attack, and that a trend exists toward obliterating levels of leadership in our organizations. Much has been written about new forms of leadership lately, about the boss who will be so focused on facilitation, so supportive, and so invisible that we won't even know who he or she is. I think we're throwing away some of the best parts of leadership, and I for one will not tolerate it.

I want to create more opportunities for leadership, more chances for more people with dreams to help the rest of us live them. The cause of death in most of our large organizations is control, not leadership; but because the two are often associated with the same people, it's easy to indict leaders on the basis of circumstantial evidence. I know there are criminals out there: leaders who control their organizations to death in the service of their own egos, who destroy more leadership than they provide. But there are many more innocent citizens who find themselves in leadership positions uncertain of what to do, of how to en-courage dreams and innovation. I'm also certain that there are many more brilliant leaders in our organizations than we recog-nize, and that our current mode of organizing will keep them well hidden, unable to contribute their genius to our success. Inflexibility makes for poor leadership and prevents those who could help from leading us out of the mess.

It's not unusual for us to think about our parents when we think about leadership. In the earliest (and Freud would say the most malleable) years of our lives, our parents were our leaders; we knew no others, we had no real basis for comparison. So we simply accepted their leadership as it was, although we often rebelled against it. We never asked how they got to be the leaders they were, or where they practiced their trade as journeymen before becoming full-fledged leaders. Good or bad, for better or for worse, most parents and kids are stuck with each other.

I was pretty lucky. I was the youngest of six kids, and by the time my parents got around to leading me, they were experi-enced. They knew what to get excited about and what to ignore. They were encouraging, but not pushy; and because they were good to me, I tried to be good to them. My father was always busy working on something: fixing the old cars he brought home, repairing the 150 year old farmhouse we lived in, taking care of the animals on our little farm outside of Chicago that he had moved to in order to get us kids out of the city. He still drove to work in the city every weekday, leaving early in the morning and not returning until dinner time. I remember the drawer full of white shirts he kept for work—every day, the same color. I didn't realize then how much he must have disliked wearing those shirts, because his love was for the outdoors and for rolling his sleeves up and getting dirty working on something with his hands. But he did it for us. On weekends, he would busy himself with projects, and we would often join him. He encouraged me to hang around, to hand him wrenches when he was under the hood, or drive the tractor when it was time to load hay onto the wagon. I never felt pressured by him to learn, but it was clear that he hoped that I would. I'm afraid I disappointed him a bit, because my love was for school. My mother was secretary to the principal; I always thought she would have made a great teacher, but she insists not. I know she taught me. No one could read a story like my mother, or make more of something out of nothing. I still don't know how she managed to feed us, or where she found the energy to do all the things she did.

I played freely in those days, traveling miles from home at times to see friends or get into more trouble than I should. There were few rules, and not much need for them. The country was safe, other than accidents that could happen to almost anyone, like the time my brother broke his arm jumping out of the hayloft. My parents worried more about my older brothers and sisters, admonishing them not to smoke and to drive carefully. Because I didn't cause a lot of headaches, I was given a lot of slack. I learned a lot of things from my expeditions with friends, some of which I shouldn't have learned; but, being older now, I think of all the lessons as valuable, helping me to strengthen and shape my values as an adult. I wouldn't have learned them if I had been made to stay home. Parents provide some of their most important leadership when they trust us to think for ourselves, to learn from experiences of our own choosing.

It's not surprising that we draw analogies between leaders in our organizations and our parents; the parallels are too obvious to ignore. Harold Geneen at ITT was an overly strict and controlling father who demanded detailed monthly reports from his direct reports, which he personally analyzed and tore to shreds. Ed Land at Polaroid was paternalistic and warm, but always saw his employees as children, not quite the equal of their parents. Some would say that John Pepper at Procter & Gamble was too permissive, and that the company needed Ed Artzt to impose tighter controls. There is a tremendous amount of parental imagery concerning founders of firms, since many organizations begin as family businesses. People talk about staying on the good side of the "old man" if he's still around, or mourn his passing when he relinquishes control. Where would we be without our parents?

Like parents, our leaders are human beings who try to sense what the organization needs most from them and provide it as best they can. However, in any large organization, there is usually a wide divergence among leaders at different levels in what they feel they should be doing to help their subordinates and the firm succeed. Some of the divergence is due to the different conditions leaders face, and some is due to what kind of people they are. Kids often compare their parents and are fascinated by the difference in behaviors and rules. How could parenting be viewed so differently by people? "How come your allowance is twice mine?" "How come you get to stay up until ten o'clock?" The same dynamic occurs in organizations and fuels hours of gossip. Some leaders get reputations as permissive, others as authoritarian. Some have lots of trouble disciplining their subordinates, while others operate on trust and seem to have excellent rapport. It's clear that there is as much variation in how people lead as in how they parent. Views about how to do each of these things are deeply held, and there is still no agreement on the one right way.

The problem with leadership is not that there is too much of it, or that it is so variable from person to person. It is that we have never learned that our employees are not our children; they are experienced, responsible adults. Shared leadership, which varies according to the needs of the situation, is not a model that we knew when we were children nor have experienced as adults. We are locked in a parental metaphor for leadership that insists that we appoint one person to lead, and others to follow, in every situation we encounter. We expect our leaders to be our parents, to take care of every problem, to provide for our needs, to care. We expect them to be omnipotent, to know everything, to always make the right choice for us, even if we don't understand it at the time. When parents are abusive or neglectful, children keep their mouths shut, because parents have the power; when leaders are ineffective or pompous, we follow them anyway, because we have given them the power. We have never grown out of our childhoods to assume roles as adults in organizations. We continue to operate with an old metaphor that we cherish dearly, despite its occasional blemishes. We know no other way.

Flexible management means more than knowing one's way around the management grid or understanding situational leadership. Flexible management is more than one way of managing, to be sure, but it's also more than one person managing. In Logan Aluminum's star-point model of leadership, each member of a self-directed work team is a leader in something. One person may lead in the quality area, another in equipment maintenance, another in scheduling, another in training, and yet another in team development. In true self-managing teams, the work to be done in managing the team is done by the team; not just to put power closer to the people doing the work who know what decisions make sense, but because it takes a lot of people to do a good job of leading in all of these areas. We simply expected too much when we asked one person to handle the budget, be a technical expert, know how to deal with conflict and grievances, be a father confessor, and handle whatever else came along, including the change program of the month. Many people are needed to handle all these things well. Figure 7-1 lists some dimensions of self management that are important for groups in production settings to master, and the stages that they usually go through in developing internal leadership.

In Stage 1, teams are still highly dependent upon leadership for decisions and direction in almost every important facet of their work. The team expects its leader to assign people to roles

	Stage 1	Stage 2	Stage 3
Role assignment	comply	assign	create
Group management	follow	participate	lead
Technology	operate	maintain	improve
Customer relations	serve	interact	enhance
Time management	fixed	variable	spontaneous
Quality control	inspect	manage	improve
Planning work	execute	participate	create
Information management	receive	process	manage

Figure 7.1   Stages of self management.

in the group, manage group discussions, teach group members how to operate technology, handle customer relations, set times for meetings, work, and tasks, be responsible for quality, plan the work, manage information, and provide whatever additional training is required. Leaders of teams in Stage 1 are constantly busy, even overwhelmed in trying to accomplish everything that needs to be managed for the group while still trying to do the rest of their own job at the same time. As groups progress in their internal leadership abilities, each of the areas of focus, such as customer relations or quality control, becomes an area of concentrated study by one or more group members, who learns about the topic on behalf of the team.

The team leader is still very involved at Stage 2, helping people to learn what they need to learn to become effective leaders in their chosen areas; but in Stage 2, people begin to perform the functions that were once performed by the leader. By Stage 3, the group is truly self-managing; in fact, the team has moved beyond where the leader was in his or her understanding of each function to the point where group members can not only perform the function, but actually improve it. Team members help create new and more effective roles for team members, lead the group in improving its process, find ways to improve the technology, work together at enhancing customer relations, spontaneously manage their own time to get their work and special tasks done, improve quality, create new plans for themselves to follow, manage their information requirements, and design their own training. In Stage 3, the leader can redirect energy to innovation, linking with stakeholders, and strategic planning.

Is there still a need for leadership or management in Stage 3? Definitely. In our democracy, we each have a vote; but we still elect leaders, who will help us all to focus on what is important, to present us with ideas and visions to stimulate our imaginations, to call our attention to the things we would otherwise forget or ignore. Our leaders are our conscience, our antagonists, our symbols of unity and hope. They provide a function we cannot provide easily for ourselves: the ability to sort out, among the many possibilities, opinions and voices that might be listened to in a given moment, what action is most consistent with our values and our dreams. They cause us to rise above ourselves, to leave behind our focus on our own needs, and to consider the good of the many. They are tie-breakers and emergency decision-makers, people whom we trust to be fair and just and unswerving in their dedication to our welfare. They are Plato's philosopher-kings, and our own Mother Theresas and Martin Luther Kings. They are the best that we could aspire to be, and perhaps more. They are people of tremendous intellect, worldly in their understanding yet concerned about the local good, too. They are people who have earned the right to lead through their courage and their self-sacrifice, their compassion and their persistence.

Few people meet these standards of leadership. When we find someone who does, or who comes close, we should help them find ways to lead us. But we should never settle for pretenders or second best when the true leaders are not to be found. The Gandhis and the Martin Luther Kings are rare, and we should treat them as such. When they are not available, we should remember that we, too, are leaders; and that while no one of us possesses the many traits of a great leader, together even a small assembly of us usually do. Our individual wisdom may fall short, our single courage fail; but our collective knowledge is expansive, and our combined resolve resolute. To have consistent great leadership, we should stop searching for great men and women; they are there, but in far too small numbers to help each of our many organizations improve. Instead, we need to look toward each other, and create a system of flexible management in which together we can develop the many talents of leadership we possess.

Is the role of the leader in organizations becoming extinct? In a traditional sense, yes; unless we are certain that our leaders possess the many qualities needed to make them truly great, we are better off without them. But better still is for us to be *with* them; not to remove them from office and send them packing, but to find new ways to use their talents and for them to help us find ways to use ours. For them to continue to lead when appropriate, but for others of us to lead at other times, when it makes sense. For different groups of us to come together to make the decisions that one person used to make because we understand the problem more fully than one person ever could; for some of us to specialize in areas where our leaders could never find the time before, and then to make our expertise available to the decision process when it is needed; and still to call on our leaders to expedite decisions, break ties, keep us on track when we get bogged down, settle arguments, remind us of our norms, give us feedback on our performance, and all the other things we may never learn to do for ourselves. It's okay to have a flexible idea of leadership: leaders who sometimes act traditionally and sometimes don't act as leaders at all, people who step into leadership roles even though they aren't usually called leaders, groups that act as leaders, and individuals that lead groups.

Flexible leadership makes sense when the world is changing, and the nature of leadership demanded by the situation shifts more quickly than a single person's knowledge or abilities ever could. In a world of change, leadership must help the organization to make the best decisions it can about things it never intended to decide, as quickly as possible. Individuals are fast decision-makers, but they aren't necessarily good decision makers. Everything we know about individuals from studies in the behavioral sciences points to the fact that leaders will be biased to filter out what they don't understand or don't like, use a response they already know instead of learning a new one, and see the world through their own values instead of understanding the views of others. It's human, and leaders are human. We can't grow leaders in a laboratory who will not have these imperfections; and, thus far, we aren't comfortable in trusting machines to replace people in leadership positions. Our only hope for rapid improvement is for all of us to get into the leadership act, helping us to manage ourselves.

THE ISSUE OF IDIOCY

As I think about the great leaders I have known or interviewed, I am thankful that they somehow found their way to the positions they held. They began their journey with passion and desire, including in most cases a passionate desire to serve others. But their passion and desire and caring alone did not make them leaders; they only became leaders in the context of an organization or group which had its written or unwritten procedures for selecting leaders. The primary objective of these procedures is to prevent the wrong people from becoming leaders; in the most blunt of cases, from idiots claiming the throne. I'll bet the issue of avoiding poor leaders has been with our species forever, even though we only learned how to write about it beginning a few thousand years ago. Plato's philosopher-kings were one solution, Athenian democracy another. The French and American revolutions were fought to free people from leadership they saw as unjust if not idiotic, and the struggle continues in Eastern Europe, the former Soviet Union, and in South Africa. Our own constitution has its idiocy prevention procedures written into it; the existence of the electoral college is a safeguard against the stupidity of the masses. In the event that democracy ever fails us, rest assured that an august body of electoral college voters will correct our short-sighted temporary insanity. Now, tell me again, how are the members of the electoral college elected?

The point is that we so fear empowering the wrong people to lead that we implement extremely thorough and complicated procedures to make certain that only great leaders take command. It is only when we violate these procedures, as we sometimes do, that people we think are idiots come to lead.

In a system of flexible management, in which many people may lead, the problem is compounded. Even though our discussions of presidential candidates is based on the misinformation we receive through biased media and uninformed but highly convicted neighbors and friends, the discussions do serve a purpose: They remind the candidates, and everyone behind the scenes, that we are watching. We are evaluating what the candidates say and what we think may influence our vote. Whether our information is right or wrong, we will vote based on what we think we know at the time of the election; so it is in the candidates' best interests to try to tell us what they really think.

In most organizations, the process for electing leaders isn't as clear, and there are fewer safeguards against bias. A much smaller, and hopefully well informed, circle makes the choice and then explains to everyone else why the choice made sense. We seldom get a full run-down on the other candidates considered, their relative strengths and weaknesses, and the full reasoning behind the choice finally made. Lacking this information, it's difficult for us to question the choice, to know if we would have decided differently ourselves. The integrity of the process depends on the integrity of the decision-makers. A good barometer to watch is the amount of secrecy surrounding the selection process: the greater the secrecy, the less the integrity. It may not be a perfect correlation, but if there's nothing to hide, then what's the need for all the secrecy?

When we introduce flexible management, we are opening up difficulties we would rather not have to think about. If each of us becomes involved in leading, then at times, the bottom quartile of people will be in charge. Idiots will reign. Sane men and women will tear out their hair, not knowing how to restore reason and order. The best and brightest will be frightened away from a system that can apparently aspire to mediocrity at best. When there are large numbers of people leading, the law of large numbers applies, which says that on any given day, leadership will be just about average. How can an organization be best-in-class with only average leadership?

One answer to this problem is to suggest that, on average, average leadership is better than idiotic leadership. Since our traditional system expects leaders to be superheroes when they can't be, and because our selection systems are hopelessly compromised, perhaps average leadership would be an improvement. At least we wouldn't keep taking sharp turns to the left and then back to the right every time we changed the person at the top.

But the better answer, I think, is not to settle for mediocrity; not even for a moment. Flexible management doesn't imply that each person should be given an equal opportunity to lead, or that groups are always smarter than individuals. If we want excellent leadership, we must define what excellence means and pursue it; we must have the strength of conviction to stick to our definitions, even when they apply to us. We can define excellence in leadership collectively, even though we may not be able to attain excellence individually. When it is apparent that we have not met our standards, we must make choices about the best thing to do in the moment, and learn what we need to do to create excellence in that area so that it is available in the future. There is no reason ever for an idiot to lead, if we agree on our definition of excellence. People who are idiots may never earn the right to lead, or they may do so only in a very small area of highly developed expertise, or as a part of a group that values their point of view if only as a devil's advocate.

Hopefully, we can agree that idiocy is a temporary and correctable condition, and that, in time, it is possible for everyone to develop excellence in some area of organizational need. I know that I have done some stupid things at times, and that, during those times, it was particularly fortunate for others that I was not in a position to lead. There have been other times that my leadership has been excellent, and still other times when my leadership *could* have been excellent if it had been permitted to show itself. If we can help each other know of our idiocy, and to learn of excellence in leadership and how to attain it, there is hope for us all.

LEARNING TO PARTICIPATE

The Colonel was an interesting man. I'd flown all night to meet with him that morning in his office in Heidelberg. To my great embarrassment, I dozed off in the middle of that first session;

but, being the great man he was, he overlooked my limitations and saw in me something of value, something that might help him to fulfill his mission.

He was a "lifer" and a short-timer; he had spent his entire adult life in the military, had risen as far as he was going to go, and had only one assignment left before retirement. He had been given command of the management information system that supported the Seventh Army in Europe, a unit that wore military uniforms but was quite different from any other unit in almost every other way. The Colonel's troops were professionals who happened to be wearing khaki for a variety of reasons. Most wore it for the benefits provided, including the training, which they knew would help them to land a lucrative civilian job after their tour of duty. Others wore it out of security, since the Army has always been a home to those who could find no other. And some wore it out of duty, as true patriots as any who could be found in the front lines, serving in the best way they knew how.

Because they performed work that the Colonel didn't fully understand (this was his first command of such a unit) he knew instinctively that playing the role of the traditional commander would be a mistake. True, he could issue orders that his subordinates would have to obey; but why would he, if the orders would make no sense and could even threaten the effectiveness of the unit and the entire Army it so vitally served? Besides, the Colonel had had enough of traditional command; he had lived under it for just about long enough, and he was tired of dishing it out. He became interested in psychology, and in motivation. He didn't know that an entire field was devoted to the study of human beings in organizations, and to organizational change, or he would have studied that. I suppose "organization effectiveness," as the Army referred to it, sounded like more spit and polish to him when he first heard the words. But now that he had discovered it, or rather that it had discovered him, he couldn't get enough.

The Army Research Institute had an office in Heidelberg, devoted mostly to the study of more traditional topics such as leadership selection and decision-making under stress. But a young Army Research Institute project officer became interested in organization effectiveness, and specifically in the benefits of sociotechnical systems design. The idea of self-directed work groups intrigued him, and he was thankful that he was stationed thousands of miles from Washington, where he might be allowed to investigate something that wasn't green or brown, and didn't fit the time-tested model of chain of command. He needed a willing client organization to host the research, and a person who could introduce the experimental intervention. The Colonel and I were chosen.

I, of course, expected the worst: a hard-core, blood-and-guts Patton of a client who would shoot me if I even mentioned the idea of people making decisions for themselves. I don't know what the Colonel expected, but I'm fairly certain it wasn't the reluctant civilian he saw sleeping in front of him.

When I recovered the next day and made as many apologies as I thought a Colonel deserved without making myself appear *overly* penitent, I asked him the toughest questions I could conceive: Would he tolerate my talking directly to his people about changing the nature of leadership in his unit? Would he be open to redrawing the organizational chart; to devoting time to training for himself and others to learn new skills; to sharing the responsibility for making a decision about what to do with his unit with me and his reports; to challenge his superiors if necessary to obtain the freedom and resources needed to try something new; to explain his actions in Washington when the time came, and help others to understand why these crazy, anti-hierarchical ideas made sense in a vertical Army? Yes.

In retrospect, convincing the Colonel that flexible management was a good idea was easy. I didn't have to convince him; he was already there. What was hard was convincing his direct reports, and the troops below them. Boot camp leaves lasting impressions on people; one of them, apparently, is to keep one's mouth shut and ears open when in the presence of a higher ranking something or other. Asking soldiers to share in their own leadership is like asking a computer to calculate the square root of love; it just doesn't compute. The resistance was greater than either the Colonel or I had ever imagined, and remained strong through the life of the project.

I remember one particularly humorous incident that captured perfectly the tension we were feeling as we helped the unit discover flexible management. A design team had been appointed to review the organization's structure and operating procedures. Team members were chosen, since most were afraid to volunteer. Once in the room, progress was dismally slow; at every suggestion of an innovative experiment, a long list of reasons was put forth to explain why the idea either wouldn't work or would be in direct violation of military law. At one point, a member of the design team blurted out that he was tired of being manipulated in this way. He knew that the Colonel had already decided how he wanted the organization to work. In fact, the soldier said, the Colonel had it all written down on a paper in his desk. I assured the private that he was mistaken, that the Colonel and I had an understanding that the whole premise of the organization we were creating was that people needed to design a system for themselves that they knew would work. It was clear from the private's remark that the group was in the dependency mode, waiting for its leader to tell them what to do; but the leader wasn't present in the room. The Colonel and I thought it best that he remain outside of the design team to allow it to function as freely as possible. But due to the group's dependency on an absent leader, it wasn't functioning at all.

When I told the Colonel that he would need to join the group in order to overcome this barrier, he was concerned. How could he be in the group and not overly influence it? He admitted to having his own biases about how the organization might be designed; in fact, he had sketched out a design that he had kept hidden in his desk until he showed it to me; or at least he *thought* he had kept hidden. If even his secret thoughts had been made public before he could speak them, then how could he say anything without overwhelming the group? We solved the dilemma in a simple yet entirely appropriate way. In the group, when he wished to be treated as the Colonel, he wore his hat. When he wished to be treated like any other group member, he removed his hat. The group, understanding the rules, knew when to challenge and when to back off. With this clarity, we began to make real progress. I thought to myself how silly it would have looked to anyone walking by to watch the Colonel taking his hat on and off and the group following his lead by shifting back and forth between salutes and pure democracy. But it worked.

As time went on, the Colonel put his hat on less and less, and the group grew stronger. One sergeant turned out to be a brilliant contributor, offering far more creative ideas than the captains in the group. The grumbling private who was once sorry to ever have put in for the unit reenlisted when his time came up. The larger unit had a hard time adapting to the design proposed by the team, and it was never fully implemented by the time the Colonel retired. The Colonel ran into some resistance from the General, and most of the policies and procedures used in the rest of the army couldn't be set aside to allow this one unit to experiment with completely flexible management. The Colonel and I, and our friend from the Army Research Institute, have moved on to other organizations, other projects. I don't know what happened to the people in the unit; I suspect that most of them have taken civilian positions. But I do know that there is a report buried deep in the Army's files in Washington that shows the remarkable progress in performance the unit made under less than ideal conditions, hinting at least at the possibility that flexible management may one day be considered again by those who insist, "That's no way to run an Army!"

If flexible management could work in the military, it can work anywhere. There is no law of the universe that compels us to live with our hierarchical, one-person-at-a-time model of leadership. We are free to try something else if we wish. Until we do, we will never know whether the current way is the best way, or if something better is out there. As Warren Bennis points out, even Max Weber, the architect of bureaucracy, had grave doubts about the effects his system would have on mankind: "It is horrible to think that the world could one day be filled with nothing but those little cogs, little men clinging to little jobs and striving toward bigger ones . . ."[1] But here we are.

To clarify the contrast between bureaucracy and flexible management, look at Figure 7–2. On the left are characteristics of bureaucracy as we have come to know them; on the right are elements of flexible management.

CONSTANT CHANGES IN LEADERSHIP

Flexible management means constantly changing who's in charge, based on the demands of the situation. At the work group level, we all have experienced this informally, from moment to moment. We don't work or think as mechanically as bureaucracy would insist; we shed our customary roles, take off our hats, and think things out together. Once we have decided something, we look toward the leader to bless our decision, because that is her formal role. Under flexible management, however, the decision of the group needs no blessing, other than to be certain that our thinking fits with what others are thinking. We don't need lead-

Bureaucracy	Flexible Management
A well defined hierarchy	Constant changes in leadership according to situational needs; can be either groups or individuals
A system of duties and rights	An evolving system of norms and values developed consensually
A set of procedures for every task	A system of processes invented participatively
Impersonality in relationships	Full expression, open debate
Selection based on technical competence	Selection based on knowledge and skills
Strict division of labor function	Temporary assignments to integrated project teams

Figure 7.2 The contrast between bureaucracy and flexible management.

ers to spend their time as messengers, carrying our decisions up the hierarchy and then bringing the good or bad news back down. We can run our own messages, by meeting with other people whose work or projects are affected by our decisions. What's more, in a group situation, we can cover much more ground quickly, with many individuals touching base with counterparts elsewhere and bringing back the news, so that decisions can be adjusted accordingly. In place of months of delay or cryptic messages from Mt. Olympus, we just talk to each other in real time. When there are resources to be committed, or decisions of strategic importance being made, we may go the extra step of calling together an integrating committee, which is charged with handling such matters. If knowledge is lacking to make the decision properly, it can be developed; but if an intuitive or rapid decision is needed, the integrating group can decide to make it, or allow a smaller group or even an individual to make it; there are no fixed rules about how leading takes place or who does it.

It sounds chaotic at first, and it is. It takes time for the system to discover how to lead itself, when to look to individuals for decisions, when to call together teams; but over time, learning takes place and people do begin to understand when to use which forum. During the transition, traditional leaders can take their hats on and off as necessary to guide the process toward quality and integrity. If as you're reading this, you're thinking, "This is too messy to ever work," then visit places where it is already working. Visit professional service firms, universities, volunteer organizations, and organizations involved in global change. Visit R&D laboratories to sit in meetings of skunkwork teams developing new products. Sense the energy and the order in the chaos. Look at the results. Understand that if flexible management can work in settings where everything is subject to change from one minute to the next, then it is actually easier to make it work in manufacturing or accounting, where things are relatively stable from day to day. Ask people how they make decisions, what keeps the institution or organization together, and why each person doesn't try to maximize his or her personal gain. Ask them why they care so much about what they are doing and why they argue so much with one another. Hear the dialogue, the challenges, the speeches by even junior people about what they believe. And then return home to your world of order and precision and listen to the silence.

EVOLVING NORMS

Bureaucracy and hierarchy are often equated; but, in fact, it is the rules and procedures of bureaucracy that give it its special stultifying character. Leaders of bureaucracies complain along with everyone else that their hands are tied; the rules prohibit their responding to the customer or the opportunity in the way that makes sense. If being customer-focused means anything, it means being willing to change the rules; but changing the rules is not something we have been taught to do. Clearly, each generation is getting better about this than the last; understanding more that changing the rules doesn't mean defying the logic and values behind them; understanding that breaking the norms is OK, but that preserving what we value about our society and relationships is important as well. Without shared ideology and values, there would be nothing but anarchy; and anarchy denies freedom rather than protects it.

Flexible management does not mean anarchy; it means people coming together to think about the rules, to question the operative norms and values that underlie the way they do things, to discuss how new customer requests or market opportunities or changes in the world might call for different norms and values. The clearer and more consensual the norms and values become, the more freedom people experience to operate within them. They can go further to satisfy the customer or pursue an innovative idea knowing that what they are doing will meet with approval even though it has never been done before. Bureaucracy dictates one set of rules based on what was believed to be true or right at the time the rules were written. Once the other elements of bureaucracy that support the rules are in place, challenging the rules is often extremely difficult. Flexible management means always being willing to discuss the rules in the face of new evidence; and to trust that, because people understand and help to develop the norms and values, they won't take money from the register simply because the rules prohibit doing so. The real truth is that rules aren't obeyed simply because they are written. They are obeyed when they are understood, and more often still when they are determined democratically.

PARTICIPATIVE INVENTION OF PROCESSES

Where bureaucracy stumbles most visibly in a changing world is in its specification of "one right way" to perform every task. The policy manual, the operations guide, the book of procedures. If work is routine, all of these make sense; there is no reason to reinvent the wheel each time we attempt a repetitive task. But in a world of constant change, continuous improvement, process reengineering, downsizing, joint venturing, and new information systems, the procedures will forever be catching up with reality. In the end, the work put into updating procedures is wasted and may carry a hidden cost by making it more difficult to change procedures when they need to be changed. Like rules, procedures are followed when people create them for themselves. Not individually, so that each person treats the customer differently; but participatively, so that collective wisdom can be applied in the moment to the task at hand. Flexible management means taking the work as it comes, putting our best thinking to work in figuring out how to do it, and then starting all over again as the task changes. Between changes, we can agree to continue to use a procedure if it is helpful; but we should always be aware that we created the procedure in the first place and can change it at will. Like the outdated lists of social rules from the last century that we all laugh at, our current procedures are mortal. Rather than putting our energy into maintaining them in their old age, our efforts are better spent finding superior ways to get the job done. Without flexible management, the notion of continuous improvement is nothing more than empty words.

FULL EXPRESSION

Our forefathers knew that attempts to stifle free speech would eventually lead to restrictions on free thinking, and that with neither free speech nor free thinking, there could be no true democracy, no real progress. Only the most secure leaders invite open challenges to the status quo; it's apparent that we have so frightened most of our leaders with our opinions that they haven't the courage to listen any longer. Bureaucracy, with its belief in master plans and omnipotent leaders, insists that there is no room for the expression of emotions in the work place. Weber did not fully intend this, of course; his restrictions on interpersonal relations were aimed at abolishing favoritism and nepotism more than free speech. Given the other elements of bureaucracy, however, little purpose for free speech or emotion existed anyway. Nothing could be changed unless the bureaucrats wanted it changed; and good bureaucrats operate on the basis of logic, evidence, and demonstrated proof, not emotionality. Faced with such obstacles to change, voices fell silent and, with them, emotion. Today, we recognize the role emotion plays in organizations—namely, in fostering creativity, commitment, spirit, competition, and cohesion. But often, we try to inject emotion through programs of one kind or another that fly in the face of the existing bureaucracy. We take people off site for a weekend and ask them to "get real" with one another; or send them off to a T-group to learn how to relate to other human beings, only to have them return to a setting that values impersonality and laughs at their touchy-feely insights. When we ask people to *feel* inside our well machined organizations, we are spitting into the bureaucratic wind.

Flexible management recognizes that human beings have emotions, and that they may be the species' best feature. Further, flexible management encourages the expression of emotions in the service of organizational improvement. There can be little energy without emotion; and in the world of change that we inhabit, we need all the energy we can get. We also *need* each other because the tasks are too big and too complex for us to figure out and do by ourselves. And since we need to continue leaning on each other, it makes sense in the long run to figure out how to work together without pissing one another off.

Emotions and logic are not mutually exclusive. I can be very emotional about my thoughts, which are based on pure logic in my own mind. The fact that others base their ideas on different logic is what makes for progress, if we can understand one another. Great intellectual debates are highly emotional, and conflicts at work can be of tremendous help in clearing the air. We have to manage emotions so that they result in productive gains, to be sure; but if we allow them to emerge more often, we can become more comfortable in dealing with them, so that we might develop skills in this area that we currently lack. Like everything else, how to use emotions productively takes time and practice; the bureaucracy would allow neither. Flexible management means getting our thoughts out there where they can be heard, tossed around, built upon, and used, instead of going home and kicking the dog. The expression of emotion is a sign that someone cares strongly about something, and we should regard it as an opportunity for improvement rather than as an attack on the system. Flexible management permits people with strong feelings about change or improvement to convene forums, and for those forums to move to action if they are compelled to do so. Emotionality is only dangerous when it is driven underground. When it has clear avenues to productive outlets, it is the engine of change.

SELECTION BASED ON KNOWLEDGE AND SKILLS

In the polynoetic organization, many people lead, based upon their knowledge and skill in relation to the task at hand. I have argued that this is the only way to fully develop and utilize the talent of people in the service of organizational success. But the question of how to determine the quality of an individual's knowledge or skills in relation to the task at hand is still open.

Many organizations I have worked with recently are moving toward some sort of peer review process; in the most advanced ones, this idea has been extended to *360-degree feedback,* meaning that each person is evaluated by his or her peers, subordinates, and superiors, and sometimes by customers as well. Multiple points of assessment make sense; what a person does looks much better or worse depending upon one's perspective, which is influenced by where one sits. Superiors may view a manager's actions as highly commendable, while subordinates are sickened by them. Who's view means more in the long run? The best answer is both, because both views have a basis in reality, even though there may be more than one reality. In flexible management, the question of assessing knowledge and skills is an important one and one that is best accomplished using multiple frames of reference.

Trist and others at Tavistock discovered some time ago that interviews were a poor way to select leaders; observing people in real or simulated situations that reflect the demands of the job works much better. Assessment centers are effective but costly and time consuming to run; and in the world of rapid change, which produces unrelenting demands for shifts in leadership, they would be much too slow. We need to opt for a compromise of sorts between simply appointing people to leadership based on quick interviews and conducting lengthy assessments. We need to let people actually lead when they think they can and then provide them with feedback that helps them learn and improve. Because we hate to give feedback, we invent bureaucratic procedures for once-a-year evaluations that we dread, knowing that we have been sitting on the news for months. Learning how to provide leaders with feedback quickly and painlessly is essential to help people learn to lead and make them more comfortable in exerting leadership when we need them to. Pausing long enough after each significant task to provide those who lead with feedback, both formally and informally, is a habit we need to develop. It doesn't matter whether we throw a party and make it fun or use short surveys to make it painless. What matters is that we do it. The one advantage of flexible management is that we don't need to confront the old hierarchy with fear of retribution from superiors; we may all get our turn in the barrel of hearing from others about our leadership, and we'll all get the opportunity to get even. If nothing else, this may help us to learn to be a bit more considerate in how we go about telling people off.

TEMPORARY ASSIGNMENTS

Bureaucracy means walls, real and imagined, between people who do different kinds of work. Specialization by function is associated with efficiency, as preached by Adam Smith. Efficiency is heightened by specialization, but it is also lowered by lack of integration. Bureaucracy was more concerned with the former than the latter, since the primary vehicle for integration in bureaucracy is the hierarchy, and hierarchy is hopelessly ineffective at accomplishing meaningful integration of people performing complex tasks in a changing environment. Flexible management assigns people to share responsibility for completion of a whole task for as long as it makes sense for them to work together, and utilizes as much of a person's time and energy as completing the task demands. When flexible management works perfectly, there is no wasted or idle time; each person is working on a meaningful task or preparing to work on the next one. Job definitions and departmental boundaries do not interfere with people pitching in to do what they know how to do to get the job done.

A flexible system of roles and responsibilities is not a new idea, and unions fear it because of the abuses suffered under slavemaster bosses who constantly drove their employees for efficiency and failed to recognize the worth of their skills. There are also questions of pay equity, when highly trained or educated specialists find themselves working alongside unskilled labor, and both are essential to getting the job done. And then there are issues of career advancement in a world where there is no ladder to climb and no guarantee of the need for one's expertise in the future. None of these issues is easy to resolve, and talking about them once or twice doesn't make them go away.

They are the subject of continuous dialogue and constant experimentation. Some general trends can be observed: As more work is done in an interdependent fashion, it makes more sense to increase the emphasis on shared rewards, such as profit sharing or gain sharing, while decreasing the emphasis on individual rewards or rewards for tenure. To enhance flexibility, it makes more sense to reward people for learning and moving around than doing the same thing over and over again. When the promotional ladder disappears, it makes more sense to reward people for the knowledge and skills they develop and for the results they achieve in utilizing them. In order to gain the commitment we need to support one another regardless of our differences, it makes sense for us to feel like we're all in the same boat together. If we want people to *act* like owners of the business, it makes sense to *make* them owners, through stock option plans or outright ownership. It seems to work well enough for Avis. At Donnelly Mirrors, where the Scanlon pay plan has been used continuously for more than 20 years, an equity committee composed of employees and managers still meets regularly to discuss issues pertaining to pay, promotion, technological improvements, and a number of other topics that ultimately affect bonus payouts. It seems that there's never a lack of things to discuss when we talk about pay. Flexible management doesn't work well within the constraints of inflexible pay systems; if we want the option of assigning people to temporary tasks, and having them be motivated to complete them successfully, we need more latitude in rewards.

Flexible management is not possible without a work force that is prepared to help lead; preparing people for participation is a necessary prerequisite. Managers cannot become flexible when they cannot rely on subordinates to manage tasks as well as they would. The capacity of subordinates and teams to be self-managing develops over time, as indicated in Figure 7–1. Managers can't become flexible instantly; when they do, the results are notoriously bad. Developing flexibility takes time and effort. When managers resist giving up power, it's usually out of a mixture of self-preservation and a real understanding of the gap between where the system is today and where it would need to be for greater self-management to work. Flexible management is not a digital concept, on or off, leaders or no leaders. It is flexible. At times, it makes sense for leaders to step in and support others as they develop skills; and, at other times, it makes sense for leaders to stand back and allow people to experiment with things for themselves. When self-preservation becomes the primary motive for not relinquishing power, that's another story; and when this occurs, more drastic measures may be needed to move managers out of control. But early on, and perhaps forever, allowing managers to maintain the ability to lead makes perfect sense. It will be confusing, and they may have to take their hats on and off to make it clear to others when they are leading and when others are leading; but, despite the confusion, helping others to learn to lead is part of what it takes to make flexible management work.

In addition to flexible and capable subordinates, flexible management depends upon flexible managers: people with enough ego strength to let go of control, to help others develop into leaders. There are many examples of great leaders in the literature but few examples of flexible managers. Since flexible management is such a new idea, it would be helpful if there were a school for flexible management, but such a school doesn't exist. One certainly won't find a course on flexibility in MBA programs, and company training courses are no better.

If there were a curriculum for flexible management, it would include studies of great coaches and mentors; of people who devote their lives to the development of others, including first-grade teachers; of people who work in inventive atmospheres such as R&D or advertising where ideas count more than the number of stripes on a person's sleeve. It would be a highly experiential curriculum, since talking flexibility and learning to actually be flexible are two entirely different things. And it would cover the classics in democracy and in psychology, in literature and in film. Those who study adult learning have concluded that in order to learn new behaviors, people need real examples of people like themselves they can emulate. So it would be helpful in the curriculum to bring in guest speakers: managers who have experimented with flexibility and learned something about it they can share with others. The curriculum should also be recursive; that is, it should be designed to do what it is attempting to teach. It should itself be flexible, and allow different individuals to enter at different points, approach learning in different ways, and complete their studies at their own rate of speed. I'm not talking about home study, because learning to be a flexible manager is not something one can learn at home; this learning requires contact with the real world and a great amount of discourse with others who are also in the process of learning. The curriculum will provide practical skills, but skills alone are not enough; theorists in the field of adult development have discovered that higher level skills are easily learned but quickly forgotten if a person fails to develop the cognitive understanding that is required to support a higher level of thinking and behaving. I can learn to recycle, but I will not do it well until I understand the linkage between my actions and the condition of the planet. With flexible leaders, it is easy to let go of control sporadically, randomly, as an experiment; but it is harder to understand when to let go of control and why, and what to do when letting go of control fails to produce the desired results, and how to handle the pressure of superiors and peers and subordinates who cry out for a return to authoritarianism in the name of predictability. Working through these things involves dialogue, experience, argument, and, finally, the development of one's own theory of flexible management. Once the personal theory is developed, it becomes implanted in the brain, where it begins to influence behavioral choices. Eventually, people change because they have convinced themselves that changing is the right thing to do. We change because we want to change, not because someone writes a book on flexible management or because our superior tells us that we need to become more flexible. In the end, it's all up to each one of us.

It's easier to become flexible when others around us are trying to become more flexible, too and, when together, our actions make the organization we work in more open to our flexibility. At some point, we may come together to redesign the organization for flexibility so that it ceases to be an albatross around our necks and instead becomes the platform for supporting our learning. The subject of how to design organizations for flexibility is taken up in the next chapter.

Fractal Organization Design
Replacing the Organization Chart

The futurist Alvin Toffler predicted that, before very long, organizations would have the qualities of a Calder mobile, shifting appearance with the slightest breeze. At about the same time Toffler was writing, Tracy Kidder penned his classic, *The Soul of a New Machine*, about the team that developed a new computer for Data General. The book has become a touchstone for those who believe in informality and team spirit as the source of competitive advantage. The good guys hide out in a basement and do incredibly creative and brilliant work, while the bad guys on the huge team with the nice offices plod along, behind schedule, on a product with no distinctive breakthroughs. Kidder describes a slice of the informal team's life in words that would make Toffler smile:

To almost everything they touched, the Microteam attached their prefix. The office that the four of them shared, sitting virtually knee to knee, had a sign on the door that said The Micropit; the room in which they held their weekly meetings was the microconference room. They gave out microawards and Carl Alsing had his microporch. One of them owned a van, which became the microbus. That winter several of them would go out riding in it on Friday afternoons, when West held his own weekly meetings with his managers. Then, in the first warm days of spring, they created the outdoor microlounge, to which they now repaired on those Friday afternoons. . . . Part of the microteam displayed a tendency to keep odd hours and play zany games. You'd expect that. Compared to that of the Hardy Boys, who were now bound by a schedule to the actual machine, the Microteam's job had an air of the ephemeral. In the main, they could write their code when they pleased, as long as they did it on time, which is to say, very quickly[1] (pp. 154–156).

The age we live in is like no other before it. The trajectory of change has carried us past a point where our knowledge and experience in building organizations is useful, to a new place where learning and flexibility are of utmost importance, and our knowledge of the past is actually a hindrance to our progress because it blinds us to new ideas and possibilities in organizing. We are victims of the industrial revolution, as choked on our notions of what is right and wrong as we are choked on the pollution we can't seem to live without. We need to clear the air, both literally and figuratively. We need to look at organizations as human creations that are subject to human intervention, rather than as entities that constrain the human spirit and mind.

We must accept the fact that organizations face paradoxes that cannot be resolved; and that when we try to resolve them through the design of the organization to favor one side of the paradox or the other, we always end up suboptimizing and endangering our future. We must believe that we actually *do* have a choice about all of this, and that we really *can* design organizations that fit their environment and our most important values. We can't pursue excellence in a straightjacket created by other people for other times. We need to break free of the past and learn what it means to organize for flexibility in a world that has no tolerance for the status quo.

This isn't a new message. We have been hearing it for some time. Elements of flexible organizing are visible in Rensis Likert's *New Patterns of Management*, William Ouchi's *Theory Z*, Elliott Jaques' *Requisite Organization*, Warren Bennis' *Beyond Bureaucracy*, Tom Peters' *Thriving on Chaos* and *Liberation Management*, Rosabeth Kanter's *When Giants Learn to Dance*, and, more recently, Michael Hammer and James Champy's *Reengineering the Corporation* and William Davidow and Michael Malone's *The Virtual Corporation*.[2-10] Of course, Eric Trist had flexibility in mind when he described the composite method of coal mining, and later when he wrote with Howard Perlmutter about the idea of social architecture.[11] The basic notion behind social architecture is that we can create organizations that reflect our values and aspirations just as architects create edifices that reflect the essence of society in their period. Perlmutter and Trist note that the predominant values influencing organizational design are those associated with industrialism: Big is better, control should be accomplished through bureaucratic and hierarchical methods, specialization maximizes efficiency, people are extensions of machinery, long-term strategies should prevail over short-term decision making, let the buyer beware, change should be avoided. Recently, however, they note a rebellion against these values, a swing of the pendulum to the other extreme, in what they call the "deindustrial paradigm": Small is beautiful, leaders are not to be trusted, people are more important than profits, protecting the consumer and the environment is more important than protecting organizations, planning is useless, change is good. Perlmutter and Trist view this paradigm as just as dangerous in the long run as the last and call instead for a "symbiotic paradigm" that integrates the best of both. The characteristics of the both/and symbiotic paradigm include: limited state sovereignty; free and regulated markets; wide varieties of partnerships among state, private, and community sectors; marriage of short- and long-term policies; participative democracy; large and small corporations; responsible individuality; harmonization of human needs and environmental conservation; joint optimization of people and technology; generalist–specialist balance; multiple channels of learning; and independence and collaboration.

What I find attractive about Perlmutter and Trist's paradigm S is not its validity or its attainability but the fact that it expresses the paradoxes that we must confront openly in society. The industrial paradigm ignored human and social needs in viewing large institutions as the solution to all problems; the deindustrial paradigm denies the need for economic and political vitality in favor of utopian return to nature, and puts human needs ahead of all others. The S paradigm recognizes the good and bad in the other two world views.

PARADOXES TO MANAGE IN ORGANIZATIONAL DESIGN

In regard to organizations in particular, I would add to Perlmutter and Trist's paradoxes the following: ownership and partnership; control and delegation; short-term and long-term; intrinsic and extrinsic; commonality and diversity; efficiency and effectiveness; focused and opportunistic; flexible and inflexible. Organization designs that fail to embrace these paradoxes have built into them the seeds of ineffectiveness, if not destruction. Traditional designs do not address these paradoxes in a balanced manner, which is the reason for some of the dissatisfaction we currently experience with the way our organizations function and the results they produce. Additional dissatisfaction with the status quo stems from our notions of what is possible that we have not yet attained; we sense that our organizations should be capable of doing more of what we know they should be doing, but we can't seem to figure out how to design them to make it all happen. I'll describe the paradoxes and ideals that we are striving toward and then offer a new way of thinking about the design of organizations.

Ownership and Partnership

The issue of ownership of organizational resources has been open to debate for some time. Clearly, the model of communism practiced in the former Soviet Union is not a model that the world will pursue again. On a much smaller scale, however, questions remain concerning the relationship of employees to their organizations. When we speak of participation, high-involvement, and high-commitment, what are we really saying? If these things are desirable, then where do we draw the line as employees become more involved and more committed? When do we say, "We know we asked you to get involved, but this issue is none of your business."? Ownership is the engine of capitalism; and, despite its many shortcomings, capitalism has proven to be the most powerful economic engine ever created. Would we forsake capitalism for employee ownership? Or should we seek a new kind of organization, one that provides limited ownership for employees while maintaining the rights of founders? Flexible organizations will be forced to face this paradox between ownership and partnership; and, in the end, neither should win out. Owners should continue to have incentive to risk their capital, and employees should be treated as full partners when we ask them to behave as full partners would.

Control and Delegation

A very closely related paradox is that of control and delegation. Maximum flexibility is attained when each individual is free to do his or her own thing; but organizational synergies are gained from sharing resources, pursuing common strategies, and working together interdependently, all of which require some form of centralized control. The flexible organization will attempt to maximize both control and delegation through the creation of integrative mechanisms that allow people to do their own coordinating. To the extent that people with local concerns are provided viable forums to discuss common needs and objectives, the wisdom of delegation can be combined with the power of centralized control.

Short- and Long-term Goals

The flexible organization will also need to be designed to deal with the paradox between short-term goals and long-term strategies. Short-term goals allow responsiveness to customers and environmental change; long-term strategies keep the organization pointed toward a vision of a more desirable future and help people make choices in the short term that allow the eventual realization of longer-term dreams. The flexible organization needs to be guided by a powerful vision that shapes the thinking of its members, but it also needs to be receptive to input that revises the vision as conditions change and new possibilities replace the old.

Intrinsic and Extrinsic

The clash between the industrial and deindustrial paradigms involves a tension between intrinsic and extrinsic values and motivation. Under the industrial paradigm, "greed is good"; in the deindustrial paradigm, trees are more important than money. In the flexible organization, the tension between working for money and working to feel good need to be brought together. Organizations like the Body Shop and Ben and Jerry's are already finding ways to make money while donating funds to causes their employees believe in. The extra motivation that is gained by knowing that one's work contributes toward a greater social good can be an important ingredient in the flexible organization. When we labor for love in addition to money, we are willing to put ourselves into our work more completely, and to work at being successful more creatively than if we feel like it's just "another day, another dollar."

Commonality and Diversity

Flexibility without commonality would produce chaos and wasted energy, as the work of one person undoes the work of another. Yet how far can we go in developing commonality in our methods and our thinking without reducing innovation? Diversity is good, not simply because it is the watchword of the '90s, but because it holds our only hope for progress. Without diversity, we would always remain the same. In a world full of change, we need more diversity than ever. The flexible organization helps diverse people find common ground, through search conferences and integration groups, through teamwork and temporary alliances, through flexible leadership and flexible people. The important difference between many organizations today and flexible organizations is that flexible organizations don't just talk about diversity or hold 3-day seminars to raise people's awareness of the need to be careful about what they say. Flexible organizations work at managing diversity to find commonality, continuously. The subject is always under discussion, and the results of the discussion hold meaning for decision-making. Diversity is more than a discussion topic; it is a part of success.

Efficiency and Effectiveness

Flexible organizations sound inefficient: People are moving from team to team, starting new projects, trying out new ways of doing things, learning how to lead. The trade-off to be gained is effectiveness; in the long run, the flexible organization will learn more than its inflexible counterparts, which will in turn create sustainable competitive advantage. Still, in the short run, the bills have to be paid; too much inefficiency for the sake of effectiveness could lead to trouble. Flexible organizations learn to build in reserves for inefficiency; for training and learning, for experimenting with new ways of doing things. R&D is not the only place where research can take place to enhance profitability; experimenting with new methods and procedures can produce big gains as well, as the stories from total quality efforts, reengineering, and work redesign have pointed out. When organizations learn to invest in flexibility like they invest in R&D, they quickly learn that flexibility provides an excellent rate of return. In a meticulous study by Barry Macy and Phil Mirvis of an intervention in one organization, the rate of return was calculated at 26 percent; less precise estimates from other organizations range toward *1200* percent. The return to be gained depends on a variety of factors, not the least of which are the quality of the intervention and the degree of inflexibility in the current organization. The rate of return on R&D investments in *Fortune* 500 companies has been estimated at between 12 and 20 percent, still far ahead of most other uses of funds these days, but no more than comparable to the gains to be made by investing in flexibility. The flexible organization will have room for investments in both.

Focused and Opportunistic

Flexible organizations create the ability to be opportunistic in pursuing new products and markets or in adopting new procedures or methods of getting the job done. But there is much to be gained from waiting for the fruits of past labors to ripen by doing a bit more of the same for a while longer. We learned from Tom Peters and Bob Waterman that it is important for organizations to "stick to their knitting." But we learned from the Penn Central Railroad and IBM that we can't just sit around and knit. Flexible organizations develop feedback mechanisms that allow them to know when they have hit the peak of the product demand S-curve, and to be more realistic in making choices about when to venture into new territory and when to stay home by the fire. Flexibility doesn't mean becoming a vagabond who never stays long in one place; it means both having established businesses and funding the development of new ones, expecting, as 3M does, that about one quarter of existing revenues will need to be replaced by revenue from new sources every five years.

Flexible and Inflexible

Although this book is about flexibility, I recognize the need for inflexibility in some aspects of the organization, such as inflexibility in integrity, in quality, in service, in trying to do one's best, in cooperation, in processes that have proven superior to everything else that has been tried. Times do change, and eventually so will our processes; but some values are more enduring and may never change. As Paul Salipante points out, inflexible values support flexibility by clarifying for people what is good and what is bad, what is open for debate and what is sacred, what is important and what is not. With clear and inflexible values in mind, people can work on changing aspects of the organization that allow greater realization of those values in practice, which I call *organizational integrity*. It's walking the talk in the way we design and manage our organizations. If we say we want to be world class, what are we really doing about it? If we say we want high commitment, how are we going to get it and sustain it? The flexible organization has a backbone as strong as steel, and it is made up of the values that are inviolate.

IDEALS TO STRIVE FOR IN DESIGN

While much of what is required to create flexible organizations remains to be discovered, a few principles can be stated. These include the creation of holographic knowledge, commitment through meaningful work, shared incentives, feedback on performance, attention to process, action through reflection, search and respond, organizational learning, assuming the best about people, and organizational integrity.

Holographic Knowledge

People need to understand what is happening in order to help the organization succeed. The more they know about what the organization does, how it does it, what is going on in the world, what the customer wants, what other people do, what shape the organization is in financially, and what the possibilities are, the more they can act without fear of causing problems for someone else. When people don't know what is going on nor understand more than their own job, they are forced to continue doing what they have always done, even though the need for change is apparent. Like a nuclear meltdown, the organization keeps on making products that are no longer in demand or delivering service that doesn't meet the customer's expectations. The more people know and understand, the more they can use their creativity and talents to help improve products and processes. Keep people in the dark, and the organization stays in the dark ages. Let in the light, and people can see where they are going.

Commitment through Meaningful Work

Would you design a boring, meaningless job for yourself that didn't utilize any of your talents or allow you to help the organization succeed? Neither would most people. Flexibility is based on commitment: commitment to do the best job you can at the current task, and commitment to change what you are doing when it becomes clear that there is something more important or more appropriate to do. The way to build commitment isn't to give speeches but rather to give people meaningful work to do: work that requires them to think, that uses their talents, that involves learning, that provides feedback, that is significant, that makes a difference to others, that requires teamwork, that commands respect. There seems to be a belief that there is a limited amount of meaningful work to be done in any large organization, and that most people will be forced to do work that is meaningless. This belief is totally incorrect and is derived from the jobs that are created in inflexible, hierarchical, bureaucratic organizations. In flexible organizations, there is no limitation on meaning; there's plenty of meaningful work for everyone.

Each person can become a specialist in one or more areas of significance to the teams he or she works with, such as quality, group process, technology, understanding the customer, planning, financial analysis, or managing change. In inflexible organizations, a great deal of meaningful work simply isn't getting done because workers' jobs aren't designed to allow them to do it. The flexible organization needs everyone's commitment to succeed, and meaningful work is the way to build meaningful commitment.

Shared Incentives

To answer the question, "Why should I change?" it helps to be able to do more than just say, "For God, Mother, and Country." Shared incentives help people see the big picture in a world that is already far too oriented toward individualism. Profit sharing, gain sharing, team incentives, stock ownership, team recognition dinners, organizational celebrations—the medium isn't as important as the message, even though the more resources that are dedicated to rewarding cooperative effort, the more likely shared incentives will actually change behavior. Work is seldom done by one person these days; we all get by with a little help from our friends. Let's quit pretending that heroes make all the difference and begin rewarding people for working together to get the job done, as mundane as it may seem.

Feedback on Performance

Every organization I have ever worked in or consulted with could improve the way it provides people with feedback on their performance. There's not much new to be said about this; people want to know how they are doing individually, as a team, as a unit, as an organization. Usually they find the information they receive extremely helpful and will take the steps necessary to do better next time. In a study my colleagues and I conducted some time ago, we reviewed 134 efforts in work redesign and found that, when feedback was improved, it never caused performance to decline.[12] Not once. Improving feedback is one of the cheapest and easiest things that can be done to improve organizational performance. Anyone who cares about the bottom line should jump on the opportunity to design feedback systems into their organizations.

Feedback is even more important in the flexible organization. People need to learn and learn *fast* what works and what doesn't. There isn't time in the flexible organization to stabilize processes, iron out all the bugs, and then develop elaborate feedback processes that tell people how well they did this year compared with last. People need to know as much as they can today, this minute. Approximations are better than no data at all. Market researchers would challenge the validity of data collected from one or two customers, and rightly so; but market research is intended for situations in which products will be around long enough to justify the costs of rigorous market research and product development. In the fast-cycle, short product-life-span world of today and tomorrow, by the time we find out through market research that people like our products, someone else has already offered them something better.

Attention to Process

In traditional organizations, the organizational chart takes precedence over everything else. People are so concerned about where their box on the chart is relative to others, and how to get from their box to one higher up, that they forget that the boxes don't do anything. In one sense, it makes no difference whether the organization chart has 50 boxes or 5000, one level or 15; what counts is what people do when they get to work. If people let the boxes get in their way, even a few levels can be problematic. If people pay attention to process, and keep focused on the goal of success rather than the size of their office or the thickness of their carpeting, the number of boxes or levels doesn't make much difference. I shouldn't have to talk about paying attention to process because completing processes is what organizations were invented to do. But the focus has shifted so much toward boxes, functions, and levels that the processes have been forced to take a back seat. Early sociotechnical systems work concentrated on restoring the integrity to whole processes that had been broken into bits by time- and motion-crazed industrial engineers. Today, Hammer and Champy insist that we reengineer the corporation around processes instead of functions.[13]

Action through Reflection

Flexibility requires learning, thinking, experimenting with new ways of doing things. Sometimes we get so busy fighting fires or solving problems that we forget to pause and capture what it is that we have learned from our experience. In one R&D organization I worked with, thousands of experiments would be run quickly because products were always behind schedule in development. But people were so busy trying to beat the clock that they recorded only the results of successful experiments; the thousands of experiments that failed were left unrecorded, waiting for someone else to repeat them since the knowledge from their failures was never written down.

Taking time out to record what we have learned is important. We forget what we learn and even how we learned it. Telling others what we know is more difficult if we don't remember much about what we went through to get to where we are. Having a history for new people to follow helps them get up to speed more quickly, and move beyond where we have been rather than recreate the history we have worked so hard to overcome.

As important as is recording what we learned, taking time to reflect is even more critical. We can *think* of things much faster than we can *do* them. We can talk with others to get their ideas or reactions to something we are about to try much faster than trying it and then waiting to hear from them what they think.

The bottom line is that we can make more progress by slowing down a bit than we can by running flat out, 17 hours a day. My observation is that our norms around work are so strong in equating work with action that reflection isn't even valued. We need to design reflection time into organizations, for individuals as well as teams and larger units, to reflect on what they have learned and how they might do things better. Reflection is a terrific way to make improvements and to actually speed up the pace of organizational change. And you thought those off-sites were just excuses for playing golf.

Search and Respond

Staying focused outside is another norm we need to reinforce through the design of the organization. We know we need to pay attention to our customers, to our shareholders, to the competition, to the world around us; but we get busy solving internal problems and, before we know it, the time we planned for looking outside is gone. We can increase the likelihood that we follow through with our plans if we commit ourselves to them publicly, by inviting people from outside the organization or unit to join us at some specified date in the future. We can also make it a part of our jobs to stay tuned in, and make what we do in this regard count when it's performance appraisal time. Looking only at internal problems is like staring at your radio while you're driving: You'll know exactly what station you are tuned to when you hear the crash.

Organizational Learning

Flexibility means developing requisite variety, being able to do things we didn't even know we would need to do until we need to do them. We can't be flexible if we're one-trick ponies, doing the same routine over and over again and learning nothing new. If we only know one thing, when we experience the need to change, we panic; we try doing the thing we know over and over again, faster and faster each time. It's like trying to speak to a person in a foreign language; before you know it, you are saying words in your own language louder and louder, as if it would help the other person to understand.

Organizations need to learn how to learn; organizational learning isn't something that you simply write into this year's annual objectives. Who is going to collect information? What information are they going to collect? How will it be used? How will we evaluate the effect of using it? How will we decide whether to do more of the same, or try something new? What experiments do we believe in? How much proof do we need? How can we remember what we have learned so that the knowledge will be there when we need it? How can we remove the barriers to individual learning? To team learning? To organizational learning? There's a lot of learning to do about organizational learning. And we aren't going to do it in a classroom, all lined up in neat little rows. We have to get our hands dirty in the real world. We have to take some genuine risks and make some substantial investments that may or may not pan out. Since we always learn by accident anyway, we need to commit ourselves to learning more *intentionally*. But so does everyone else. If we can't learn intentionally, it may be that being accident prone is to our advantage; at least we'll know more than the other guy. But it's a relatively painful and expensive way to learn.

Assume the Best about People

In designing the flexible organization, assume that people will want to grow, that they are interested in learning and capable of tremendous development over time. Assume that people want to help the organization succeed with all their hearts, and that they will give every ounce of their energy trying to make it so. Assume that people will act in trustworthy ways, and that they really do share common values and objectives. Assume the same things about people that you assume about yourself. If you do, there will be occasional disappointments; but there will be more frequent pleasant surprises, even miracles. Little things, like people cleaning up after themselves; and big things, like people finding a way to win a multimillion dollar account away from a competitor by taking the time to really care about the customer. We know enough about the Pygmalion effect to make this rather bold statement: People will behave almost exactly as we expect them to. Why expect the worst?

Organizational Integrity

Walk the talk. Create a design that is evidence you are serious about flexibility. Don't talk about flexibility and then fall back on the same old boxes and levels that have been used before, all the while saying, "This time it will be different. We've issued instructions to all our managers to behave more flexibly." It won't happen. Change the design. And be *changed by* the design. Live what you say, and model the behavior you hope to see from others.

So what does a flexible organization look like? Unfortunately, the limits of our current publishing technology don't permit me to depict a dynamic, changing flexible organization on this page very well. Our methods of communication, based as they have been on static representations in two dimensional space, contribute to the difficulty we have in imagining how organizations could be different. When we draw an organizational chart, we see what is on the piece of paper: a fixed pattern of lines and boxes, arranged in equal-appearing intervals depicting a neatly designed organizational machine. When we behave in the organization so depicted, we take on the characteristics of its representation. We limit our activities to what fits within our box and confine our purview to the appropriate levels of issues, despite our intelligence, information, or abilities. We use the chart to defend our positions and to attack others who seem to be overstepping the bounds of their authority. We look on the chart for leadership, and we find it easily in the current occupant of the box above ours. The thinking behind the chart is neat, orderly, unchanging, and *completely inappropriate*. To draw an organization as a chart is to destroy the organization's flexibility, and condemn those who would improve the organization to forever face resistance from those who find the chart their comfort in times of change.

Yet to draw no chart is to trust in the miracle of creation occurring every day. With no guidance, people invent their own charts; and what seems like a good idea to one person is poison to another. Individual charts drawn in a vacuum rarely produce the synergy that chart-burners desire; the boundaries don't get in the way, but there are no paths for people to follow in finding more productive ways to get the job done. Anarchy and flexibility are not synonymous. Dave Brown points this out in his work on "underbounded organizations," which, because of their lack of structure, face problems as serious as their overly structured counterparts.[14] In politics, Paulo Friere notes that the overthrow of dictatorships frequently leads to even greater repression by the new regime. Since no model other than dictatorship is known in some cultures, people are simply unprepared to behave as responsible citizens in a more democratic society and consequently take advantage of the anarchy produced by revolution. To maintain its hold on power, the new regime is called upon to do something about the troublemakers, and a new cycle of repression and fomenting of revolution begins. As the threat to power intensifies, so does the repressive behavior of the incumbent regime, which now appears to be the same as or worse than the one it replaced. Anarchy foments continuous, uncontrolled instability in organizations; flexibility maintains order, even though that order is fluid. While specifics may change, patterns remain stable. We have a peaceful transition in government every four or eight years because the process is designed to allow people to influence government, even as political issues constantly change.

It is important to have a picture that represents the design of the flexible organization but any picture drawn here would be more static and misleading than informative. The whole idea behind the flexible organization is that it changes as it faces new situations that call for new organizational responses. Yet to say that there is no chart at all is also misleading because there are agreed-upon processes to allow the organization to change without anarchy; we might call this *controlled change*.

In the flexible organization, we don't need to face anarchy with every change because we know that some ways of organizing work better than others in certain situations, and that some people are more knowledgeable about some topics than others and therefore are better suited to lead us in discussion when their topic is focal. Constancy of leadership need not be provided by a single individual or group, as long as there are processes in place that ensure a thoughtful transition from one form to the next. Just as our constitution provides a framework within which contemporary lawmakers can revisit past decisions and tackle emerging new challenges, the structure of the flexible organization is a set of agreements that empower people to behave in a flexible fashion, but always within the bounds of control provided by those agreements.

In the flexible organization, the sizes of teams or units may vary, or they may remain constant for a long time, if we agree there is no need for change. An individual's power may grow to immense proportions for a brief moment, and then shrink to nothing in the next, as the focus of the organizational challenge changes. Leaders may change quickly if many people are prepared to lead and the situation calls for it, or leaders may stay in place for a long time if things seem to be calm for the moment. Always, though, there are mechanisms for people to help the organization question its assumptions about the world and adapt its architecture to the reality of the current situation. There can be no dependency on a single great leader for all time, because times change. But there is room for great leaders to lead, when the time is right. There are no rules about span of control, number of levels, or length of office; there is only the challenge of deciding, based on the framework provided by the guiding agreements, what is to be done when and for how long. If the outside world demands that a CEO be named, it may be appropriate to do so rather than confuse investors or customers. What the CEO does with her office is a matter to be determined internally through dialogue with those who apply the principles. Or, if it is apparent that people in the organization have not yet developed the capacity for flexible leadership and still need to depend on the strong hand of a single individual to prevent anarchy, a CEO may be appointed for internal reasons.

Flexibility isn't something you wish into place, or that you create by drawing a few lines on a piece of paper, or by burning the organizational chart. This whole book is about changing the entire system and each of its many components to make flexibility possible; like athletic agility, flexibility is a quality that is earned through hard work and dedication.

The design of the organization should address the paradoxes mentioned earlier and provide avenues for pursuing ideals such as holographic knowledge and organizational integrity. Current designs don't allow this; whether they are based on functions or projects or a matrix of both, on divisions or geographical regions, or on cost centers or business units, our current organizational designs are too inflexible to adjust to the level of change we are experiencing today. A new design for flexibility must be a contemporary design that fits the wisdom of our age, not some past era in which we were fascinated with machines and obsessed with stability. We have graduated from the industrial revolution in our technology and in our society, but not yet in our thinking about organizing. It is time to take a step forward.

FRACTAL ORGANIZATION DESIGN

As in the past, our notions of what is possible in designing structures of any kind are shaped by advances in the physical sciences. As we learn of new materials, discover secrets about the structure of the atom and the universe, and learn new laws of relativity, we begin to change our thinking about the world we live in. We invent geodesic domes and plastic, airplanes and computers. We reconfigure the physical space around us and the things we do with our time. We learn new talents, discover new capabilities in ourselves, and develop a deeper appreciation for the things about ourselves and our world that we cherish and hope will never change. All of this new thinking, led by advances in the physical sciences, changes our lives and our notions about what is possible in organizing.

One of the most exciting developments to emerge from the physical sciences recently is the discovery of the fractal, which is a basic building block of highly complex and chaotic-appearing systems. As chaotic structures are created by computers running programs that are based on nonlinear equations and used to generate images, scientists have discovered that the images created contain an innate order. At each higher level of magnification, the same pattern of shapes and colors emerged from what at first appear to be totally free-form images. These basic repetitive patterns are what we now call fractals. Order in chaos. Meg Wheatley has described the implications of the physics for management in her book *Leadership and the New Science*, so I needn't review the details here.[15] Instead, I'll concentrate on the implications of fractals for the design of flexible organizations.

In the local restaurant where we eat breakfast, an antique quilt hangs on the wall. Its design is based on fractals, although the person who made the quilt wouldn't have known that fractals existed or that that was what she was doing at the time. Each geometric shape in the quilt is repeated, first on a tiny scale, at the level of individual diamonds of varying colors, and then on larger and larger scales until the quilt is covered by them. Smaller diamonds make up larger diamonds, and these diamonds create larger diamonds still. Not every diamond is the same; the small diamonds are made up of different colors and patterns of cloth, and the middle-size diamonds are in turn composed of different combinations of these smaller diamonds. Still, the resulting work is not a picture of chaos, but of order; the middle-size diamonds vary in color and appearance but have enough similarity to elements of other middle-size diamonds that there can be no mistaking that they belong to the same quilt. The overall effect is

beautiful and mystifying. The quilt at a glance seems a patchwork of different colors and textures of bits of cloth, sewn together into a large diamond shape; but, upon closer scrutiny, the
larger diamond is made up of smaller diamonds, each of which
is made up of still smaller diamonds, which share an unmistak-
able lineage and family resemblance. There is order in the chaos,
a pattern of relationships and rules, which, when applied to the
quilt-making process, produces an organized total effect. Each
mid-size diamond is a holographic piece of the whole structure;
in it is the code that enables the rest of the quilt to be assembled,
for the quilt to grow or shrink in size, and to vary its combination
of colors and textures to suit its local tastes, while not falling out
of line with the rest. Once the pattern and colors and textures are
decided, there is room in the quilt for local variation; autonomy
at lower levels of organization does not produce anarchy in the
whole, as long as it follows the same shared rules.

By analogy, the small diamonds in the quilt are individuals in
organizations. They may vary in color or texture in many different ways, but they are suited to fit in the larger structure of the
organization. They share certain basic values, possess shared
meanings and knowledge, and understand they have a place in
the pattern. Moreover, the talents, skills, perspectives, and knowledge they possess are duplicated in other individuals in other
parts of the organization, just as identical diamonds appear in
mid-size diamonds in other parts of the quilt. There is agreement
on the critical skills, abilities, ideals, and beliefs that the organization needs to attain excellence in its mission, and these are
found in individuals throughout the organization. The critical
characteristics needed for success are not held tightly by one
person or even by one unit of the organization; one diamond of
the quilt is not made of totally different material than all the rest.
Rather, the characteristics needed are distributed among individuals throughout the organization, where they can be called
upon by local units to make decisions that need these inputs and
also that help to keep the local unit thinking and acting as part
of the whole. Not every individual is the same, and not every
subunit contains the same ratio of different types of people or a

complete inventory of the characteristics of people in other parts of the organization. Some units are made up of many of the same kinds of people, and others contain relatively few of those people; yet each unit contains enough of a mix of people or abilities or knowledge to fit into the whole. I've tried to convey these ideas in Figure 8–1.

Occasionally, individuals who share similar thoughts, skills or knowledge come together to think about their shared concerns in a more concentrated fashion, to explore the issues they are most able to explore in depth with each other in order to advance the state of their knowledge or improve the processes they perform on behalf of others. At other times, large assemblies

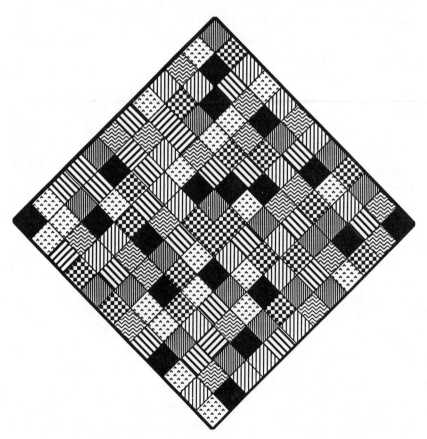

Figure 8.1 Fractal organization design.

that comprise the entire range of diversity in the system are brought together to focus on the whole organization, playing the role of the quiltmaker who can survey her work and make certain that the overall pattern of the quilt is emerging as planned. From the perspective of the individual piece or mid-size diamond, the emerging pattern of the quilt may not be obvious; but when the pieces are juxtaposed with one another, the pattern emerges.

Individuals are themselves fractals; they each possess some level of understanding of what the system is trying to accomplish and help it to do so by developing some degree of mastery over certain types of business, technical, and social skills that are relevant to the organization. Individuals differ in the combination and mastery of their skills, and in the values and perspectives and creativity they bring to the organization. As individuals comparing notes with one another, they may find more diversity than commonality, more arguments over what should be done than agreement. But when the organization is surveyed as a whole, the pattern of shared skills and beliefs begins to emerge. Even though an individual may know relatively little about steelmaking, for example, and a lot about accounting, that person still knows more about steelmaking than does an accountant working for an airline. The intersection of knowledge and beliefs may not be great between the steelworker and the accountant, but it is sufficient to bind them into the same organization, the same quilt. It would help the organization to be more flexible if a few people in the accounting department understood a lot about steelmaking, and others in the steelmaking department knew a good deal about accounting. Then, the two functions could work together more easily in introducing changes in accounting procedures that reflect what is happening in the steelmaking operation without destroying the integrity or effectiveness of the organization in the process. It's important to note that not every steelmaker needs to be an expert in accounting, any more than every accountant needs to understand steelmaking; each function needs to contain shared sets of knowledge, but each person in the organization is not expected to know everything that every other person knows. Each middle-size diamond in the quilt is different, yet the basic integrity of the quilt is maintained because of the appearance of some combination of similar individual diamonds in different middle-size diamonds throughout the quilt.

In organizations, individuals have the advantage of mobility, unlike the inanimate diamonds on the quilt. Thus, it is possible for mid-size units of organizations to acquire diversity through the temporary inclusion of individuals with different characteristics. Each unit need not contain a permanent representative of every other type of person in the organization in order to obtain holographic knowledge or multifunctional abilities. The need for different types of people, knowledge, or abilities can vary from unit to unit based on its local needs without violating the integrity of the overall pattern of organization. Each unit of the infantry may not have the same list of people and equipment as every other unit; those fighting in the jungle may have different people and equipment than those fighting in the desert. Yet both have access to the resources of the larger organization and can change their composition if they fight their way from the jungle to the desert or vice versa. What makes fractal designs flexible is that the units can be of different sizes and compositions, can be formed and reformed as needed, and each element contains knowledge of the whole system, as illustrated in Figure 8–2.

As the basic building block of the fractal organization, the more flexible individuals are, the more flexible the overall organization becomes. Yet again, not every person needs to be a jack-of-all-trades, and some people will master skills in depth and then be made available to others who cannot take the time to learn to perform them with the same level of ease. The surgeon and the receptionist need never trade places in the fractal organization; although, over time, each may assist the other in relevant ways at the intersection of the talents, abilities, and values. In meetings of larger holographic representations of the whole system, the receptionist and surgeon may find that they have equal voice in addressing the assembly of their peers on shared concerns pertaining to the health, future, or governance of the

Fractal units can be of different sizes and compositions

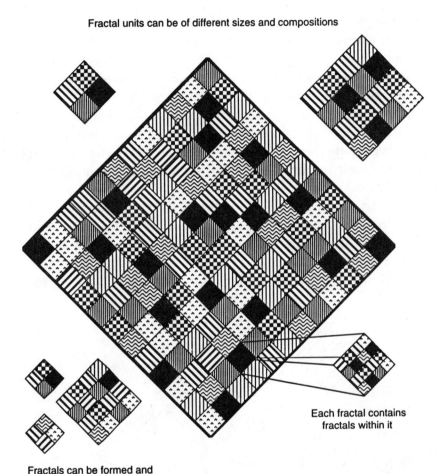

Each fractal contains
fractals within it

Fractals can be formed and
reformed as needed

Figure 8.2   What makes fractal organization designs flexible.

entire system. Despite the dissimilarity in their individual orientations, each has a perspective that is valid and enough shared concern about the whole to listen to one another's point of view. In the fractal organization, it is the assembly pattern of individual pieces that share some similarities that creates the overall effect of order, not the fact that each piece of the whole is exactly like each other piece. Simplistic designs for self-managing teams have missed this point in their insistence that every person learn how to perform every other person's job. This does not take into account the need for specialized knowledge, differences in abilities or stages of development, or varying local conditions. Instead, the flexible organization is based on an inventory of talents and shared skills and values, which are assembled over and over again into varying patterns that allow local responsiveness without altering the fundamental pattern of the whole. When experts need to be drawn together to focus on an issue that requires many people with the same expertise, fractal design permits their resources to be easily marshaled, as indicated in Figure 8–3.

Also in contrast to the quilt, organizational mid-size units can vary in size without destroying the symmetry of the larger whole in which they reside. Plants or divisions of unequal size are perfectly allowable; and, over time, the size of a particular unit may shrink or grow depending on business needs. Within each

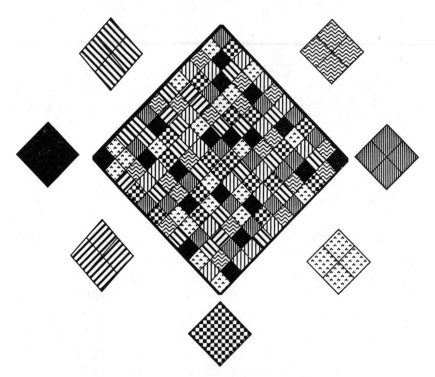

Figure 8.3   When needed, concentrations of expetise can be created.

unit, the ratio of different types of skills, abilities, or perspectives may also vary, in the short and long term. When problems arise that require skills in greater numbers than the unit possesses normally, the unit may swell in size temporarily to accommodate experts from other parts of the organization who rush in to help out. Then, when the problem is solved, the experts diffuse to their original locations. Much of this moving back and forth may be more a matter of focus than actual physical relocation, with the assistance of telecomputing technology that allows for virtual colocation. The length of duration of assignments to different units by different individuals is determined by business needs rather than by staffing tables, career progression rules, or other arbitrary conventions. Performance evaluations are made continuously, by peers who share similar skills and by internal or external customers who receive the efforts of a person's labor. Unit performance is judged by the next higher aggregation of units to which the unit belongs; and the system as a whole is governed by a unit that is itself a representation of the whole.

To perform the function of the quiltmaker, who provides the inherent logic used to assemble different units into the whole and holds in her mind the vision of the entire system of parts in relation to one another, organizations need to assemble a body that can understand the whole organization. In traditional organizational design, it is assumed that a small group of top-level decision-makers is capable of understanding everything important that is happening inside and outside the organization, process all of the information based on their understanding of the capabilities of people throughout the system, and make appropriate decisions regarding the deployment of resources and direction of effort. In an organization of any size at all, this assumption is ludicrous and needs to be put to rest. In addition to the impossibility of knowing everything about everything at one point in time, we need to add that, unlike the quilt, the pieces of the organization are constantly changing, as is the environment in which the organization functions. The quilt has hung on the wall of the local restaurant for years, and other than becoming a little more dingy, it hasn't changed very much. In the same period of time that the quilt has hung on the wall, some of our largest and most respected organizations have tumbled, while new upstarts have attracted attention and resources. In the time since the quilt was made, trade centers have shifted, wars have been fought, countries have formed and dissolved, and computers were invented. To expect even the most brilliant people to know about everything, and to continue to understand everything as everything changes, is to fall into psychological dependency, to hope for salvation from a father figure, to believe and trust in authority as the only hope for mankind. Psychological dependency is the result of emotional overload, of fear of the unknown that cannot be comprehended by a single mind. When our minds cannot grasp the whole of something, we simplify it to make it appear understandable and manageable, and then adopt similarly simplistic solutions to cope with it all. We wind up managing nonsystemically, only partially understanding what it is we are doing, and knowing even less how to predict and manage the consequences of our actions. We place ourselves and our systems at peril and create more of the anarchy and chaos that we thought we were preventing. It is time to develop ways of managing systems that are as complex as the systems we must manage and to put to final rest our emotional dependence on father figures as the source of salvation for us all. Our only hope lies in our combined wisdom, and in the power of our multiple perspectives being brought to bear on the challenges we face.

The fractal organization, unlike our current high-performance, high-commitment organizations, does not rely on different types of structures for the top of the organization than those used at the bottom. In high-performance, high-commitment organizations, multiskilled, self-managing teams are good for the shop floor, but nowhere to be seen at corporate headquarters. In fractal designs, the units at corporate headquarters are patterned after the rest of the quilt, and may even be staffed by individuals who come from other parts of the system on a temporary basis. What is important, as in the polynoetic organization for knowledge work, is getting the right knowledge into the places where it can affect important decisions. In the fractal organization, the right knowledge includes not only technical information about products and services and news about the environment, but also values and beliefs and perspectives. As the organization faces continually changing circumstances, and as its individual units develop new capacities or understandings, values, beliefs, and perspectives provide the overall pattern logic that holds the organization together and keeps it on course. Like the threads that stitch the quilt together, values, beliefs, and perspectives hold people's thinking in place and provide the boundaries that guide individual actions. Meg Wheatley writes about meaning in organizations as the counterpart of "strange attractors" in physics that place limits on what at first appears to be chaos. Meanings help people know what is acceptable and what isn't, what is worth striving for and what is best left alone. To be truly meaningful, beliefs and values cannot be decreed by one group for the whole; we can't write vision and value statements, hang them on the wall, and expect things to change. Beliefs and values must be created, tested, and recreated continuously, with the direct involvement of the people and units that make up the organization. Incidentally, they always have been; we only delude ourselves when we believe that, as managers, we are setting the pattern that others will follow. In fact, individuals and units do those things with which they agree or are forced to do, and ignore the rest. Much more of what actually happens day to day in a work group is determined by local choice than by executive order.

Organizations live in a world of constraints and opportunities. Laws and regulations must be obeyed, and even momentary advantages seized. In complying with constraints and exploiting opportunities, people are sometimes asked to do things that they would rather not, and sometimes things that conflict with their basic values. For the organization to survive in the real world, there must be ways for the organization to prevail upon its fractal units to do things that, of their own accord, they might not. The traditional response to this problem is to create control structures that are reward- and punishment-based. Break the law and expect fines or imprisonment; exploit an opportunity and expect fame and fortune. In traditional systems, we trust that those in positions of authority will make decisions in the best interests of the survival of the system, as individually distasteful as these decisions may be. We expect people to rise above their individual beliefs and values in order to allow the system as a whole to prosper.

In fractal designs, we rely not on individuals for this superhuman ability, but on the wisdom of the representational whole to decide what is best for all. While I may wish that a certain law didn't exist, and even choose to ignore it individually and face the consequences if I am ever caught for violating it, in the fractal organization I am not given that freedom of choice. My membership in the organization provides both rights and privileges; I am responsible to my peers for my behavior. The choices we make are collective choices, made with the perspective of the welfare of the whole system in mind. I can't grow my fractal of the quilt, or forget to comply with regulations pertaining to the whole, without the agreement of other fractal units. The pattern of the whole must be preserved in order to ensure the well being of my unit and all others. We talk about cooperation and mutuality in traditional designs, but we reward aggressive individuals who seek to maximize their own gain at the expense of others. We preach organizational integrity and organizational citizenship, but we reward those who find ways to evade the rules in order to succeed. We view living within the rules as cumbersome and even perilous to our future. Certainly, some rules are wrong and need to be changed; but most rules provide opportunities for flexibility and potential competitive advantage to those who learn better ways to play the game while still functioning in accordance with them. In any event, the rules apply to traditional and fractal organizations alike; the only question is how the organization chooses to govern its internal compliance behavior. Traditional organizations rely on authority, rewards, and punishments; fractal organizations rely on common agreements and peer review.

As new business opportunities emerge, new skills and abilities may need to be added to the mix of those available. In traditional organizations, it is not uncommon to treat new businesses as completely separate undertakings from the rest; to establish free-standing units with almost entirely new personnel and perhaps different organizational policies, procedures, and cultures. Here, the problems of not sticking to the knitting begin to emerge as traditional decision-makers find themselves unable to understand or influence the behavior of the new organization except through the most crude and ineffective applications of brute force.

In the fractal organization, new businesses are begun with a core unit of resources that represent both the existing and new sets of characteristics, skills, and beliefs. After a short period, the new organization also begins to supply people who are knowledgeable about the new organization to work in the existing organization, to assist in the integration of the parts into the pattern of the whole. Thus, growth in the organization involves the creation of new fractals, modeled after the old, as well as transformations in the old fractals to incorporate elements of the new. The integrity of the overall pattern is maintained but modified, everywhere at the same time. The extent of the modification to the existing fractals and overall pattern will depend on the significance of the changes introduced by the new unit. New values, new technology, new business skills, new social skills associated with new cultures may all shift in small or very noticeable ways depending on the magnitude of the change. Some fractals may change more than others, because they deal more directly with the new unit. If the change introduced by the new unit is important to all the existing fractals, change will be more pervasive. The question is not whether the new unit should be free-standing or integrated into existing operations; it is how best to create the sharing of knowledge and resources and values that must take place for the new unit to flourish in the larger context of the whole.

In very large organizations, or in organizations with many highly differentiated units, the task of governance may require a number of fractal units coordinating different topics that require system-level attention, and which in turn are linked through representatives into a fractal that performs an integrative function for the whole system. Again, the nature and permanence of membership in each of these fractals will be determined by the needs of the organization, in the context of its environment.

The idea behind fractals is not to create a new form of organizational prison, a new chart to be bound within. Fractal design is intended to allow maximum flexibility in what people do and learn, within the minimum framework of commonality that is needed to guide their actions toward common goals. Specific design choices about what the fractals look like, how permanent or temporary their membership is, how many fractals there are, how large or small they are, how much formal leadership is provided, how people are compensated, and a host of other decisions must still be made by organizational designers to fit the needs of the specific organization and its environment. Fractals are a new way of thinking about design, a new medium with which to work; but local artists still must do the quilting.

CHAPTER
9

Getting There
Making Systemic Change Happen

The gremlins of change are throwing wrenches into the gears of organizational predictability. Just when we thought we had things under control with work redesign and quality, along come reengineering and diversity management. And then there are all those things we never did learn how to manage very well: turnover, global competition, new product introductions. Gremlins *must* be responsible, since we can seldom find people who are anxious for these changes to occur. Most of us prefer the status quo.

The fact is, the status quo is an illusion. We have never been in a state of complete respite from change and we never will be. The closest we can come is what the biologists call *dynamic homeostasis*, which is a characteristic of all living systems. Living systems, you and me included, are constantly in motion and changing. Our hearts are beating, we breathe air in and out of our lungs, and we digest last night's dinner. Meanwhile, as we are doing these things, more subtle changes are taking place in our bodies: We are growing older, and signs of this eventually show up in ways we all wish we could avoid. We fight to maintain the status quo through diet and exercise; but the process of aging continues anyway, and we are eventually forced to accept its consequences. Thus, it appears to us that we are neither changing nor even in motion, but in fact we are in constant motion and continually changing. This is the essence of dynamic homeostasis.

Organizations experience dynamic homeostasis, as well. Their productive hearts beat to produce materials and services, they breathe members in and out every day, they digest the raw materials fed them today and that they will have to consume again tomorrow. As they are doing these things that appear routine, they are changing. People and capital resources are getting older, equipment and strategies are wearing out, and ways of competing that have been successful in the past are becoming continually less effective. Fortunately, organizations, in contrast to us mere mortals, can replace all of their essential body parts over time and thus keep on ticking. But the desire to deny the constancy of change may cause the organization to simply replace its parts rather than redesign itself to live in a new age. Instead of viewing change as a natural part of organizational life, organizations resist change in thousands of subtle ways. When hiring a new person to replace one who has departed, we look for someone with the same talents and even the same personality. When machine components wear out, we look for replacement parts instead of replacing the whole machine. When our markets begin to shrink, we redouble our efforts to capture market share instead of seeking new business opportunities. In the most extreme cases, we ride our organizations to their inevitable demise, knowing full well that bold and innovative moves are required to save them but being unable to convince ourselves to take the necessary steps.

In organizations we compound the problem by building our

fear of change into our human, technical, and managerial systems. This makes these systems far more resistant to change than they should be, and causes the organization to become stronger than those who would help it to survive. A simple example of this is the introduction of a more efficient piece of equipment, such as a new computer that replaces manual methods of bookkeeping. In order to operate the computer, a person must be hired with or trained in the necessary skills. Thereafter, the operator has a vested interest in seeing that the computer system continues to operate in the same way; this makes their job secure and important. Beyond the operator, others in the system become accustomed to receiving the reports the computer produces; they become familiar with their appearance and comfortable in their ability to interpret their meaning. Other reports are derived from these reports, and regular decisions are made on the information all these reports provide. Managerial layers are added to integrate these decisions and to provide course correction to the organization if the information points to something that needs attention.

To change the system, many aspects of the status quo must be undone. A new computing system will require retraining or even outplacing the computer operator, which the operator may resist. Then, the new reports generated by the new computer will have to be explained and new methods of interpreting them discovered. These new interpretations will change the other reports being used by managers, who must develop new criteria for decision-making and action taking. Then, and only then, will the new computer make a difference in the performance of the system. But as every information systems person knows, the new computer shouldn't make *too* much difference, because the best changes in systems are those that people hardly notice. And so it goes throughout the organization: Every time we try to introduce new equipment or methods, new policies or procedures, new products or new managerial techniques, the organizational fear of change causes us to transform opportunities for improvement into efforts to preserve the status quo. In the end, with each person and department resisting change, the organization becomes more powerful in preserving the status quo than any individual or group within it, including the CEO and her direct reports.

THE GRINDING OF THE GEARS

Maine's economy is slow right now, like the rest of the Northeast. There isn't a lot of industry, but there is a lot of commerce, particularly in the form of antique stores. It seems that almost every other house has a sign out to sell something, from antique cars to antique furniture. Some of it looks like junk to me, but people don't seem to care. Because it's Maine, the tourists buy it anyway. If it comes from Maine, it must be historically significant. I let Mary talk me into stopping at an antique store the other day, since it was on the way to a fly fishing shop that I had been anxious to check out. Fair is fair. As these things often go, it turned out that I was the one who bought an antique and Mary who picked up some fishing tackle. What caught my eye was an old Elgin National Watch Company gold-plated pocketwatch that was of true railroad vintage, with a beautiful face, intricate gears, and the initials "LH" handsomely scripted into the back of its inside cover. I was captivated by it as I held it in my hand, wondering to whom it once belonged, and to what places the man and watch had traveled together. I thought how elegant it looked and felt, and how hopeful this person LH must have been; hopeful concerning the future of his employment, the future of the railroad. How certain he was that there would always be a need to tell the precise time, to know exactly when to pull in and out of the station. To purchase such an expensive and durable watch, he had to feel that his job would last, and that having the proper time would be important for many years to come. The watch has the power of truly classic antiques to create haunting images of lives and years gone by. When we hold an object like this in our hands, we are reminded of our own mortality, of the faith we have in the present, and in the future; of how much we want to believe that things that are important to us won't change, that the people we love will be with us forever. Yet, there in our hands is the truth. Change is happening all around us, and *to* us, no matter how strongly we push it out of our consciousness in order to carry on with our daily routines. The pocketwatches we leave behind are symbols of our love of life, and the medium we choose to pass along our message of how much we loved living from one generation to the next.

As I looked at the watch, I began to think of organizations as expensive, old-fashioned pocket watches. Except that organizations may never have run as well as the watch that belonged to LH, because the gears inside organizations were never designed to work together in the first place. Let me explain.

At the heart of the watch is the production system: the people and equipment that are used to produce the goods or services that keep the customers coming in the door. For a long time we believed that the technology in use was the planetary gear, that people could be trained, reshaped, or replaced as necessary to fit the needs of technology. But more recently we have discovered that *both* people *and* technology are planetary gears; that there are essential things people do—such as think, solve problems, and innovate—that technology cannot do, and that these human processes are just as important to the system's running well over time as is the work performed by the technology. A problem in most organizations is that the teeth on these two planetary gears don't mesh. When they designed the equipment that created the jobs that people would eventually be asked to perform, the designers didn't think about the people who would do the work. Most technical systems are designed to operate in a routine fashion, and in fact they operate at peak efficiency only when people do exactly what the technical designer envisioned. But, as all of us know, people seldom behave precisely as we expect them to; and, in some cases, they flat out refuse to do what the technical system demands. When work is designed for maximum technical efficiency, human beings typically suffer; and, as human beings do the things they typically do to avoid suffering, the system as a whole operates at less than optimum output. Furthermore, when change is introduced, human and technical systems react at different speeds. New equipment is easy to install, but it takes a long time to train people to operate it properly. On the other hand, people with ideas for improving the system find that the system resists their input, as technical changes are often costly or difficult to make. People and equipment are the heart of the watch. They drive all the other gears, but they are two different kinds of gears that often try to turn at different rates of speed, and sometimes even in opposite directions.

Surrounding the planetary gears are the second-level gears that provide direct support to the productive system: engineering, maintenance, production planning, sales, accounting, personnel, customer service, training, first-level supervision. Each of these support mechanisms is a gear, and each is designed with slightly different teeth. Over time, the people who occupy these roles file the teeth down to make it easier or better to do the job from their perspective and expect the rest of the gears in the system to adjust accordingly. With all the gears changing only slightly but simultaneously, the sound of gears grinding becomes louder and louder over time. Different gears try to exert influence over the others and, for a time, other gears do start to adjust; but then changes come along that set individual gears turning at different rates of speed, and the system is thrown out of sync again.

Third-level gears are trying to manage the fit among the first and second level gears. These include finance, human resource planning, marketing, research and development, public affairs, legal departments, and middle management. Like the second level gears, these are gears of unique design, turning at rates of speed determined from their own point of reference. And, like the other gears, they occasionally try to turn in opposite directions, as they detect problems with what the other gears are doing, attempt to respond to some external disturbance, or try to introduce innovation.

Fourth-level gears, which include top management, strategic planners, and boards of directors, attempt to keep the whole system moving. They are like the winding mechanism of the watch that turns the spring that gets everything else going. But each of these is of different design, as well. Top management may want to tighten the spring, while the board wants to loosen it. Strategic planners may want the gears to turn in one direction while management and the board want them to turn in another.

Meanwhile, while all this grinding of gears and stopping and starting is going on, the gremlins of change are throwing wrenches into the works. Turnover, diversity, global competition, recession, reengineering, downsizing, new regulations, flextime, day care, health benefits, managerial succession, stockholder meetings, CAD/CAM, joint ventures, breakdowns, all disrupt the system at some level; and, because the gears are all interconnected, each eventually disrupts the entire system.

Despite the never-ending parade of new gremlins, we try to pretend that the most recent gremlin is the last. If we can just get the gears to turn in unison in response to this latest wrench, maybe there won't be any more wrenches, at least for a while. Maybe the gears can finally begin to figure out how they should fit together before the next big change comes along. Or maybe the strategic planners can figure out how the whole watch is supposed to work and tell each of the gears what they should be doing. Maybe we can get some coherent leadership from the top to the bottom and from gear to gear that helps us to mesh better together. Then maybe, if we're lucky, we'll be so good that we won't have to change any more for a long time. But why would we want to stay the same? Getting everything running smoothly may be the worst thing we can do in the long run; we'll be afraid to change things if we ever get it right. We know this, but it doesn't keep us from trying to make each gear fit with each other gear, one at a time, while other gears are already creating changes that will undo the work we have just done.

In the first consulting effort I ever undertook, a first line supervisor lamented, "Why do we need to undertake this change right now? We've been through so much change recently, what we need is a break. Let us catch up with the changes we have already started and then maybe we can find the energy to do this right!"

On the one hand, his plea made sense to me; it was clear that people were feeling burned out and that changing more was the least desirable thing they could imagine doing at the moment. I didn't want to add to their burden by introducing yet another program to be completed. On the other hand, I knew that I hadn't invited myself in to his organization; I was there because there was a real need for the organization to continue changing, and that to avoid change would only lead to greater problems in the long run. Like a good soldier asked to charge yet another hill, the first line supervisor tightened his belt, straightened his helmet, and led the attack once again. He knew, as I did, that this war had no end.

Managing change doesn't really need to feel like fighting a war, but we make it that way, partly to find sympathy for the difficulties we experience, and partly because we just don't know another way to feel about it. Much of the blame for how difficult the process of changing organizations is rests on our own shoulders. We don't know how to approach change in ways that make it more manageable and less traumatic. We repeat the same process of changing over and over again, hoping that each time we go through it will be our last, rather than experimenting each time with ways to do it differently that will help us to do it better the next time.

Our organizations compound the problem because, like the watch, they were never designed for change. The watch was designed to do just one thing: to tell time, as accurately as its fine gears and hands would allow.

I'm reminded of Joel Barker's film on paradigms, particularly the segment about the Swiss watchmakers who disregarded the leap in timekeeping technology introduced by Texas Instruments and later by the Japanese. The Swiss had dominated the watchmaking world for years, with processes for perfecting the manufacturing of gears that no one could match. When semiconductor technology proved cheaper, more accurate, and convenient than mechanical gears and springs, the Swiss were caught off guard and never regained the market share they lost. Today, Swiss time pieces are statements of elegance and beauty: future messages to the next generation of antique collectors.

As semiconductor technology evolves, we expect our watches to do more and more things for us. Not only to tell time linearly, but to act as chronographs, counting down or up on command. We want to know the time in any time zone in the world instantly and to be able to use our watches as calculators. Some watches are designed to include depth gauges for divers, while others incorporate altimeters for pilots. Some include miniature video games to keep us entertained when we are more interested in passing the time than telling it. In the future, we will expect our watches to carry voice and video transmissions, shades of Dick Tracy. I'm sure they will find a way to build in a small fax, or at least allow E-mail hookup to my computer. The technology is flexible, and it invites change.

The watch that belonged to LH could never aspire to these things. It was a fine piece, but it was designed with a single function in mind. Its gears and springs and hands could no more be adapted to create a video game than a brick could be made to fly. It simply wasn't designed with change in mind.

Some organizations are good at changing. They have learned that trying to make the gears fit together better one at a time is a waste of energy. They have discovered that multiple changes are required simultaneously and that, to accomplish simultaneous change, the organization has to be designed out of semiconductor chips instead of gears.

At the level of core work, this means building an organization from flexible technology and flexible people and managing these flexible components in a highly interactive, flexible mode. Multiskilled teams of people who really understand their technology and who can work directly with customers, designers, suppliers, and each other to perfect the quality and services provided help create the ability for simultaneous change. But multiskilling alone is not enough; managing multiple changes simultaneously also demands learning many new things at the same time, and figuring out how to use what has been learned.

Organizations that undertake massive change efforts, in which every person goes through the same lockstep training and tries one new thing all at the same time, are lurching at change. We have accumulated enough evidence to know that this approach to change simply doesn't work as well as we hoped it would. Even if the training is effective, which it often is not, people quickly reach the point where they begin to apply the training to solve discrete problems, which is like changing just one gear in the system. Before they know it, these organizations are back in the mode of having many people filing down individual gears, and the gears end up not fitting well together. A series of massive programs that focus on one set of gears at a time (compensation, quality, reengineering) does no more good; the problem of fit is simply raised to another level, between one system and another. All the systems need to change at once.

THE SEMICONDUCTOR PARADIGM

The barriers to changing all the systems at once are resources and integration. Changing everything at once requires abundant resources, in order to learn about what needs to be changed and how to change it. Because these changes must be made in reference to one another to avoid the watch problem, integration is as important as changing each component in the long run, and integration also takes time and energy.

To free up the energy needed in the system to accomplish simultaneous change and still achieve integration, we need to make the paradigm shift from gears to semiconductors. The old paradigm is one of control, centralized decision-making, and functional specialization. The whole system is divided into gears, and each gear assigned a specific function to perform; then, because each gear is ignorant of the way the whole system is supposed to work, the organization is controlled via layers of hierarchical management. When change is needed in the old paradigm system, it must work its way down through the hierarchy, across functions, and then back up the hierarchy again for integration. Somewhere during this process, the system either becomes overloaded or simply breaks down: Components refuse to change, others try to change too much, and management tries to handle the resulting confusion and disagreement. Often, the confusion and disagreement escalate through the hierarchy, with managers disagreeing with one another about what to do to fix the system. At this point politics take over, and the change is defeated. In some old-paradigm systems, strong champions of change at the highest levels force change to occur throughout the system by demanding evidence of innovation from each of their subordinates; but even these changes are short-lived, as they affect single components of the system that can't keep operating in the new way while the remaining gears are still working in the old.

The semiconductor paradigm distributes the responsibility for change over the entire system. Each group and all its members have a responsibility for learning about change and helping to integrate what they learn into the rest of the system. Instead of single massive efforts affecting one part of the system, many multiple efforts are occurring simultaneously, with different members of a single work group involved in five or 10 learning and change activities simultaneously. Each person learns something on behalf of the group and then helps the rest of the group to learn it. Because other members of the group are involved in learning about other changes, the need for integration is apparent and immediate. Adjustments to experiments are made instantly at the work group level so that no time is wasted in implementing changes that don't fit the integrated plan. Changes that require integration across departments or functions are made by people who are from those departments or functions nominally, but who may spend as much time in other departments as their own. Integration is a real requirement for successful change, and the organization is designed to reduce barriers to movement and learning so that people can learn to integrate for themselves instead of depending on the hierarchy to make decisions for them. Because the activity level required of people is much higher than that in old-paradigm systems, people are supported in their development as citizens and agents of change. Further, they are rewarded as much for helping to improve the system as they are for maintaining it. Change becomes a significant measure of organizational success and is translated into individual develop-

ment plans and appraisals. In the simultaneous change paradigm, everyone learns all the time, and each person is a change
agent.

As the need for greater integration or resources to support
particular changes becomes apparent, ad hoc integration groups
are formed to manage "projects." Projects are staffed by a core of
knowledgeable "experts" who may leave their roles at any level
in the system to work on the project full time until it is completed. The core of experts is supported by individuals from
throughout the organization who act as messengers to and inte-
grators with their own groups or departments. Once projects
reach fruition, overall integration groups made up of knowledgeable individuals from the core teams of the various projects
approve the implementation of projects or recommend changes
to help them fit better with other changes underway. Once projects
are implemented, the core resource group disbands, and members may resume their usual roles in the system, or find themselves working on another project for change.

The resources needed to fuel simultaneous change are ob-
tained from two sources: one, underutilized talent that is blocked
from making contributions by the old-paradigm organization;
and two, from gains in efficiency produced by successful projects.
As projects bear fruit, it is quickly discovered that time spent in
improvement activities, if undertaken properly, can become self-
funding. That is, the success of the efforts will free up more than
enough time to continue to undertake improvements. Once the
upward spiral begins, more and more significant changes can be
handled simultaneously, resulting in greater gains in efficiencies
and profitability.

PREPARING FOR CHANGE

Getting there takes time and preparation as indicated in Figure
9.1. What's essential? First, making certain that you understand
why the effort is worthwhile. If you don't know why you're
bothering to change, change will become a lower priority as

1. **Preparation**
   Search conferences
   Clarifying the need for change
   Developing individual capabilities
   Negotiating stakeholder expectations

2. **Analyzing strengths and weaknesses**
   External analysis
   Internal analysis
   Goals for improvement
   Specific measures to assess change

3. **Designing new organizational sub-units**
   Increasing individual capabilities
   Increasing sub-unit capabilities
   Increasing systemic integration

4. **Designing projects**
   Search conferences
   Deliberation planning
   Improvement projects
   Learning projects

5. **Designing work systems**
   Perfecting core processes
   Identifying appropriate technology
   Processes for measuring performance
   Processes for including the customer
   Integration with other units
   Individual and organizational learning
   Designing reward systems

6. **Designing support systems**
   Identify needs for support
   Create integrating mechanisms with projects

7. **Designing integrative mechanisms**
   Determine integration needs
   Allow integration mechanisms to evolve

8. **Implementing change**
   Planning for implementation
   Assigning resources
   Developing interim change indicators
   Diffused learning
   Forming multiple change project teams
   Forming change integration teams

Figure 9.1   A model for complex system change.

other urgent agendas arise. Because change, like exercise, is something we can always put off until later, we tend to not do it at all. Preparation involves knowing the difference between where you are and where you really need to be, and knowing the difference between changing and continuing to let other agendas take precedence. The first step in understanding the need for change may be a benchmarking study, as in the case of Xerox; or, it could be a search conference that brings together the people and knowledge to make an assessment of where the organization truly stands. Less involved ways of sensing the health of the organization (such as reviewing this year's sales in comparison to last year's) also work, but usually not as well as an event that crystallizes for everyone the significance of the effort that is about to begin. It's easier to change when there's an obvious threat, but, as I said before, there are many examples of companies that have changed simply because they knew it was what they needed to do to stay number one.

The event that crystallizes the need for change should involve as many people as possible, and communications should capture the message that emerges for the rest. A shortened version of this message, even to the point of a single phrase, image, or word, is helpful in reminding people of the goal during the steps that follow. For Ford, it was "Quality is job one." Do you remember GM's? Neither do I, and neither did a lot of other people at GM who knew that change was necessary but didn't know what goal to pursue.

Preparation also means helping people get ready to participate, as I discussed in Chapter 3. The process of change I'm advocating begins with helping people prepare to behave differently. In this case, the new behavior is participation in thorough analysis and tough decisions. People must understand why they need to change, how to do it, and what's in it for them. They need to practice new behaviors, first in safe settings and gradually in deeper water. Preparing people needn't take a long time, but the tendency to skip this step altogether or speed through it superficially makes me nervous. Neither employees nor managers are ready for what comes next. The quality of their preparation may mean the difference between their acceptance of change and success in changing versus resistance and failure.

Preparing people can take many forms. Training sessions that review the ideas behind flexible organizations help. So do video-tapes and visits to other companies. But there has to be more to the preparation than just brainwork. People need to begin *behaving* differently, and this requires an iterative combination of discussion, practice, and more discussion. The process begins with discussion, because people need to share their fears and concerns before they can approach learning something new. Then, practice with new behaviors provides firsthand data to work with, rather than conjectures about what the change will involve. Thereafter, because what is learned is often difficult, more discussion is required to deal with the temporary resistance that occurs as people try to learn any new behavior. Then, more practice, more discussion, more practice, and so on until people begin to feel more comfortable doing what is necessary.

Practice can involve things as simple as public speaking or group process observation, and as difficult as shifting authority for decision making based on expertise. The essential ground to be covered includes:

1. Individual skills (such as speaking, participating, sharing ideas, critiquing, facilitating, leading, managing conflict, managing diversity, working in groups);
2. Technical skills (such as understanding the design and operation of the technical system, how to maintain it, how to improve it, what it takes to produce quality products or services, or, in non-routine systems, the key elements of the knowledge base and how they fit together); and,
3. Business skills (such as understanding the needs of customers; what drives the financial health of the company; understanding the strategy; and knowing what to do to help the business succeed).

Because many organizations have provided training in these areas already, a review is all that is really necessary to get things moving, *providing* that the training was done well in the first place. If people fail to demonstrate these skills during the change process, take time out to start over again. We can wish for change to be easy, but we can't expect our wish to be granted without the proper preparation of people.

Preparation also means preparing stakeholders, such as higher level management or the board, customers, or suppliers. Time and effort put into changing will have payoff for them, but probably not immediately. One organization I know of worked at change for *nine years* before it achieved the improvement it had targeted. This organization prepared its stakeholders for a long haul, and kept them appraised of progress along the way, such as it was. Even though a single 9-year effort sounds excessive, I'll bet the slow, steady process of change produced more meaningful results than a series of nine 1-year programs would have. The Topeka pet food plant has been changing for more than 20 years, and the good news is that it is still changing. In the early years, change would have been smoother with better preparation of some of the plant's stakeholders; but, on the positive side, the stakeholders have been supportive of the plant's continuing quest for excellence, and they have demonstrated their support by providing capital for expansions and allowing the same plant manager to stay in place for most of the plant's history. Stakeholder preparation is key in creating the right support for undertaking a quality change effort.

Spend time preparing. Overprepare if necessary. Don't proceed without the knowledge of why you are changing, the readiness of people to change, or the support you need to undertake a quality effort.

ANALYZING STRENGTHS AND WEAKNESSES

Whether via a search conference, benchmarking, industry analysis, or other method, the next step in the process of change should be to compare the organization to some external standard. Depending upon how much work of this kind has been done previously, this analysis can be either extensive or cursory. Enough external referencing has been done if there is agreement on the current strengths and weaknesses of the organization and, derived from this, an ambitious agenda for improvement.

Internal analyses are helpful, too, especially those that allow input from employees concerning the technical system and organizational concerns. Attitude surveys are helpful barometers but usually don't provide the rich, detailed insights gained through interviews, focus groups, or search-conferences that, as Marv Weisbord says, "get the whole system in the room."[1] The "fast-cycle full-participation" approach I mentioned in Chapter 3 is a terrific way to generate both data and commitment to change in a short period of time. In one instance, we took advantage of a planned 3-week shutdown of a manufacturing plant to conduct an entire sociotechnical system redesign process involving all members of the organization and key external stakeholders. This same process, utilizing the traditional design team approach I outlined in *Designing Effective Organizations*, might have taken anywhere from six to 18 months and still not have generated the data and enthusiasm we observed using the fast-cycle method. In another case, we used a variation of the fast-cycle approach to collect data quickly from everyone in an organization with widely dispersed units, then relied on a design team to pull the data together and create the new design. Both approaches worked much better than I expected, given the compressed time frame. Given the results we have observed, I'd be reluctant to return to the traditional method of analysis and design. As the pace of change accelerates, these fast-cycle intervention methods may provide us with a change process that meets our "need for speed" without sacrificing quality or commitment.

A final outcome of the analysis of organizational strengths and weaknesses should be the adoption of specific measures to assess the change. Even in nonroutine settings, it is possible to compile a list of indicators that are supportive of high perfor-

mance; and targets should be set for the effort to produce significant gains in these indicators.

A NEW DESIGN

Once the preliminary analyses are completed, changes in the
structure of the organization can be suggested. At this point in
the process of change, the idea is to create organizational units
that are designed for flexibility and can meet the needs of the
competitive market or the expectations of external stakeholders.
Later, the units created in this step will work out details of how
they will function, how many people they will need, and so
forth. At this stage, the proposed new design is a rough-cut,
macro-organizational design that is intended to free up energy,
resources, and creative thinking. Most often, the design will
focus on "projects": complete processes or businesses that serve
a specific category of customers, which will be assembled and
reassembled as either new projects emerge or older projects lose
vitality.

Although creating a new design requires analysis, participation, and a dose of creative insight, the easiest way to configure
the organization into projects versus departments is to answer
the question, "Based on our analyses, what are the most important things for this organization to accomplish during the next
five- to-10 years?" The answers to this question usually point
toward toward the key projects that should be created. Remember that in the flexible organization the creation of projects does
not impose boundaries or a division of responsibility; people
may well be involved with multiple projects. For example, if two
of the most important things for the organization to accomplish
in the next five years are one, to maintain the current operations
in good working order and two, to introduce a large number of
new products, it is possible that a number of people would be
involved in each of these two projects. In more complex or global
organizations, the design may be a matrix of projects that include
both customer and geographical orientations.

Following the principles for designing flexible organizations, the macro design will deemphasize centralized authority and empower decision making by those with knowledge in a more flexible but highly integrated organizational structure. Even the boundaries of the major projects created at this stage are subject to change as learning occurs in the detailed design process.

DESIGNING PROJECTS

Once the overall design of projects is adopted, individuals involved in various projects can bring together the resources they need from inside and outside the organization to plan the details of their work. Thinking in terms of projects instead of organizational design is important at this stage because it avoids the tendency for leaders and others to seek security for themselves by drawing boxes on organizational charts and then locking themselves inside. The project metaphor implies that everyone is in the project together, and that roles are subject to change based on project demands. Nevertheless, roles are important in projects, as are plans and processes. Planning key deliberations for the project is one part of this step; as deliberation-planning proceeds, the need to draw on external (to the project) resources becomes clear, and the self-sealing tendency of projects is avoided. Project design must incorporate how strategies will be developed, work completed, resources allocated, activities integrated, finances looked after, people recruited and developed, laws obeyed, linkages with other projects and other parts of the organization accomplished, compensation determined, and success measured.

The task of designing projects requires the participation of the core team members of the project, their supporting cast, key customers, and external stakeholders. The design process I use takes people through a series of steps and questions not unlike the design process used to create the projects in the first place. Search conferences are often useful at this juncture, as are visioning exercises, customer focus groups, and interviews of key stakeholders. Following the clarification of mission and vision, the project core team, joined by others at appropriate times, works through a series of questions concerning the design of the project, a process that normally requires seven-to-10, 2-day sessions over several weeks or a few months. The output from these sessions is an agreement on the key processes, deliberations, and roles that will facilitate the completion of the project. The core project team then empowers other project team members to design the actual work processes that will fulfill the project's goals.

To be clear about this, let me say that projects can vary in size from a few to thousands of people. The size of the project does not affect the need for the core project team to adopt a project focus, although in larger projects involving thousands of people, the analysis and design process will be more involved and may take longer to complete. A single project team may bring together large parts of what were once research, manufacturing, and marketing departments to focus on a single customer or process; or a project may consist of 10 people trying to figure out a better way to conserve natural resources across the organization. We know that large projects are possible for our success with the Apollo space program. To hear the insiders tell it, it was only when the goal of landing a man on the moon was accomplished and the organization began to formalize what had been a flexible, informal project atmosphere that success, creativity, and motivation began to wane.

Large projects are complex to manage, but trying to use formal organizational methods to manage complexity is exactly the wrong thing to do. The only way to manage complexity is with flexibility; the organization must be at least as flexible as the variation in what it is trying to learn and apply.

Everyone in the old organization will find a home on some project team and perhaps on many project teams. Concerns—raised by heads of functional departments—about losing technical depth are handled either by creating functional "learning projects" or through less formal integrating vehicles, such as networks or monthly meetings for people in different specialties. Although projects typically have a shorter time orientation than functions, human development is very much a project responsibility. Members from across projects serve on integrating teams that focus on organization-wide issues such as career development, project assignments, project creation, resource allocation, and so forth.

The project organization is not new to large engineering firms, nor is it completely new to manufacturing. When 3M spins off a business unit to develop a new product such as Post-it Notes®, it is creating a project. Managers who work in the new unit may or may not spend the duration of their careers in the new business unit, and the new unit continues to receive whatever support it needs from the rest of the organization, including other business units. Although 3M still has many traditional elements of organizational design, it is better than most at encouraging internal diversification and flexibility through the formation of project-like subunits.

DESIGNING WORK SYSTEMS: PROJECTS WITHIN PROJECTS

Within each major project, work is performed: Products are manufactured, ideas are developed, customers are served. The best way to carry out these activities should be decided by people who are experts in the work: namely, the people who perform the work. Assisted by whatever expertise they require, project members design high-performance, high-commitment, self-managing systems that are efficient and effective. Recognizing that many of its people have never previously experienced work in this kind of high-performance system, the organization may need to provide project members with assistance and educational input from internal or external consultants to analyze their work and develop design options. But, because commitment is fundamental to the success of work systems, the key decisions must be owned by the people who will do the work.

The design of work systems begins with perfecting the core tasks or processes to be performed. This consists of identifying the appropriate (and flexible) technology to be utilized, the activities that must be performed to operate that technology, and the roles that people will play in completing those activities. Beyond the operation of technology, the design of the work system will also include processes for measuring and monitoring performance, obtaining feedback from customers and other stakeholders, integrating with other parts of the work system, and individual and organizational learning. Each major process of work becomes a project in its own right, dedicated to the manufacture of a product or the performance of a service dedicated to an internal or external customer.

In order for the work system to function flexibly, it is important to build communication and integration mechanisms into the parts of the work system. Maintaining the project mentality at the level of the work system allows people to move to where their experience, expertise, or assistance is most needed, rather than being locked into fixed jobs or roles. The minimization of hierarchy speeds decision-making and enhances commitment to actions that teams decide to take.

Once the work system is designed, rewards should be created to emphasize flexibility, learning, performance, citizenship, teamwork, and customer service. The specific details of the reward system should themselves be made flexible and adaptable to local needs. Even within the same project unit, different work systems may employ different reward systems; however, an integrating rewards management team maintains a perspective on the functioning of the whole project and provides guidance to teams whose reward systems may otherwise work against the achievement of overall goals.

Since the hierarchy no longer serves as the path for career development and increases in pay, reward systems that offer elements of ownership, profit sharing, or gain sharing make more sense in this context. The Mondragon system in Spain, which is an employee-owned manufacturing cooperative employing almost 100,000 people, provides some interesting ideas in the compensation arena. For example, employees make a capital contribution when they join the organization. (The organization will lend the employee the money if the employee can't afford to make the payment.) Then, this contribution and all profit-sharing payments are held for employees, in accounts which they cannot withdraw until they terminate their employment or retire. When they do so, they *must* withdraw their funds from the organization so that the decision-making within the firm remains in the hands of the current "owners." While employee cooperatives have enjoyed only modest success in the United States, the fact that they exist and succeed elsewhere provides evidence that different kinds of relationships between employees and organizations are possible, and that reward systems can in fact be designed that fit those different relationships. When U.S. managers complain about the motivation and commitment of their work force, a fair amount of the blame should be placed on the nature of the employment contract between individuals and the organization and on the compensation system that constantly reinforces the feeling that employees are little more than expendable extensions of equipment.

DESIGNING THE SUPPORT SYSTEMS

Once the core work systems are designed within the project units, decisions can be made about the creation of centralized support services that offer economies of scale or simplify the contacts between the organization and key external groups, such as government regulators. The press these days is full of urgings by one author after another to obliterate centralized staff functions altogether. These authors insist that centralized services should become decentralized to better serve those they support, or contracted out to other organizations who can perform these functions with greater efficiency. There is no question that most U.S. and European corporate staffs are too large and inefficient compared with, say, the Japanese; but I think we are in the midst of another pendulum swing on this one, and centralization of support functions still makes sense in some cases. Often the problem is not in how large or small are these centralized staffs, but in how they conduct their business. Rather than helping the organization to succeed by augmenting organizational flexibility in decision-making, centralized staffs often gain influence by playing the role of traffic cops who set and monitor policies that produce tremendous inflexibility. For example, I've heard managers plead with corporate lawyers to tell them what they *can* do, not what they can't; and I've heard other managers beseech the industrial relations staff to quit explaining how relations came to be so bad between the organization and the union and to start doing something to improve them. Once centralized functions are created, they tend to develop their own operating cultures and even goals. The trick is to develop expertise within the project groups to interface with these units and provide guidance to them. Integrating teams composed of members from both the projects and the centralized staff functions can make plans, set goals, and provide guidance to the centralized functions. If the resources are available, rotation from the project organizations through central staff functions—and vice versa—helps to provide important learnings to people moving in both directions. Where resources do not allow for rotation, effort must be made to maintain the link between the central organization and the project organizations. The breakdown of communication and the formation of strong centralized staff units signals the beginning of the end of organizational flexibility.

DESIGNING INTEGRATIVE MECHANISMS: KEEPING IT ALL TOGETHER

Biologists have interesting debates about the advantages and disadvantages of skeletal structures for evolution. Clearly, both species with skeletons and without them have survived the evolutionary culling-out process. Those with skeletal structures tend to be stronger and are more able to exert force on their immediate surroundings. Those without skeletal structures are more flexible, and tend to survive by going with the flow. Insects, which seem to hold the best chances for survival in the very long run, have exoskeletons: They wear their integrating mechanisms on the outside, while we keep ours hidden from view.

Most of our organizations seem to be designed after our own anatomy: Heavy skeletal structures, depicted on the organizational chart, keep our organizations upright and integrate organizational limbs and systems into a coherent working whole. But is this structure the only way to go, and is it the best of the others we might consider? I would argue that, for flexibility, integration should be accomplished with less bulk and more brain; especially given the temporary, far-flung, loosely interconnected nature of organizations in these globally interesting times. If integrating mechanisms don't keep pace with the changes in the organization, what are they integrating? The old with the new? The dead with the living?

Designing integrative mechanisms that truly integrate rather than simply control is the greatest challenge and need in organizational design. Helping people to understand, holographically, what is going on and how they fit in is of paramount importance in utilizing resources fully and effectively. Control-oriented integrative devices, like the old skeletal hierarchy, ignored urgent messages about the need for change from lower in the organization in favor of simplicity and consistency. Local adaptation was routinely blocked by policies, demands for uniformity, and lack of support for innovation. There was a master plan, and the parts needed to fit in.

Today, the master plan is a burdensome constraint on flexibility and responsiveness. Many smaller plans, developed by people "on the front lines," work better, provided they are integrated into a coherent whole through appropriate integrating mechanisms. What makes an integrating mechanism effective?

First, it needs to collect and disseminate information. Integration mechanisms cannot function without knowing what needs to be integrated, and they are useless if they don't provide information that helps others to redirect their thinking or activities. The integration mechanism must act in real time, since integration that occurs after decisions have already been made and resources committed is too late. The integration mechanism should have a memory, to help provide guidance to current decisions based on past organizational learning as well as a vision, to help the integrative decisions made today lead in a direction that will still work tomorrow. The integration mechanism must understand the language and perspectives of the parts of the organization it is integrating, and it must balance diverse points of view in reaching conclusions so that the whole system maintains its viability rather than just its strongest parts. Finally, the integrative mechanism must be capable of influencing the actions taken by people in the system; it must have legitimacy in the eyes of those affected by its decisions.

On a macroscale, the United Nations is an interesting case study of a global integrating mechanism; while often lacking the power to influence the actions of member states, the U.N. clearly has become a more focal mechanism for integrating the concerns of its member nations regarding international conflict, environmental issues, and global development. Despite its many imperfections, the U.N. acts, for the most part, as a nonhierarchical integrator of global interests.

On a microscale, the office secretary or administrator plays an important integrating role in many organizations. The secretary has the information that parties need to initiate action, and although he lacks formal authority, his advice is frequently sought and taken.

The need for integration is so great in most organizations that formal and informal integrating devices are everywhere: formal meetings, informal chats around the water cooler, the company newspaper. People know how to get the knowledge they need or at least the best knowledge available. Communication studies show that, in fact, the hierarchy supplies only a small portion of the information used by people throughout an organization to make day-to-day decisions; much more information comes through informal channels. So designing integration mechanisms is not very difficult after all. People will invent them as the need arises, if the structure is flexible enough to allow them to do so. Those integrating mechanisms for which there is an obvious need can be created participatively and involve different people over time, as long as there is enough stability of membership in the integrating group to allow the memory of the group's previous decisions to be preserved. In the future, the need for integrating groups to be collocated and even to maintain a stable membership may be obviated by the design of information management and communication systems that provide real-time access to databases of information pertinent to the discussion at hand. The old hierarchy would strain and eventually break under the load of information processing that can be accomplished by today's computer-based integrating systems; and, with practical artificial intelligence just around the corner, electronic integrating devices will take organizations yet another leap forward. The organization of the future will be polynoetic and designed fractally, utilizing many different integrating mechanisms and supporting some of them electronically. If a skeleton remains, it will be a skeleton that provides strength without constraint, like the exo-skeletons of ants, or a flexible skeleton that allows the organization to bend when it needs to bend. The basic elements of the skeletal structure will be agreements among members regarding processes of thinking and deciding, alongside a series of self-designing project-oriented units, as indicated in Figure 9.2.

IMPLEMENTING CHANGE

In the new physics, there is talk about systems entering chaos, and then dissipative states, which allows them to form new patterns of temporary stability in higher level (more complex) states of existence. One could argue that the world has been undergoing this kind of chaos and then resettling ever since the invention of the atomic bomb. For the first time in our history, we have the power to destroy our entire species at once, and to take most of the rest of the living things on Earth along with us. The chaos this invention created has been tremendous; and, as we all know, there is no way to turn back, to put the knowledge we now have back in the bottle. Our only course is ahead, toward a world

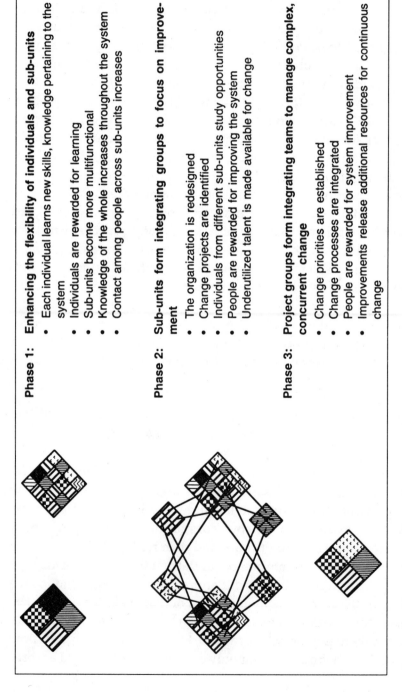

Phase 1: **Enhancing the flexibility of individuals and sub-units**

- Each individual learns new skills, knowledge pertaining to the system
- Individuals are rewarded for learning
- Sub-units become more multifunctional
- Knowledge of the whole increases throughout the system
- Contact among people across sub-units increases

Phase 2: **Sub-units form integrating groups to focus on improvement**

- The organization is redesigned
- Change projects are identified
- Individuals from different sub-units study opportunities
- People are rewarded for improving the system
- Underutilized talent is made available for change

Phase 3: **Project groups form integrating teams to manage complex, concurrent change**

- Change priorities are established
- Change processes are integrated
- People are rewarded for system improvement
- Improvements release additional resources for continuous change

Figure 9.2   Three phases of complex system change.

that must find ways to exist amidst the greater complexity of our interrelated actions and consequences. We seem to be settling into a state of relative calm within this chaos, although at any moment more chaos could emerge and overload the system. It has taken us a long time to begin to learn to live together in peace, and apparently we still have much to learn. Even with all our lives at stake, we could not accomplish the transition from a hostile world to a peaceful one quickly; a lot of sorting out had to take place, and is still taking place. So when we want our organizations to change, we should remember that significant change, even when it is desirable, takes time.

Planning for implementation is important, and it's usually more fruitful than wishing for change to happen or writing memos declaring that the change will take place by a certain date. Planning helps to clarify the work that must be accomplished to make change real, and the time and resources that will be required to support that work. Planning usually involves the assignment of responsibility as well, in this case responsibility for leading the change process rather than responsibility for making decisions. The job of the process leader is to help the system become capable of designing and leading its own process of change, but this comes only after some time; it is therefore necessary to assign process leaders at first. Initially, while the system is still learning and people are developing new competencies in participation, integration, and self-management, a great deal of structure, guidance, and support is needed. If the leaders of the old system simply abdicate power, much time and effort will be wasted while people try to figure out what the new organization should be like and their roles within it. This energy is more productively spent on learning and making the new organization a reality.

Implementation planning also means developing success measurement methods that allow calibration along the way. The system needs to continue to benchmark externally and to develop new, close-to-home measures that people can use to make sure they are on track with the implementation. Implementation is a slow, uneven, and messy process that often requires recycling through design and implementation several times before a good working organization is created. Measurement helps people keep their eye on the eventual target and not to settle for more minor improvements simply to leave the messy part of change behind. Change is messy, and the flexible organization will eventually become used to the mess. The organization chart may never provide perfect clarity about roles and reporting relationships in the flexible organization, but it won't constrain people from doing what they need to do to help the organization succeed, either.

In changes that involve the introduction of many new ideas simultaneously, managing the burden of change will require spreading the load over many people. Rather than institute lock step training programs for everyone, flexible organizations encourage individuals to learn on behalf of one another, and teach others as opportunities arise to apply their learnings. At every level of the organization, many people are involved in both doing and changing during the implementation stage; and, because implementation is particularly demanding, a higher level of integration must be sustained than would normally be the case. Unfortunately, there are no shortcuts; spreading the load over many people makes change more manageable, but its effects will still be noticeable. As each person learns, the potential of the organization increases; and as everyone learns, the organization will begin to make progress. Eventually, the system will be transformed; it will reach a dissipative stage in which the combined potential of its members is released to allow a new way of operation to appear feasible for the first time. Once tried, the only path is ahead, toward more of the same. Further implementation produces greater rewards, and obstacles give way to the gathering force of change.

Because the system begins to function differently during implementation, it's important to include the key stakeholders in frequent sessions to discuss what is happening and what differences they should expect as they interact with the organization. Sometimes, organizations become so involved with implementing new designs to better serve their customers that they forget to check with the customers to see if the changes are meeting their needs. Often, as one organization is implementing its changes, the customer's organization is changing as well. The only hope lies in organizational flexibility, not in what we see when organizations take one giant leap forward at a time, only to refreeze their design into yet another soon-to-be-obsolete configuration.

Many questions are raised about the order of implementation of various aspects of changes in organizational design and processes. Should the compensation system change first, to provide incentives for people to change, or should the compensation system be left alone until the new design can be clarified? In order to make a clean break with the past, should the structural changes be made before people are comfortable with the new processes; or should people be left in their old jobs until they are ready to perform their new ones? Should the current management lead the transition effort, or should a new team, which is more representative of the whole organization, be formed to manage the process? These and other questions have no right or wrong answers, but they are important to address and decide based upon local conditions.

The majority of unsuccessful change efforts fail at the implementation stage. Whether these late failures are due to underestimating the degree of difficulty of the implementation, last-minute resistance to change, changes in leadership, or simply being overwhelmed by other pressing agendas isn't clear; but late failure happens often enough to cause me a great deal of concern these days. Implementation planning doesn't prevent these late failures, but it may reduce their risk of occurrence. When more energy is put into implementation planning, people seem to recognize better what needs to happen and be more committed to making it so. Implementation planning clarifies who is supposed to do what when, and it helps people take the first steps toward greater flexibility.

CHANGING EVERYTHING AT ONCE

The approach I have just outlined is comprehensive. It's like starting with a clean sheet of paper and inventing the organization all over again. But at the same time it isn't. The knowledge and experience that have helped the organization to succeed in the past is drawn upon to invent the future. The reputation, relationship, and contracts that have evolved over many years remain intact, as does most of the technology and physical plant. While new information systems and improvements in technology may accompany other changes, the largest changes in this approach are clearly in human systems, in the talents and flexibility of people and the relationships among them.

Taking the blank-sheet approach frees the organization from the tyranny of past agreements among people concerning the way things have to be. It also allows us to change many things about the organization simultaneously, rather than piece at a time, through one program after another. The blank-sheet approach makes it possible to change everything all at once, by involving many people in redesigning different parts of the system simultaneously and integrating their work through multiple integrating groups. The old, hierarchical organization simply couldn't handle this amount of change in such a short time. Its control systems and information channels would quickly become overloaded, and the gears in the watch would start to grind on one another. But, with everyone involved in helping the organization to change, the organization becomes polynoetic and able to manage simultaneous transformations in many of its operating processes and structural configurations. Changing everything all at once takes a tremendous leap of faith, but following the conservative route of changing one thing at a time on a "pilot" basis virtually guarantees that nothing significant will ever change. I'm sure LH saw many improvements in the quality of rail service during the many years he held his gold watch, and I'll bet that he was totally bewildered by the decline in the number of passengers boarding his trains. When LH was riding the rails, we didn't know how to change organizations all at once. The world LH lived in changed gradually, almost imperceptibly from year to year. There was no need for a flexible organization in the early years of the railroad, so an organization structure as solid as the steel rails was created to run the system.

When times did change, the system had never developed the capacity to change, even though many single improvements were introduced over the years. The rails of the organizational structure led to oblivion, and LH most likely rode them loyally to the end.

LH probably wouldn't appreciate the polynoetic, fractal organization; like many of his era, he might resign before giving it a try. I can almost hear him say, "It's no way to run a railroad." For LH, and many like him, the idea of changing everything all at once would be frightening; perhaps too frightening. We all make calculations in our lives of whether change is worth our bother, worth the upset we will incur. While LH may have concluded that changing everything at once would be too difficult to bear, it's possible that an apprentice conductor may have felt differently. The apprentice would have liked the organization to survive and, with a full career potentially still ahead, may have been willing to take more risk to change it. It's one of the tragedies of our current norms of organizing that the people with the least desire to change are those with the greatest influence in the system. In order to change everything all at once, we need the support and understanding of our senior employees and leaders, and they in turn need our support during the period when everything looks messy and uncertain. All of us find comfort in what has been and are at least a bit frightened about the unknown. We must learn to overcome our fears, or face the fact that we will find ourselves holding ever tighter to our gold watches, wishing that change would leave us alone, even though we know that the gremlins of change are out there. If we listen closely, we can almost hear the echoes of the steam engines, and the sound of a wrench grinding in the gears.

Chapter 10

The Human Experience
Managing As If Change Mattered

Recently, during a trip to Chicago on business, I took time to visit the small farm near Hinsdale where I spent my early youth. I hadn't set foot on the property for 30 years, although I had occasionally driven past it. This time, I parked the car on a narrow gravel road that runs along the side of the farm and walked through the bushes where the fence used to be, into my past.

Someone had just mowed the hay that grew there, and the strong smell of the sweet grass brought back thoughts of the days when my family used to mow the hay on hot summer days like this one. I realized that, within the shape and contours of this field where we once grew hay or corn or pastured horses, were now held the remembrances of my childhood. Here my father had taught me how to throw a baseball, my sister told me stories she invented about animals and elves that lived in the tall grass and woods, my brother jumped his motorcycle over the make-shift pitcher's mound, lost control, and crashed into the chain link fence that served as a backstop, leaving him with diamond-shaped impressions on his face for a week.

A little farther along was the place where the 150-year-old farmhouse once stood, long ago burned to the ground in a fire caused by kids playing with matches. There was no trace of the house now; only a depression in the ground where the cellar had been. The rest was covered in deep grass and even small trees. A stranger looking upon this scene would never know a house once stood there, or how it looked, or the many things that occurred within its walls. I imagined archaeologists digging up the site, wondering about the lives of the inhabitants, their habits, and customs. I thought about all the things their digging wouldn't tell them, such as the time my brothers and I tried to coax one of the horses into the kitchen to surprise our mother, or how high the mound of presents was every year under the Christmas tree, or how my friends and I would make forts of the hay bales in the barn. There were so many things the archaeologists would never know, but I knew.

As I walked in the warm summer sun under the brightest blue sky I've seen in 30 years, through the grass where the house and barn once stood, I felt suddenly and deeply saddened. I wanted my family back. Although they are all still alive and I see them occasionally, it's not the same. I wanted my family back as they were then, even with all the things I found irritating about being the youngest of six children. I wanted to sit at the dining room table again and see each of them there, focused only on each other. I wanted my sister to tell me more stories and finish those she only began. I wanted to climb into the bunkbed above my brother and to know that, if a storm came, my parents' bedroom was just a few steps away.

In a few more years, only the trees will remain to remind me of my youth; and, eventually, even they will give way to the scythe of time. Then, the contour of the land will be the final stimulus to my memory. Being the youngest, it's quite possible that the knowledge the archaeologists seek will pass with me.

I would like nothing better than to stop this process from proceeding; to freeze time where it stands now or, better still, to reverse it. But I know I cannot. Change is relentless, a product of forces in the universe scientists haven't begun to understand. I am powerless against it. And so are organizations.

We can all wish that change didn't steal our youth, our families from us. We can hope that the organization we have come to know will remain as it is, and our place in it secure. But our place in organizations cannot be secure, any more than I could be secure in knowing that my parents' bedroom was only steps away. We can't resist change, or hope to outlast its constant eroding of what we hold dear. We cannot deny its effects upon us, physically or emotionally. We must instead find the courage to view change as a stimulus, as a partner and even an engine on our journey.

Scientists may one day discover that change is a single, gigantic, cosmic joke; another imperfection in the grand plan, another sign that the universe is more the product of chaos than intention. Whatever its source, change grabs us all by the collars and yanks our faces forward to confront it, no matter how hard we resist. Our lives, despite long periods of stability, are ultimately patterned around the changes that affect us and other people and institutions around us. We have some choices about the patterns our lives take, but no choice about change; and, ultimately, the pattern of each of our lives is more similar than it is different.

We distinguish our lives when we find the courage to endure change and create ways to work with the changes that are occurring around us so that they make others more hopeful about them, even to view them positively. We waste our lives when we use all of our energy to hold change at arm's length.

In the time it has taken me to write this book, the world has changed again in important ways. Canada has had two new prime ministers, the United States has a new Supreme Court justice, the U.N. has taken on a greater role as the world's peacekeeper, and, I'm sad to report, both Eric Trist and Calvin Pava have passed away. Perhaps, even in the time it has taken you to read this book, events have transpired in your organization that will influence your destiny and that of your peers. Creating an organizational capacity to understand what these changes mean and the flexibility to respond to them is a matter of some urgency. Change isn't waiting for us to prepare for it; every day we delay is a day we fall further behind.

Of course, we're used to falling behind. We've become almost comfortable with our false sense of security. We believe in our invulnerability, or in the grace of God; we hope that we will be spared, as we have been in the past. We believe that, somehow, we will survive without changing, because we have gotten away with it before. We think we can get away with it again.

How important it is to wake up, to take action, to become more flexible, depends on the specifics of your organizational and personal situation. Maybe your organization can sleep through this one, and the next one, and the one after that. Or maybe it can't; maybe the next one is the change that shouldn't be ignored. Maybe now is the time to begin developing the flexibility your organization will need to deal with the change that is coming tomorrow. I can't say; you probably can't either.

As a general policy, defying the reality of change isn't a wise thing to do. Most people would agree that being ready for change is preferable to not being ready; but, apparently, being ready isn't easy. Being ready takes time, energy, and effort; and, even more, it takes confronting our fear of change, our hate for what it does to our lives. Increasing organizational flexibility begins at a personal level, perhaps in the heart of a single individual; perhaps in your heart. But it must end as an organizational act.

A single, flexible-minded individual can't do much to make an organization flexible, in the short run. The gap between individual and organizational acts is very wide; crossing it may be unimaginable to you. It would be wonderful to have an ally, especially a powerful one, to help you along your journey. It would be better still if everyone could hear the message of change at once and begin the journey together, all at the same time. But, for now, you may find yourself alone.

I think about how Dr. Lown must have felt on his flight to the former Soviet Union, beginning his personal mission to end the threat of nuclear war between two superpowers. A single individual, a private citizen, an uninvited guest. How often did he doubt his ability, question his mission, even question his own sanity? Human change begins with actions taken by human beings, by a single individual. In your organization, you may be that person. Where do you begin?

When Dr. Lown left for the Soviet Union, he did more than pack his bags and make a reservation with a travel agent. He didn't plan to go to the middle of Red Square and start shouting at the top of his lungs until somebody listened. He had a strategy: He identified a key individual he wanted to influence, a person he could arrange a meeting with, who might be able to influence others. In this case, it was the Soviet's chief medical officer and personal physician to members of the Kremlin, Dr. Eugeni Chazov. Lown developed a case for change that he would present to Chazov; in this instance, a personal appeal from one physician to another to help prevent the biggest medical catastrophe in history. Lown didn't demand that Chazov do something; he simply appealed for help. Chazov was skeptical; he suspected that Lown was a CIA operative and worried that the KGB would find this visit and conversation troubling. If the CIA were to invent a plot for weakening Soviet resolve, it would look exactly like this. A single private citizen, attempting to make contact with a well placed Soviet official. An appeal to compassion, rather than a demand to disarm.

Chazov left Lown sitting in his hotel room for a full day after their first meeting. Lown was certain that Chazov was receiving instructions from the KGB. In fact, Chazov was discussing the situation with his family, asking them what he should do. Finally, it was Chazov's daughter who cast the deciding vote. She agreed that it was much too risky, much too complicated to do what Lown had asked her father to do; but for the sake of her daughter, Chazov's granddaughter, he must proceed anyway. As much as she loved her father and wanted to protect him, she knew the importance of what was at stake. Chazov agreed to cooperate with Lown in presenting medical arguments for the end of the Cold War. Together, they succeeded in beginning the thaw in relations that made the movement toward peace possible.

Lown was respected; he had a plan; he appealed to Chazov rather than demanding change. If it is up to you to start the change in your organization, you may want to consider what you can learn from Lown and other Nobel peace prize winners. Unless you have an army at your disposal and can use it to force revolution, you may find that you are compelled to use more peaceful tactics: working within the system while you challenge its limits, being bold but not reckless, confronting authority rather than defying it, holding discussions instead of throwing rocks, developing a case for change that you invite others to participate in voluntarily instead of demanding that they change. Introducing organizational flexibility requires that you be flexible, too.

It used to be that we couldn't expect to see meaningful change in our lifetimes. In the middle ages, a person might devote his entire life to building a cathedral, knowing that he would probably die before it was completed. A person could even define the significance of his life by undertaking endeavors that would not be appreciated for generations to come.

Today, the pace of change has quickened, and we need not despair that we will never see the fruits of our labor. Our organizations need to change and change fast, and they know it. We can help them to change by making them more flexible, designing and managing them as if change mattered.

Footnotes

CHAPTER 1

1. Mirvis, P. (Ed.) 1993. *Building the Competitive Workforce: Investing in Human Capital for Corporate Success.* New York, John Wiley & Sons.
2. Pasmore, W. 1988. *Designing Effective Organizations: The Sociotechnical Systems Perspective.* New York, John Wiley & Sons.

CHAPTER 3

1. Weathersby, R. 1981. "Ego Development." In A. Chickering & Associates (Eds.), *The Modern American College.* San Francisco: Jossey-Bass, p. 51–75.
2. De Tocqueville, A. 1956. *Democracy in America.* In R. Heffner (edited version, 1956). New York: Penguin. Original work published in 1835.
3. Locke, E. A., & Schweiger, D.M. 1979. "Participation in Decision-making: One More Look." In B. Staw & L. Cummings (Eds.), *Research in Organizational Behavior,* 1: 265–339. Greenwich, CT: JAI Press.

4. Lewin, K. 1947. "Frontiers in Group Dynamics," *Human Relations*, 1: 5–41.

5. Lewin, K. 1948. *Resolving Social Conflicts*. New York: Harper and Brothers.

6. Roethlisberger, F., & Dickson, W. 1939. *Management and the Worker*. Cambridge: Harvard University Press.

7. Coch, L., & French, J.P. 1948. "Overcoming resistance to change." *Human Relations*,1: 512–532.

8. Locke, E. A., & Schweiger, D.M. 1979. "Participation in Decision-making: One More Look."In B. Staw & L. Cummings (Eds.), *Research in Organizational Behavior*, 1: 265–339. Greenwich, CT: JAI Press.

9. Vroom, V. 1960. *Some Personality Determinants of the Effects of Participation*. Englewood Cliffs, NJ: Prentice-Hall.

10. Lowin, A. 1968. "Participative Decision Making: A Model, Literature Critique, and Prescriptions for Research." *Organizational Behavior and Human Performance*, 3: 68–106.

11. Dachler, H.P., & Wilpert, B. 1978. "Conceptual Dimensions and Boundaries of Participation in Organizations: A Critical Evaluation." *Administrative Science Quarterly*, 23: 1–34.

12. Locke, E. A., & Schweiger, D.M. 1979. "Participation in Decision Making: One More Look." In B. Staw & L. Cummings (Eds.), *Research in Organizational Behavior*, 1: 265–339. Greenwich, CT: JAI Press.

13. Neumann, J. 1989. "Why People Don't Participate in Organizational Change." In W.A. Pasmore & R.W. Woodman (Eds.), *Research in Organization Change and Development*, 3: 181–212. Greenwich, CT: JAI Press.

14. Dachler, H.P., & Wilpert, B. 1978. "Conceptual Dimensions and Boundaries of Participation in Organizations: A Critical Evaluation." *Administrative Science Quarterly*, 23: 1–34.

15. McGregor, D. 1960. *The Human Side of Enterprise*. New York: McGraw-Hill.

16. Loevinger, J. 1976. *Ego Development: Conceptions and Theories*. San Francisco: Jossey-Bass.

17. Fromm, E. 1941. *Escape from Freedom*. New York: Avon Books.

18. Argyris, C. 1957. *Personality and Organization*. New York: Harper and Brothers.
19. Argryis, C. 1964. *Integrating the Individual and Organization*. New York, Wiley.
20. Lowin, A. 1968. "Participative Decision Making: A Model, Literature Critique, and Prescriptions for Research." *Organizational Behavior and Human Performance*, 3: 68–106.
21. Lewin, K. 1951. *Field Theory in Social Science*. New York: Harper and Brothers.
22. Emery, M. 1982. The Search Conference. Canberra, Australia, unpublished.
23. Weisbord, M. 1992. Discovering Common Ground. San Francisco, Berrett-Koehler.
24. Kanter, R.M. 1982. Dilemmas of Management Participation. *Organizational Dynamics*, 11: 5–27.

CHAPTER 4

1. Trist, E., Higgin, Murray, H. and Pollock, A. 1963. *Organizational Choice*. London, Tavistock Institute.
2. Woodward, J. 1958. *Management and Technology*. London, Her Majesty's Stationery Office.
3. Emery, F. 1963. "Some Hypotheses about the Way in Which Tasks May Be More Effectively Put Together to Design Jobs." Document No. T176, London, Tavistock Institute.
4. Badarraco, A. 1992. The Knowledge Alliance. Cambridge, Harvard University Press.

CHAPTER 5

1. Herzberg, F. 1968. "One More Time: How Do You Motivate Employees?" *Harvard Business Review*, 46, 53–62.
2. Zuboff, S. 1988. *In the Age of the Smart Machine: The Future of Work and Power*. New York, Basic Books.

3. Hirschhorn, L. 1984. *Beyond Mechanization*. Cambridge, MA, MIT Press.

CHAPTER 6

1. Vroom, V. 1960. *Some Personality Determinants of the Effects of Participation*. Englewood Cliffs, NJ: Prentice-Hall.
2. March, J. and Simon, H. , 1958. *Organizations*. New York, Wiley & Sons.
3. Argyris, C. 1985. *Overcoming Defensive Routines*. Needham Heights, MA, Allyn Bacon.
4. Wensberg, P. 1987. *Land's Polaroid*. Boston, Houghton Mifflin.
5. Asch, S. 1952. *Social Psychology*. Englewood Cliffs, NJ, Prentice-Hall.
6. Bradford, D. and Cohen, A. 1984. *Managing for Excellence: The Guide to Developing High Performance in Contemporary Organizations*. New York, Wiley & Sons.
7. Peters, T. 1992. *Liberation Management: Necessary Disorganization for the Nanosecond Nineties*. New York, Alfred Knopf.
8. Ibid.
9. Peters, T. 1987. *Thriving on Chaos: Handbook for a Management Revolution*. New York, Harper Collins.
10. Wheatly, M. 1992. *Leadership and the New Science*. San Francisco, Berrett-Koehler.
11. Argyris, C. *Knowledge for Action*, San Francisco, Jossey-Bass, 1993.
12. Stacey, R. 1993. *Managing the Unknowable*. San Francisco, Jossey Bass.
13. Berquist, W. 1993. *The Postmodern Organization*. San Francisco, Jossey-Bass.
14. Handy, C. 1989. *The Age of Unreason*. London: Business Books Limited.
15. Pava, C. 1983. *Managing New Office Technology: An Organizational Strategy*. New York, Free Press.

CHAPTER 7

1. Max Weber, as quoted in Bennis, W. 1993. *Beyond Bureaucracy: Essays on the Development and Evolution of Human Organization*. San Francisco, Jossey-Bass.

CHAPTER 8

1. Kidder, T. 1981. *The Soul of a New Machine*. Boston, MA, Atlantic, Little, Brown.
2. Likert, R. 1961. *New Patterns of Management*. New York, McGraw-Hill.
3. Ouchi, W. 1981. *Theory Z*. Reading, MA, Addison-Wesley.
4. Jaques, E. 1989. *Requisite Organization: The CEO's Guide to Creative Structure and Leadership*. Cason Hall & Company.
5. Bennis, W. 1993. *Beyond Bureaucracy: Essays on the Development and Evolution of Human Organization*. San Francisco, Jossey-Bass.
6. Peters, T. 1987. *Thriving on Chaos: Handbook for a Management Revolution*. New York, HarperCollins.
7. Peters, T. 1992. *Liberation Management: Necessary Disorganization for the Nanosecond Nineties*. New York, Alfred Knopf.
8. Kanter, R. 1990. *When Giants Learn to Dance*. London, Unwin.
9. Hammer, M. and Champy, J. 1993. *Reengineering the Corporation: A Manifesto for Business Revolution*. New York, Harper Collins.
10. Davidow, W. and Malone, M. 1992. *The Virtual Corporation: Structuring and Revitalizing the Corporation for the 21st Century*. New York, HarperCollins.
11. Perlmutter, H. and Trist, E. 1986. "Paradigms for Societal Transition," *Human Relations*, 39,1, 1986, pp.1–27.
12. Pasmore, W., Francis, C., Haldeman, J. and Shani, A. 1982. "Sociotechnical Systems: A North American Reflection on Empirical Studies of the Seventies." *Human Relations*, 35, 2, 1179–1204.

13. Hammer, M. and Champy, J. 1993. *Reengineering the Corporation: A Manifesto for Business Revolution.* New York, HarperCollins.

14. Brown, L. 1983. *Managing Conflict at Organizational Interfaces.* Reading, MA, Addison-Wesley.

15. Wheatly, M. 1992. *Leadership and the New Science.* San Francisco, Berrett-Koehler.

CHAPTER 9

1. Weisbord, M. 1992. *Discovering Common Ground.* San Francisco, Berrett-Koehler.

Index